# Praise for *Six Disciplines for Excellence*

"Wow, now I get it! For the first time this approach puts together all the key pieces needed for working on my business…"

—LYNN CHILD
CEO, Aardvark, Inc.

"I've never read a book that was so tailored to small businesses…it's a unique tool for enabling small businesses to effectively manage operations."

—TERRY TERHARK
Founder, The Right Thing

"Six Disciplines is unlike anything I've seen for small businesses. It's a book. It's a methodology. It's technology. It's a coaching system. It's something you'll be hearing a lot more about."

—ANITA CAMPBELL
Small Business Trends

"I really liked this book because it is simple and practical. It is easy to read, relevant to most companies, and thorough."

—ROB MAY
The Business Pundit

"This hands-on book goes beyond the fluff that many other business books serve up, and offers a real world business plan."

—SARAH BOSCH
Business Opportunities Weblog

"One of the more enjoyable books I've read on small business success."

—DR. ROBERT RAUSCH
CEO 1 Executive Energy

"The Six Disciplines™ Methodology synthesizes and integrates the most fundamental elements of strategic planning, quality management, integrated organizational learning, business process automation, people performance management and measure-driven improvement—and offers a systematic and practical "business-building" approach for small businesses to continually improve and sustain business excellence."

—THE CEO REFRESHER

"*Six Disciplines for Excellence*, by Gary Harpst, is a great example of how to use common sense to build a business."

—BUD BILANICH
The Common Sense Guy

"Six Disciplines Corporation provides Internet technologies to successfully implement the methodology unveiled in the book *Six Disciplines for Excellence* by Gary Harpst."

—Small Business Computing

"Any small business owner with 100 employees or less will find a great deal of practical insight from reading *Six Disciplines for Excellence* that will be very helpful in an attempt to build a successful business."

—TREVOR M. HALL
Instructor at Viterbo University, MA in Servant-Leadership

"These people mean business and have a desire to truly help other companies. Their ideas are sound and proven. Their business model for Six Disciplines is fascinating. If you work especially in a small organization that is struggling with growth and lack of direction, get the book and just give it a try."

—SKIP ANGEL
Chief Technology Officer, Integrated Services, Inc.

"Well-written with great substance...*Six Disciplines* is actually a small business owner's manual."

—PATRICIA DRAZNIN
Owner, Writing to Go
Columnist, *Fairfield Weekly Reader* and *The Iowa Source*

"Nobody helps you figure out how to manage the company to get results in such an easy-to-understand way."

—LINDY LOPEZ
President, Research for Action, Inc.

"This book shows me how I can systematically move my business from existence to excellence. I can do this!"

—JOHNNY WARREN
Co-Founder, Cornerstone Management

# Six Disciplines
## for Excellence

*Building Small Businesses
That Learn, Lead and Last*

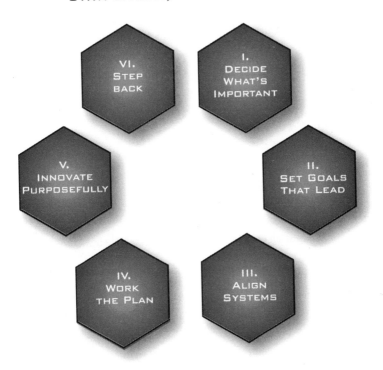

## GARY HARPST

Synergy Books

Six Disciplines for Excellence: Building Small Businesses that Learn, Lead and Last
Published by Synergy Books
PO Box 80107
Austin, TX 78758

Produced in association with Six Disciplines Corporation.

For more information about our books, please write to us, call 512.478.2028, or visit our website at www.synergybooks.net.

Library of Congress Cataloging-in-Publication Data

Harpst, Gary.
 Six disciplines for excellence : building small businesses that learn, lead and last /
Gary Harpst.
    p. cm.
Includes bibliographical references and index.
 ISBN-13: 978-1-933538-81-5 (pbk. : alk. paper)
 ISBN-10: 1-933538-81-3 (pbk. : alk. paper)
1. Small business--Management. 2. Organizational learning. 3. Creative ability in
business. I. Title.
HD62.5.H37345 2007
658.02'2--dc22

                              2006102590


                         10 9 8 7 6 5 4 3 2

# Contents

# Foreword

Achieving a rare kind of business excellence—lasting, sustainable excellence—is not easy. Although there are many different types of books, business improvement methods and tools, one approach hardly ever works in all cases. We still must take the time to sort it out for ourselves and pick out which parts work for our business.

As we attempted to create the right business model for our organization, we integrated various quality methods and systems (Baldrige, lean, TQM, balanced scorecards, etc.) into our culture, trying to take our company to that next level of performance. During our journey, we borrowed the best practices from various sources and used the most appropriate ones to improve our performance.

On this journey, I was introduced to *Six Disciplines*.

My initial reaction when I found out about *Six Disciplines* was: "Wow, where was this ten years ago?" The *Six Disciplines* program integrates business practices so that organizations develop and execute their plans. And it does this in a way that empowers and challenges associates to align their activities with company goals throughout their day.

The *Six Disciplines* methodology brings structure and simplicity to the processes essential to managing our business. We have been using the *Six Disciplines* process for nearly two years and have achieved noticeable results. Sustainable improvement has occurred through the help of the Six Disciplines Leadership Center and our coach. We now do meaningful strategic planning that provides goals and individual plans aligned throughout our organization to the mission, vision and values of our company. Tracking performance, measuring results and identifying areas requiring additional resources has become much more efficient and effective. Probably the most important benefit of all is that *Six Disciplines* helps us learn how to execute better and better year after year.

*Six Disciplines for Excellence* is a book with a lasting impact. It's a handbook that describes not only what it takes to achieve that rare level of excellence but the specific steps of how your business can take advantage of it. The unique difference in the *Six Disciplines* methodology is that in addition to the text, which provides an outstanding blueprint for sustainable excellence, it is supported by useful deployment tools and an extraordinary coaching program.

Simply put, I'd recommend *Six Disciplines* to any business leader who wants to achieve a sustainable level of organizational excellence.


PAUL WORSTELL
President, PRO-TEC Coating Company
2007 Malcolm Baldrige National Quality Award Recipient

# *Hancock Engineering*

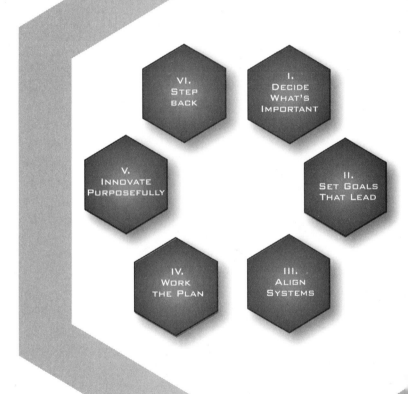

VI.
STEP
BACK

I.
DECIDE
WHAT'S
IMPORTANT

V.
INNOVATE
PURPOSEFULLY

II.
SET GOALS
THAT LEAD

IV.
WORK
THE PLAN

III.
ALIGN
SYSTEMS

*"I told him business had never looked so good. He congratulated me and then gently told me the hardest part was ahead—building an organization that would stand the test of time. . . ."*

BRIAN JENKINS,
HANCOCK ENGINEERING

# Hancock Engineering

Brian Jenkins, who had founded Hancock Engineering twenty years earlier, was walking to his car after lunch when he bumped into Steve Denton. While in college, Steve had interned at Hancock, but they hadn't seen each other in years. "Steve, I heard you started a printing business a few years ago," asked Brian. "How's it going?"

Steve smiled and said, "ScriptRight is doing great. We have twenty employees and are growing. But managing the business is more of a challenge as it grows and I could use some advice. Can we get together?" Brian responded, "Sure, come on over to my office Saturday morning."

When Steve arrived, Brian took him on a tour of his 75-person office. Then Brian asked him about ScriptRight. Steve began, "I started ScriptRight nine years ago. We struggled the first few years and I wasn't sure we'd make it. Then we turned the corner. We're growing at a healthy pace and profits are better than average in our industry."

Brian said, "Sounds like you're doing great. I'm curious as to why you want to talk to me."

Steve replied, "Even though things look pretty good, something isn't right. I can feel it. It seems we're not all on the same page in terms of priorities. We don't have the same sense of teamwork we had. I've promoted and hired new managers but, if anything, the communications challenges have increased as we have grown.

"Bumping into you the other day reminded me of a remark you once made, that growing businesses eventually outgrow the very skills that made them successful in the first place. And that it happens so slowly, most business leaders don't realize it until they're in deep trouble. Makes me wonder if I'm missing something."

Steve continued, "The things I hear about Hancock Engineering made me want to talk to you. Your customers say great things about your people, the quality of their work and the integrity of your firm. Hancock's ability to consistently deliver on its promises makes it stand apart. Some of your competitors have told me they're no longer in the same league. My fear is we're not going to figure out how to reach that level. I already see signs that make me nervous."

Brian replied, "Your sensitivity is unusual. Most business leaders who make it through the survival stage don't realize the magnitude of the challenge ahead. Some refer to it as learning how to work *on* your business instead of *in* it. Years ago, a business mentor helped me begin to grasp this concept.

"We'd grown to about your size and I told him business had never looked so good. After congratulating me, he gently said the hardest part was ahead—building an organization that would stand the test of time. It would need to survive changes not only in markets, technology, and competitors, but also changes in the leadership and in the company itself. He gave me a book that helped explain what he meant. That's when I began thinking of myself not as an *engineer of buildings* but as an *engineer of a business*. The difference is huge.

*The first few years were an incredible struggle and I wasn't sure we were going to make it.*

"What makes Hancock Engineering distinctive today is the result of a journey that began with his comment. As I'd said, our business was healthy and growing. We worked hard to maintain good client relationships. We frequently had 60-hour weeks at crunch time. However, sometimes I sensed our team was burning out, and the atmosphere wasn't as much fun. After our headcount got above fifteen, it seemed something fundamental changed. But I thought this was normal.

"I began thinking about what it would take to have a business two or three times our size that was so well-managed I could cut back on my involvement if I wanted to. Then I realized I didn't know how. It had taken years for me to become proficient at engineering, but no one had prepared me to build a *business* that could do excellent engineering, regardless of size, and function so well it would even work without me.

"As I read through the book my mentor gave me, I discovered a systematic approach for working on the business itself. Having spent my professional life learning to use a defined process for building a building, having a systematic way to build an *enduring business* appealed to me.

"We decided on a step-by-step program for working *on* the business. The principles were pretty basic. In fact, they were all things I'd heard about but wasn't taking seriously. The programs combined a little strategic planning and some continuous improvement practices, along with business process automation and measurement. Last of all was performance management to help individuals learn and grow in their ability to connect with company priorities.

"Much of the weakness in these areas shows up gradually as an organization grows. Growth adds stress in such a way that what works with ten people may be fatal with thirty or fifty. As we moved forward, there were times it felt overwhelming, so we slowed down and focused on one piece at a time. There were some things people resisted, but gradually we all began to see how these pieces worked together.

> *I stopped thinking of myself as an engineer of buildings and began thinking of myself as an engineer of a business. The difference is huge.*

"Over time, our leaders began to do a better job of setting priorities, and our people began to connect their daily work with those priorities. We learned to communicate with each other more effectively. Gradually people became more self-managed, taking responsibility for identifying roadblocks and resolving them.

"Looking back, I realize how far we've come. Our quality has continued to improve and, with it, client satisfaction and profitability. As our reputation grew, our ability to attract better people improved as well.

"Don't get me wrong. Building and sustaining a solid business is always a challenge. We have to put out fires occasionally, but we're always learning how to get better. This makes our team much more resilient, innovative and nimble. We now have two or three other people on our leadership team who could run this business successfully, because everyone understands the way we set priorities and execute them."

Reaching for a book behind him Brian said, "I could spend hours describing how we got here, but I think it would be better for you to read *Six Disciplines for Excellence*—it will save us both time. I'll warn you that when I first read this, I was a little overwhelmed with how much we weren't doing, and yet for the first time I could see an organized way out of the proverbial 'swamp.'

"After reading it, come back and I'll describe in more detail what it was like to implement these disciplines. We'll give you both sides of the story. I'll even let you talk to the biggest skeptic we had in this whole process. I can tell you this: we're now a completely different kind of company."

Taking the book, Steve said, "Thanks. You've given me a lot to think about—I'll call you next week."

To be continued . . .

# Who This Book Is For

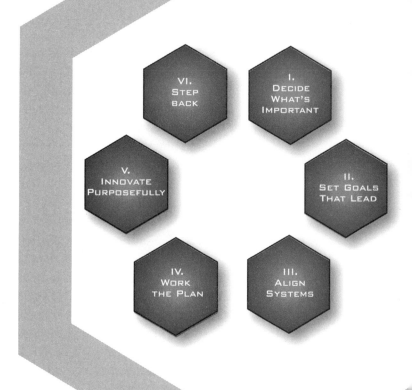

*When it comes to achieving excellence, figuring out the right things to do isn't nearly as difficult as continuing to do them over the long term.*

## The Idea

The idea behind *Six Disciplines for Excellence* crystallized at the Grouse Mountain Lodge in Whitefish, Montana on a warm, cloudless day in July 2001. I was a guest speaker at a business improvement conference being held at the lodge. During the frequent outdoor breaks, I asked people what they were learning and whether the conference was useful to them.

*The problem for most of us isn't knowing what to do, it's doing it.*

Thinking about my questions, Eric, a conference attendee, looked beyond me to the mountains in the backdrop of the lodge. He repeated what I'd heard from several other small business leaders: "This material is outstanding . . . but I probably won't be doing anything about it two years from now."

After hearing this comment several times, it finally dawned on me that when it comes to achieving excellence, *figuring out the right things to do isn't nearly as difficult as continuing to do them over the long term.* The depth of this challenge sunk in when I realized how pervasive the problem is. We face similar problems in our personal lives with fitness, finances, relationships, etc.

Paraphrasing C.S. Lewis, "The key to understanding ourselves and the universe we live in is realizing that people know what to do and don't do it." All you have to do is read the daily newspaper or look in the mirror and you know that this is true. Facing this naked truth was actually my "crossing of the Rubicon."* It was when I became passionately committed to the idea of Six Disciplines. That passion is directed toward helping small businesses not only *achieve* excellence, but *sustain* it.

This book describes six fundamental disciplines that help people learn how to overcome the obstacles that stand in the way of every growing business. The *Six Disciplines Methodology* (the Methodology) is different from other business improvement approaches in several ways.

---

\* The Rubicon was the river that formed the boundary between Gaul and the Roman Empire in 49 B.C. Caesar's decision to cross this river with his army was an act of war from which there was no turning back.

First, in contrast to the content of most business books, which focus 80% on principles and 20% on implementation, this book's content *is focused 20% on principles and 80% on implementation.* Remember: the problem for most of us isn't knowing *what* to do, it's doing it.

> Six Disciplines *distills and integrates what were designed as separate best practices into one cohesive whole.*

Second, the Methodology is *designed specifically for small businesses.* Whereas most best-selling business improvement books target large organizations, the focus of this book is small businesses. Examples abound throughout this volume; they were drawn straight from the experiences of many small business owners and entrepreneurs like yourself.

Third, the Six Disciplines Methodology is the first methodology to *distill and integrate what were designed as separate best practices into one cohesive whole.* It integrates various portions of strategic planning, continuous improvement, integrated learning, business process automation, performance management and quality management. We've stripped out concepts not needed for small businesses, and we've peppered this "synergistic mix" of best practices with time-tested truths and empowering tools, effectively unifying the "best of the best." Thousands of hours of research and more than 25 years of trial and error in business are the bedrock of the Six Disciplines Methodology, giving it a unified, 'hands-on,' experience-based quality.

Finally, this approach differs because, unlike older approaches, it is *designed with the Internet in mind.* Sustaining improvement requires each worker to learn how to align his or her work with company goals every day. For those who know how to use it, the Internet enables all workers everywhere to implement the best practices that can transform a company. The resulting achievements would have been undreamed of just a few short years ago.

## Not for Everyone

This book is not for everyone. It's for the *small* business: Aardvark, Inc., Cornerstone Management, Research for Action, and The Right Thing. These businesses typically employ 10 to 100 people and are found in every metropolitan city and every small town. They are often unknown outside their business area, but they collectively form the backbone of the economy. By specifically gearing the Six Disciplines Methodology to small business owners and entrepreneurs, and by offering it as a simple set of disciplines to understand, adopt, and apply, we're paving the way for small businesses to continually get better.

*This book is NOT for those who are looking for a quick fix. It is more of a "long-term fitness program," not a fad diet.*

Small businesses have many of the same challenges as larger ones. These include cash flow, recruiting and keeping good people, finding new customers and servicing them. On top of all that, they have to grow the business, deal with ever-changing technology, and keep an eye on the competition. And, as they say, "all before lunch."

What makes these challenges different for small businesses is finding answers within their time and resource constraints. This book is for those businesses that have all the challenges listed above, but don't have strategic planning departments, fully staffed HR organizations, large IT functions, and competitive research analysts to attack their challenges.

This book is *NOT* for those who are looking for a quick fix. The Six Disciplines Methodology is more of a "long-term fitness program," not a fad diet. This book *is* for those small businesses that have passed the initial stage of basic survival and are already good at what they do. These small businesses hunger to improve their current success in lasting ways and are willing to make the long-term investments required to do so.

In the first chapter, we probe what excellence really means and examine how the best small businesses differ from the rest, based on market research. We wrap up this section by reviewing some of the main barriers that stand in the way of small business excellence. Following that, we explore the importance, challenges, and advantages small businesses have.

In the main part of the book, each of the Six Disciplines is described, along with examples of how to implement them. Great efforts have been taken to ensure that the typical small business owner will understand the step-by-step approach described. At times, it may seem as though the number of things you are *not* doing is overwhelming; by the end of the book, however, your hope will be renewed as you begin to see that there is a systematic way to work on your business, making it an enduring success.

## How We Got Here

The Six Disciplines didn't suddenly materialize that day in Montana. They're the synthesis of many things learned from the expertise of numerous others, and my own experience, over the past 30 years. A brief history will give you a sense of the underpinnings of this book.

My first ten years of work experience were divided between two large organizations, which provided great insight into their strengths and weaknesses. Then, in 1980, two friends and I formed a software business known as Solomon Software, which focused on providing microcomputer-based accounting and business management software to small businesses.

*All my years of experience have taught me that the greatest attribute for any business leader is perseverance.*

It was a very successful business that grew to almost $60 million in sales and more than 60,000 customers over a period of 20 years. Because of industry consolidation, the Solomon business was sold and is now a part of Microsoft.*

Being co-founder and CEO of Solomon provided a tremendous learning experience for me. As a start-up, we struggled through the normal things most small businesses go through, from cash flow to people issues. We also worked with hundreds of small businesses that sold and supported our products, and tens of thousands of small businesses that were our end customers.

---

* In 2000 Solomon Software, the largest privately-held company in its market, merged with Great Plains, the largest publicly-held company in the same market. Shortly thereafter, acquisition discussions began with Microsoft for the combined company.

All my years of experience have taught me that the greatest attribute for any business leader is perseverance. As long as you keep trying, you'll keep learning. We experienced the highs of rapid growth and the lows of near bankruptcy, and both taught us much about what to do and what not to do.

We made lots of mistakes that cost us dearly. But we also did many things right. We were surrounded by creative and committed people who never quit. We sought the best advice we could get from consultants and other business people, and I personally read every business book I could get my hands on. It was in this real-world learning laboratory that we tested many different ideas. We found many that worked and many that weren't practical for a small business.

Following are some of my favorite resources and what I've been able to learn and adapt to small businesses:

From Michael Porter's many writings, I learned what "strategy" really is.

From Stephen Covey (*Principle-Centered Leadership* and *The 7 Habits of Highly Effective People*), I learned how to help individuals be more effective, and how to base business decisions on enduring principles.

From Michael Gerber (*The E Myth Revisited*), I learned about the confusion of roles all entrepreneurs go through as the business grows, and how they must transition from working *in* the business to working *on* it.

From Robert Kaplan and David Norton (*The Balanced Scorecard*, *The Strategy-Focused Organization*), I learned the value of communicating strategy to all levels of the organization, and getting organizations to develop the ability to focus on strategy execution as a core competence.

From Peter Senge (*The Fifth Discipline*), I learned the importance of approaching learning from a systems perspective.

From Jim Collins (*Built to Last, Good to Great*), I learned the importance of defining enduring values and living by them.

From Al Ries (*Focus* and several other books), I began to grasp the power of focus and the difficulty of saying "no."

From the Baldrige National Quality Program, I learned a great deal about how to manage for excellence systematically.

And finally, from the Bible, I learned how work fits into life and its purpose, and timeless truths about honesty, integrity, vision, diligence, stewardship, respect, priorities, wisdom, and character.

As a result, for the first time, a clear blueprint is offered in the pages of *Six Disciplines for Excellence* which shows small business leaders a step-by-step process for building an "Olympic" mentality where "the best just keep getting better."

The sale of Solomon opened the door that allowed the formation of the Six Disciplines team to pursue its passion of helping small business owners and operators achieve and *sustain* excellence.

Assembling a gifted team of experts who knew, respected and trusted each other, we began simplifying and integrating everything we'd learned about how to successfully operate a small business.

Over a period of four years, we invested fifty man-years of work and $10 million putting together a systematic, practical methodology that any small business leader with a genuine commitment to excellence can use. This methodology is described in the pages of this book.

# *Excellence*

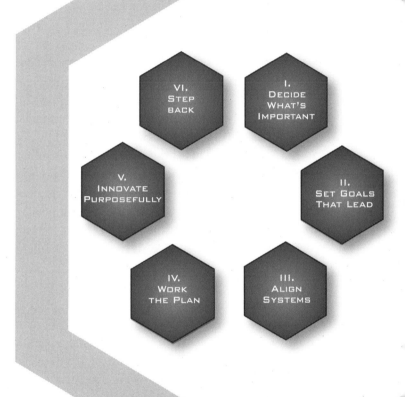

*Excellence, like beauty, is in the
eye of the beholder. . . . If you're
serious about pursuing excellence,
you must decide what excellence means
for your organization.*

## In the eye of the beholder

Excellence, like beauty, is in the eye of the beholder. Different people have different standards of excellence. If you're serious about pursuing excellence, you must decide what excellence means for your organization. You also need to be prepared to have your definition change, because as you learn and grow, your expectations will change as well. For businesses, it's useful to think of excellence in terms of two broad categories. The first is *customer excellence* and the second is *business excellence.*

*The point isn't that all businesses should be franchised; the point is that all businesses would benefit from taking the same holistic approach to excellence.*

*Customer excellence* has to do with those attributes that are of direct interest to customers, such as quality, price, reliability, taste, speed, etc. This is the type of excellence that wins product reviews and is featured in advertisements and promotional material. One of the primary functions of business strategy is choosing the dimensions of excellence in which the company will pursue leadership. For example, some businesses may focus their efforts on price leadership, some on full service, or some on convenience.

In contrast to *customer excellence, business excellence* is more transcendent and includes characteristics which are valued and highly desirable, regardless of business type: growth, profitability, predictability, longevity, etc. Business excellence and customer excellence are mutually dependent, because neither can be sustained without the other. In other words, satisfied customers drive business success and business success enables investment to satisfy customers.

We can learn much about achieving excellence—not only for our customers, but for ourselves—by taking a lesson from franchises.[1] The franchising concept has been wildly successful over the past 40 years. The appeal of a franchise is rooted in two promises. First, there's a very clear promise to the customer that's reflected in the brand. What comes to mind when you think of Starbucks?

Second, there's a promise to the business owner (franchisee) of a well-considered and proven business model that delivers on the customer promise. The result is two-fold. It delievers something of excellence to the customer—a steaming hot, fresh-brewed cup of coffee. It also delivers something of excellence to the business owner—a predictable return on investment, established business procedures, employee training, staffing plans, marketing strategies and interested customers.

The point isn't that all businesses should be franchised; the point is that *all* businesses would benefit from taking the same holistic approach to excellence that franchises take. Franchised businesses recognize that there really are *two* products—the product or service which the customer buys, and the business which the investor buys. The goal of *Six Disciplines for Excellence* is to help business leaders work on their businesses so *they* can be as satisfied with their businesses as their *customers are* with their products.

# Learning, Leading and Lasting

We believe excellent small businesses should have three primary attributes. First, they should be learning organizations. Individuals in the organization should be like members of an Olympic team, where the best keep learning how to get better.

Second, excellent organizations should have clearly defined areas in which they have chosen to be leaders, and they should be relentless in their pursuit of those areas.

Third, the ultimate mark of business excellence is the ability to sustain success—to handle the difficult times well and to continue to grow stronger and better. As you read on, you'll learn a step-by-step approach that helps your organization *learn*, *lead* and *last*.

## Learning

Because the standards for excellence we pursue in business continue to change, the ability to learn is an essential capability. Learning is the pathway to continually increasing levels of mastery. Even more basic than that, however, is the intrinsic motivation and satisfaction that comes from learning.

In *The Fifth Discipline*, Peter Senge says it this way:

> Real learning gets to the heart of what it means to be human. Through learning, we re-create ourselves. Through learning, we become able to do something we never were able to do. . . . This, then, is the basic meaning of a "learning organization"—an organization that is continually expanding its capacity to create its future.

He goes on to point out that the best word to reflect what's going on in learning organizations is the Greek word *metanoia,* which means "a shift of mind."

Metanoia is *not* about the pursuit of surface knowledge or knowledge of mere academic interest. Metanoia is a new truth that reasonates within you; it changes the way you think, what you do, and in some ways, who you are. This word is used in the Bible to describe the deep changes that come about in those who become followers of Jesus. Hence, the "shift of mind" found in a "spiritual rebirth" is *the* extreme illustration of what all learning is about: finding and applying new truth.

The leaders of a learning organization must help its members do the difficult work of choosing what the purpose and strategy of the organization are, and recognizing how they individually and collectively can contribute to that purpose. In a sense, organizations and individuals are both on a life-long quest to learn what they want to become and to figure out how to pursue that vision. The best leaders have a knack for fostering, by their own example, the kind of open environment where people have gained the courage to continually learn and be changed by what they learn.

> *Real learning gets to the heart of what it means to be human. Through learning, we re-create ourselves.*

For learning organizations to reach and expand their potential, they must help individuals do the same. *The following pages are filled with practical approaches for transforming small businesses into learning organizations.* Such organizations, essentially, are dedicated to helping their people learn how to work together as a team, how to contribute as individuals, and how to achieve their full potential.

## Leading

During a recent meeting of the school board (of which I am a member), we were interviewing candidates for an open position. "Susan" (not her real name) was one of the most energetic and passionate individuals I've ever come across in an interview, anywhere. She frequently referred to "excellence" in her answers to our questions: "a desire to be excellent;" "a desire to encourage teachers to be excellent;" "a desire to encourage students to be excellent;" etc.

At one point, someone in the meeting finally asked Susan, "What's your definition of excellence?" There was silence, and then a stumbling answer about "attitude" and "effort" and "enthusiasm." Although I believe Susan clearly has a passion for excellence, she hasn't yet determined what *it* is. As stated earlier, achieving excellence begins with deciding what excellence means to you or to your organization.

*The reality of life is that we can't "have it all," and if we try to get it all, we end up getting very little.*

I remember, as CEO of Solomon, year after year, I'd write goal statements like, ". . . to be the leader in the accounting software market." Over the years, we learned we needed to be more specific in terms of defining our leadership. What types of leadership did we want (full services, price, convenience)? In what markets (type of company, geography, etc.) did we want to lead?

One of the most difficult parts of being a "leading" organization is making choices between one path of leadership and another. Most of us are reluctant to make such choices, because it eliminates options and it holds us responsible to succeed in that one chosen area.

In his book, *The Call*, Os Guinness describes a similar challenge for graduate students making career choices. He says, "Graduate students confront it (the challenge of choosing a path) when the excitement of 'the world is my oyster' is chilled by the thought that opening up one choice means closing down others."

The reality of life is that we can't "have it all," and if we try to get it all, we end up getting very little. Oh, how hard it is to say "yes" to the areas we want to lead in, and to say "no" to the others. The courage and wisdom to do so is one of the major factors that separate leading organizations from the rest of the pack.

We, as business leaders, do great damage when we stir up the passions people have for pursuing excellence if we haven't yet figured out what our business strategy is—what dimensions of leadership the organization is going to pursue. General conversation about excellence *without focused directions for action* just gives people a spark of hope that's quickly dashed, because passion that's not applied to a purpose doesn't lead to excellence.

In summary, committing to excellence means committing the organization to being a leader in some area that's important to customers, and then pursuing that leadership relentlessly. The Six Disciplines Methodology is designed to help organizations *choose the areas in which they want to lead and, more importantly, to help people align their creative talents and their energy toward that purpose.* With the proper focus and clarity, the potential of the organization will be unleashed and expanded for the benefit and reward of both the customers and everyone in the organization.

## Lasting

There's a big difference between an "excellent book" and an "excellent author." The evaluation of a single book is self-contained; it stands on its own. We would normally think, however, of an excellent author as one who wrote over a long period of time and demonstrated the ability to produce excellent books on a repeatable basis. We've all witnessed or participated in moments of excellence: a great round of golf, a superb musical performance, or a terrific sales quarter. However, a great round of golf isn't the same as a great season of golf, nor is it the same as a great career in golf.

If the ultimate measure of business excellence is learning and leading for a long time, then how long is "enough?" Is success for ten years enough? Twenty years? Fifty years? In their best-selling book, *Built to Last*, authors Jim Collins and Jerry Porras studied businesses that survived at least 100 years, in order to learn more about enduring companies. In the end, this question of "how long" is one only you can answer.

When it comes to improvement methodologies, whether for businesses or individuals, experience teaches us to be skeptical. During the last few years that I was leading the Solomon organization, I co-facilitated Stephen Covey's *The 7 Habits of Highly Effective People* for the whole company in about 25 small-group sessions.

This three-day training got rave reviews from our team members. I had notes from wives thanking us for helping their husbands. We had requests from employees' spouses to attend. The book by the same name has been on the best-seller list for almost 10 years. The bottom line is that *Seven Habits* is filled with good principles and practices that help make individuals more effective, both personally and professionally.

*Passion that's not applied to a purpose doesn't lead to excellence.*

However, I've made it a practice to ask people who were in one of my sessions if they're still following the prescribed approach. Some lasted a year, some two, but no one I've spoken to lasted three years. Remember what Eric said at the business improvement conference in Whitefish, Montana? "This material is outstanding—but I probably won't be doing anything about it two years from now."

This fellow isn't alone. We've *all* undertaken programs we didn't stick with—whether a quality program at work or a fitness regimen at home. He was simply expressing the largely unspoken *and* unresolved sentiment—or is it dilemma?—of millions.

Seeing such a pervasive pattern begs the question "Why?" As you read on, we'll begin to answer this question and show you what to do about it.

# How the Best Differ from the Rest

In trying to better quantify factors that contribute to excellence, we surveyed more than 300 small businesses (each with 10 to 100 employees) that included a range of service, product and project-oriented companies. The participants, who were all owners or senior leaders in their organizations, rated their businesses on many different areas of performance.

For this analysis, we evaluated organizations based on a combined factor of growth and profitability. We thoroughly analyzed the results and looked for areas where the lowest- and highest-performing organizations were the most different. We found several areas where the contrasts were significant (see figure below). Let's review the top five, in order of importance.

## % Difference in Characteristics of Highest- Versus Lowest-Performing Small Businesses

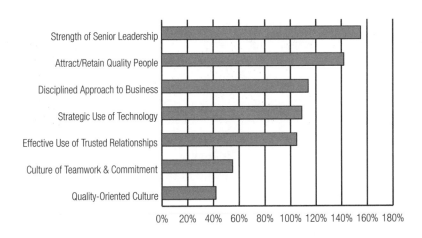

## 1. Strength of the Leadership Team

In our research, the leaderships teams of top-performing organizations rated 155% higher than the lower performers. There were two primary factors evaluated in this rating. The first was *the ability of leadership to define a clear vision* for the company. For full effectiveness, the vision needs to be well-defined and explained in a way so people connect with it and are motivated by it.

*People go in the direction leadership is walking, not pointing.*

The second major factor was *appropriate involvement of leadership in leading and supporting projects that are strategic to the organization*. People in organizations (and everywhere, for that matter) read the *actions* of leadership to determine what's important and what's valued. Strategy statements and posters by themselves are ineffective.

One client expressed it this way: "People go in the direction leadership is walking, not pointing." The research suggests that the leadership of high-performing organizations know where they want the organization to go, make sure everyone else understands the direction, and are visibly engaged in helping the organization move in that direction.

## 2. Attract and Retain Quality People

Top-performing organizations are rated 142% stronger at attracting and retaining high-quality people than the lowest performers. Finding people, motivating them, compensating them, keeping them focused, and keeping them satisfied are always hot topics in focus group research and in conversations we have with business owners. This is one of the most dynamic challenges for all businesses. The best small businesses have figured out that success in this area starts with recruiting.

It's very hard to overcome a hiring mistake, and excellent businesses leave nothing to chance in making their hires. In addition, the top small businesses use the strength of their leadership teams, their stability, their sense of purpose, and the quality of people around them to retain people once they're on board.

## 3. Disciplined Approach to Business

For some people, the old-fashioned idea of being "disciplined" is a turn-off. But that's not so for the top performers. They're rated 114 % stronger than the lowest performers when it comes to taking a disciplined approach to business. Instead of "shooting from the hip," top-performing small businesses take the time to plan well in advance for changes that are likely to affect their organizations. They do so because the people in the higher-performing organizations truly believe that planning is a critical factor in achieving company success, as opposed to just being a "high overhead exercise."

However, top performers are also very *practical*, in that they value *planning* more than voluminous *planning documents*. Eisenhower said it this way: "In preparing for battle I have always found that plans are useless, but planning is indispensable." High-performing small businesses work at being realistic; they "sweat the details." They're careful about not forming or setting their expectations until they've learned enough about the situation at hand to know whether or not those expectations are reasonable. They have a culture where people don't go off "half-cocked." They're disciplined about the commitments they make.

## 4. Strategic Use of Technology

High-performing organizations give more emphasis than lower-performing companies to using technology to impact the business in strategic ways (109 percent more, according to our analysis). Underlying this rating is the greater use of long-term technology plans aimed at delivering competitive advantage.

Such organizations have developed a culture that figures out ways to deploy technology, not for technology's sake, but to better serve their strategy. They're also willing and able to invest to make it happen. This investment includes not just the technology itself, but the training to make sure they maximize the utilization of the technology.

## 5. Effective Use of Trusted Relationships

Another area where high-performing organizations stand out is their ability to utilize the expertise of external organizations. Top performers are rated more than 100 percent stronger than the lower-performing organizations in this area. Because of their size, small businesses have more generalists than specialists in their organizations and, as a result, can make decisions quickly, while keeping overhead costs lower.

High-performing small businesses have learned to supplement their internal expertise by building trusted relationships with the right types of organizations. This allows them to cost-effectively buy the amount of expertise they need when they need it. One example from our research indicated that high-performing organizations rate their satisfaction with the business advice they get from their external CPA much higher than low-performing organizations.

We believe there are three primary reasons why such organizations are more effective using outside expertise. First, high-performing organizations are stronger financially and can afford to hire the best. In addition, they can afford to make contractor selection mistakes and learn from them. Some of my toughest learning experiences in business have been related to picking the right (or "wrong") advisors.

Second, high-performing organizations have a clearer picture of where they want to go. They have a clear vision and strong leadership, and are disciplined in their approach to business. All these factors make it easier to focus a consultant or advisor on something specific. Ill-defined projects are a guaranteed formula for failure.

Third, high-performing organizations have stronger learning cultures that allow them to do a better job of listening to and applying expert advice. This feeds on itself: the more they listen and learn, the better they perform, and the better they perform, the better advisors they can hire.

All these factors together give top-performing small businesses the great advantage of being able to utilize outside talent when needed.

## Other Factors

Other contributing factors to top performance turned up in research: attitude, teamwork, commitment, quality-oriented culture, etc. They all play a part, but the five just described highlight the areas of greatest difference. As you read through the *Six Disciplines for Excellence*, you'll come to understand how to develop further each of the characteristics of top performers in a step-by-step way. But first, let's examine in the next section some of the barriers to achieving the durable kind of excellence we're all striving for.

# Barriers to Lasting Excellence

It has been my experience, in working with many types of small businesses, that the barriers that keep us from achieving the kind of business excellence that *lasts* are deeply rooted and won't be removed with "quick fixes." Stephen Covey, after reviewing the success literature over past centuries, makes the following observation about such approaches:

> I began to feel more and more that much of the success literature of the past 50 years was superficial. It was filled with social image consciousness, techniques and quick fixes—with social band-aids and aspirin that addressed acute problems and sometimes even appeared to solve them temporarily, but left the underlying chronic problems untouched to fester and resurface time and time again.[2]

Following are six fundamental barriers to excellence that, if not addressed on an ongoing and systematic basis, will cause organizational performance to decline.

## 1. Poorly Understood Strategy

Most organizations have a strategy*, but most people in most organizations do *not* understand what that strategy is. When people don't know where the organization is going, they're like Alice in Wonderland:

---

\* When referring to an organization's *strategy,* we mean its mission, values, vision, strategic position, long-term goals and near-term goals that collectively answer the most fundamental questions about who the company is, where it's headed, and how it will get there.

Alice came to a fork in the road. "Which road do I take?" she asked.
"Where do you want to go?" responded the Cheshire cat.
"I don't know," Alice answered.
"Then," said the cat, "it doesn't matter."[3]

This well-known exchange makes it obvious that if we want our people to take the right road, we must make sure they understand where we're going. One study[4] revealed that 85% of leadership teams spend less than one hour per month discussing strategy. Is it any wonder people don't understand strategy?

It must be clear that this barrier isn't focused on the quality of the strategy itself. Studies indicate that up to 90% of strategies fail due to execution.[5] A terrible strategy could produce terrible results, but experience teaches that most of us are better at formulating strategy than getting people to understand it.

Strategy-related warning signs:

❑ Mission, values, and vision are just "window dressing;" your people don't connect to it.

❑ Goals don't communicate who, what, when and why.

❑ Goals aren't balanced among financial, customer, production and people assets.

❑ An inability to say "no" to all but the essential priorities of the organization. Saying everything is a "high priority" in reality means nothing is.

❑ The strategy isn't written down.

❑ Equating *volume* of strategy documentation with strategy *quality*. Three or four pages are enough.

## 2. Weak Strategy Execution

My first job out of high school was working at a factory that produced plastic containers for products like chip dip, cottage cheese, etc. The engineering department would design the cups to customer specifications, balancing cup size, required wall strength, weight and cost.

A different group of engineers designed, maintained and set up the machines for new product lines.

To be a success, this company had to know how to engineer cups *and* the machines to produce cups. So it is with a business. You must not only work on designing the service or products your customers want, but you must *also* work on the business (the *machine*) that produces them. Just as a machine has a blueprint, the business strategy serves as a blueprint that tells how the business should work: what and how much it needs to produce, how fast, how many resources should be used to run it, how to maintain it, etc.

One of the major barriers to achieving lasting excellence is how little formal effort organizations put into learning how to *execute strategy*. One author refers to this ability as "making clocks instead of telling time,"[6] another "being strategy-focused,"[7] another "working *on* the business instead of *in* it."[8] Whatever you call it, this capability is critical, because service offerings and product lines come and go, but the *core competence to define and execute a strategy is forever*.

Warning signs related to not being "strategy focused":

❑ People don't understand the difference between working *on* the business and *in* it.

❑ There's no defined process for working *on* the business itself.

❑ The target customer isn't clearly identified, nor are the promises being made to the customer.

❑ People don't understand the strategy, and goals communication is infrequent and inadequate.

❑ People, systems, processes, policies and/or capital are not aligned with the strategy.

❑ Creative energy is low. People don't see how to contribute, nor do they see how to tap their own creative abilities.

❑ Reward systems are misaligned with goals. Incentive systems aren't working.

## 3. Unchecked Organizational Entropy

Webster's Dictionary defines *entropy* as "a measure of the degree of disorder in a system." Physicists have determined that "entropy"always increases and available energy always diminishes in a closed system. A layman's example of this can be demonstrated by placing an ice cube in a glass of warm water. The law of entropy states that the ice melts as the heat of the water is transferred to the frozen water, and eventually the temperatures of the two forms of water equalize. Think of the ice cube as having *order* (the crystalline cube), which came from the energy applied in a freezer. A melting ice cube is the process of equalizing the degree of disorder between the water and ice.

*Once a small business makes plans, the chaos of everything changing around it gradually erodes those plans, like the warm water melts the ice.*

Businesses are "systems" and they're subject to forces similar to entropy. Once a small business makes plans, the chaos of everything changing around it gradually erodes those plans, like the warm water melts the ice. An organization must have a systematic and ongoing way to offset these forces, or it will eventually become ineffective to the point that its survival will be at stake. Or, using a different analogy, Stephen Covey once said, "We are too busy driving to get gas."

The first step in dealing effectively with the forces of organizational entropy is to become aware that it's going on and to begin applying offsetting forces to counteract it. In other words, we need to regularly put in some gas.

Organizational entropy warning signs:

❑ A lot of red tape is required to get things done—it takes too long or costs too much.

❑ Inadequate time is allotted for planning.

❑ People don't know what's expected of them.

❑ People aren't held accountable for their responsibilities.

❑ Results aren't measured, so decay goes unnoticed or unchallenged and learning is inhibited.

❑ Inadequate resources are allocated to keep systems/processes working properly.

## 4. Lack of a Systematic Approach

According to Peter Senge,[9] "vision without 'systems thinking' ends up painting lovely pictures of the future with no deep understanding of the forces that must be mastered to move from here to there."

> *Vision without "systems thinking" ends up painting lovely pictures of the future with no deep understanding of the forces that must be mastered to move from here to there.*

We're so surrounded by "systems" that we don't really see them. Our bodies are a system of systems—circulatory, respiratory, and digestive—all tightly integrated to work as a whole. Businesses are "systems," but with the added complexity that they're changing every day in ways we may not understand.

When a business is started, there may be one person in whom all the "systems" reside. Because they're all internal to one person, they may not even be discretely recognized. Sales, marketing, production, accounting and sweeping the floors are all handled by one person. There are no misunderstandings. Ten years later, however, there may be separate departments for each of these functions.

*Thinking holistically about the business*—how to make all its components, people, processes, policies, key measures, assets and strategies work together to meet the promises made to customers and other stakeholders in a repeatable and predictable fashion—*is key to achieving lasting excellence.*

Warning signs regarding lack of a systematic approach:

❑ Critical business processes are missing or poorly defined, e.g., planning, recruiting and training.

❑ Processes aren't measured, so there's no way to evaluate the effectiveness of new ideas.

❑ People don't understand the measures that are critical to company performance or their own.

❑ Trended data necessary to support long-term learning are either absent or insufficient.

❑ Basic information about the behavior and satisfaction of stake-holders (customers, team members, vendors, etc.) is unavailable.

❑ The business feels like it's in chaos most of the time.

## 5. Impractical Implementation Methods

Small businesses don't have large, dedicated staffs devoted full-time to strategy, planning, learning or IT (Information Technology). As a result, improvement methods and systems that aren't designed for small businesses become too cumbersome for them to implement. They require too much investment to learn, and the ongoing cost of using them is too great. That fact does *not* stop sales forces from hawking their wares at the front doors of small businesses, or the over-eager entrepreneur from attempting to implement the "latest and greatest" in his company.

Many small business leaders have learned the hard way that using consultants and processes that serve large companies often result in long, expensive projects that don't provide a very good return on investment and waste a lot of time. The moral is: *small businesses need to choose wisely when deciding to implement improvement methods and systems, focusing on "fit" rather than "form."*

Warning signs regarding use of impractical methods include:

❑ Systems and processes that produce lots of paperwork. Small businesses need increased understanding, not increased paperwork.

❑ Systems and processes that don't fit together well—information is missing or hard to get, resulting in a lot of work having to be redone.

❑ Approaches are loaded with unique and complex terminology, instead of terms that have plain meaning for all who use them.

❏ Methods and processes are focused primarily on *setting* direction, not *executing* it.

❏ There's a "big bang" approach to implementation, instead of a "learn as you go" approach.

## 6. People Are Not Engaged

An "engaged worker" is one who's personally committed to the goals of the company. Unfortunately, "90% of the time, what passes for commitment is compliance."[10] However, people have tremendous reservoirs of endurance, creativity, passion, energy and enthusiasm for the things they believe in.

If you can't get the people in the organization engaged in moving beyond product excellence to business excellence, then no improvement approach can last. Therefore, an approach that's going to work over the long haul *must engage the individuals in the organization.*

Warnings signs of people not being engaged:

❏ Poor understanding about how an individual's work connects to the purposes of the company.

❏ Poor, limited communication with team members about the purpose of the organization, its strategies, challenges, strengths, weaknesses, etc.

❏ Expectations aren't properly set in the minds of all staff members, resulting in disappointment, frustration or resentment.

❏ There's an imbalanced focus on short-term achievement, instead of long-term thinking.

❏ People are hired who are not aligned with your mission and values, resulting in a weakening of company culture.

Although small businesses have some unique barriers to achieving lasting excellence, they also have some distinct advantages. The next chapter explores those advantages.

## CHAPTER TWO

# *The Small Business Advantage*

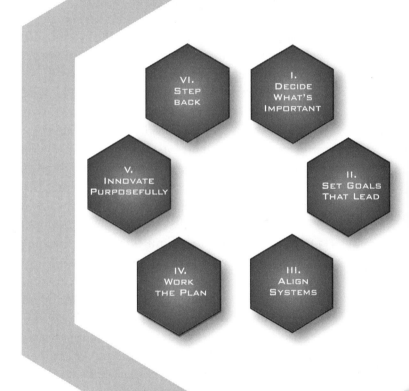

*Small businesses are different than large businesses . . . having to leverage differences is what competitive advantage is all about.*

## The Importance of Small Businesses

Several years ago, a friend told me that people who start businesses are heroes. Although that was the first time I thought about it, I've hardly stopped thinking about it since. There are few opportunities to do more good in life than through a well-run business, large or small.

The importance of small business owners grows clearer when you realize that small businesses are the spawning ground for our whole economy. More than 400,000 new businesses starting every year. 98% of all businesses in the U.S. have fewer than 100 employees, and those businesses employ 40 million people, generating sales in excess of $5 trillion![1]

These numbers dramatically demonstrate the vital role every small business plays. But the idea of a small business owner being a "hero" hits home even *more*, when you think about the impact made on a smaller scale. Business owners give individuals—real people with names and faces—a chance to provide for their families, and an environment where people can learn and grow and express their God-given creativity and talents.

*80% of all new business start-ups are out of business within five years.*

Most people will spend half their waking hours at work. To a business leader who takes the risk of owning and building a business, this is both exciting and sobering. It's exciting because of the great opportunity to do something meaningful in the lives of other people. It's sobering because of the responsibility it implies, derived from the understanding that oftentimes a single decision may significantly affect the lives of many others. Those who take this stewardship seriously truly *are* heroes!

## The Top Challenges of Small Businesses

Even though small businesses collectively generate $5 trillion in sales in the U.S., the biggest challenge of an individual small business is "survival."

*80% of all new business start-ups are out of business within five years.* And if that doesn't get your attention, 80% of the 20% that survive the first five years don't survive the second five![2] That means, on the average, 960 out of 1,000 businesses that start this year will *not* be around in 10 years. This is proof that you're in an elite group if you've just survived (let alone "thrived")! *What makes it so hard?*

After working with thousands of small businesses for many years, we've learned that the top issues small businesses struggle with can be grouped into the following general categories:

1. **Financial Issues**. Includes finding adequate funding, getting billings out on time, collections, and credit management. In a word, a top problem is CASH.

2. **Customer Issues**. Includes understanding what the customer really wants, finding enough of the right kind of customers and keeping them happy, so they don't turn to competitors.

3. **Production Issues**. Varies by type of business. In general, businesses of all types struggle with being able to give customers what they want, when they want it, at the price they want it, and at the highest quality levels. Doing this predictably and repeatedly is a tremendous challenge.

4. **People Issues**. Includes finding the right people, keeping them happy, compensating them, motivating them, training them, and getting them to deliver quality work.

5. **Limited Resources**. Small businesses usually don't have large cash reserves, dedicated research departments, fully-staffed IT functions, strategic planning functions, etc., to address challenges or opportunities.

6. **Growth**. Growth brings the challenge of change. It's one thing to get good at something when you can hone your skills through repetition; it's a completely different challenge to get good and stay good when the rules of the game keep changing with regard to competition, customer expectations, globalization, people issues, finance, technology, etc.

At times, these challenges can be daunting, indeed overwhelming. It's encouraging to know that the struggles we encounter every day are normal. *All* small businesses face them. And like other "heroes," we continue the fight because the cause is worth it.

## The Small Business Advantage

Those who have worked both in small and large organizations have a much better appreciation for how fundamentally different large companies are from small ones. Each has its strengths, and the savvy small business owner understands what those are and takes advantage of them aggressively. They include:

### 1. Connecting People to Purpose

People are creatures of emotion and reason. The best performers want to belong to an organization that's on a mission, and they need to see how they're contributing to that mission. Small businesses have an enormous advantage in their ability to help people connect to the purpose of the organization, AND enable them to see that what they're doing is contributing to that purpose in a meaningful way.

*The biggest problem with communication is the illusion that it has taken place.*

This importance was hammered home to me in a lunch meeting with "Sandy," who recently moved to a much larger organization. She commented, "It's just not the same. I feel like a number. It seems like nothing I do will make a real difference in anything. And if it did, it probably wouldn't be noticed."

Another businessman understood how to use this advantage. He set up a 50% profit-sharing program in which a portion of the profits was retained by the employees themselves and the remainder was given away *by the employees* to charitable causes. This small team was one of the most productive, spirited and lively groups I've ever known.

## 2. Effective Communication

Someone wise once said, "The biggest problem with communication is the illusion that it has taken place."[3] The larger the organization is, the greater this *illusion* becomes. As organizations grow, communication challenges grow, as well; in fact, they grow dramatically faster (exponentially) than the organization headcount does. To illustrate this, the following table shows that when there are only three people in an organization, there are three possible communication combinations (persons A&B, A&C, or B&C). However, if you grow a 3-person organization to 25, there is an 8-fold increase in the number of people but a 100-fold increase in the communications combinations! A 100-person organization is *33 times* the size of a 3-person organization but *1650 times* more complex from a communications perspective.

| # PEOPLE | # POSSIBLE DIFFERENT INTERACTIONS | INCREASE IN PEOPLE | INCREASE IN COMMUNICATIONS COMPLEXITY |
|---|---|---|---|
| 3 | 3 | - | |
| 25 | 300 | 8 x | 100 x |
| 50 | 1,225 | 17 x | 408 x |
| 100 | 4,950 | 33 x | 1,650 x |
| 1,000 | 499,500 | 333 x | 166,500 x |

Organizations respond to this increased complexity by creating business units, divisions, departments, groups, etc. In other words, more layers. When you add to this challenge the fact that experts believe that 55% of communication takes place through nonverbal body language, it becomes clear how great an advantage it is to be able to gather everyone together in one place quickly and easily.

## 3. Timely Decision-Making

Decision-making is also dramatically different in smaller organizations. As organizations increase in size, the leadership team moves from *generalists* to *specialists* who are responsible for a particular business area. Because top decision-makers in a larger organization are more insulated from the day-to-day activities of the company, they no longer have the first-hand knowledge to make decisions without the input of several other *specialists*. The result is slower and often lower-quality decisions.

> In smaller organizations, a much greater percentage of employees work with customers directly.

In small businesses, however, there are fewer decision-makers, and they're so close to customers, employees and daily operations that they can get a sense of whether a decision is right or wrong very quickly.

## 4. Customer Intimacy

In smaller organizations, a much greater percentage of employees work with customers directly. This includes the leaders in the organization, who frequently are still involved in closing sales or supporting clients. This kind of closeness to customers means the people in the company know customer issues and they can spot changing market needs earlier. And because their decision-making is more timely, they can act on those trends earlier.

## 5. Attracting Team Members

Small businesses don't have to take a back seat to larger organizations when recruiting top people (and they *shouldn't*). The advantages already discussed—connection to purpose, effective communication, timely decision-making, and customer intimacy—when explained very carefully to all candidates, can provide a great draw to the most talented prospects. It's important to recognize that many people who haven't worked in large companies may not understand these advantages. Yet for people who *are* experienced in larger organizations, the advantages will be obvious and often quite welcome.

The point of all this isn't that small businesses are *better* than big businesses, but that they're *different* than big businesses. And learning to leverage differences is what competitive advantage is all about. Yet many small businesses don't consciously develop strategies that use their advantages. As you read on, you'll begin to see how the Six Disciplines Methodology helps small businesses systematically take advantage of their strengths.

## CHAPTER THREE

# The Six Disciplines Methodology

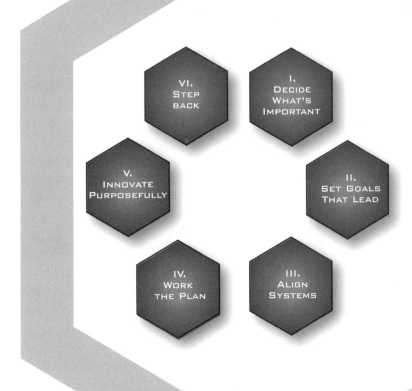

*The Six Disciplines Methodology puts together, into one integrated step-by-step process, what has formerly been thought of as different disciplines.*

Have you ever played golf? Those who have know that hitting a golf ball well involves doing several basic things right. First, you must select the correct club for the shot you're making; next, you must address the ball properly, placing yourself the right distance from the ball and aligning yourself to your target.

After that, you must grip the club correctly, and finally, you must swing the club on the right club path, keeping your left arm straight in the backswing. You may then execute a well-paced downswing so that your hips and arms lead your wrists through the contact with the ball.

For those of you who've tried it, you know it isn't easy, because you MUST do ALL these things TOGETHER exactly right every time, or the ball won't go where you want it to (trust me, I know).

Overcoming the barriers to lasting excellence in business is even more challenging. This is because you must not only learn to do several different things *all at the same time* but, unlike golf, you must do them with a *group of people* instead of by yourself.

In addition, in business if you want *lasting* excellence it is not enough to get good results, you must know what causes those results. Such knowledge is a prerequisite for responding to the relentless changes that all businesses face. To help organizations understand how sustainable their current performance is, we have developed the Business Excellence Sustainability Model.

| Business Excellence Sustainability Model | | | | | | |
|---|---|---|---|---|---|---|
| **MAJOR DISCIPLINE AREAS** | **CAPABILITY LEVELS** | | | | | |
| | UNDEFINED (0) | DEFINED (1) | ALIGNED (2) | MEASURED (3) | IMPROVEMENT (4) | PROVEN (5) |
| **I. Decide What's Important** (mission, values, vision…) | | | ✓ | | | |
| **II. Set Goals That Lead** (1 to 5 year goals, with measures, targets…) | | ✓ | | | | |
| **III. Align Systems** (processes, policies, people, technology…) | ✓ | | | | | |
| **IV. Work the Plan** (individual plans, measures, review, assessment…) | ✓ | | | | | |
| **V. Innovate Purposefully** (problem solving, idea ownership, recognition) | | ✓ | | | | |
| **VI. Step Back** (competitive, industry, stakeholders, measures) | | ✓ | | | | |

The *rows* in this model represent major categories of processes that most businesses need in order to function well. (for a more complete analysis these categories would be broken into much more detail than shown here). The *columns* represent levels of capability within each of these process areas—the levels range from "0" to "5" and are described below:

> **Undefined** (0)—not defined at all, poorly defined or if defined, not followed. Heavy dependency on the individuals doing the work. If those people are unavailable the capability is gone.

> **Defined** (1)—Processes are defined in writing and executed consistently. However, the objectives of the processes are not evaluated against company priorities, so the degree of alignment is not known.

> **Aligned** (2)—Process objectives were designed to align with the long-term priorities of the company and are monitored so that they stay aligned.

**Measured (3)**—Measures for determining the effectiveness of the process are defined, captured and presented in trended fashion for the purpose of evaluating proposed innovations to the process.

**Improvement (4)**—The interaction of well-trained people (who understand company priorities) with defined, aligned and measured processes stimulate on-going improvement and integration of best practices.

**Proven (5)**—Level 4 has been achieved for five consecutive years, proving that Level 4 improvement is sustainable through the inevitable changes in people, business priorities and market conditions.

Even most high performing small businesses will score low on this model because all too often their success is based on the heroics of a handful of amazing people. "Star performers" that know what to do themselves, but they haven't developed repeatable approaches that others can use to achieve similar results. For small businesses this isn't surprising because most start-ups achieve their initial positive cash flow through the heroics of a few people.

However such a mode of operation can't lead to the kind of excellence that lasts because either those key individuals eventually leave the organization (sometimes unexpectedly) or more frequently the organization grows to the point that the capacity of such individuals is totally consumed. They either burnout or their quality of work drops.

Another challenge, that's not obvious, is the interdependence between the rows (major process areas). All of these processes are interrelated and you can't get to level 5 in one process area and be at zero on another. Therefore progress in one area has to be synchronized with progress in another.

The Six Disciplines Methodology is just that—a synchronized, systematic approach for building your business to the point that you can sustain excellence. It puts together into one integrated step-by-step process, what has formerly been thought of as different disciplines—strategic planning, quality management, integrated learning,

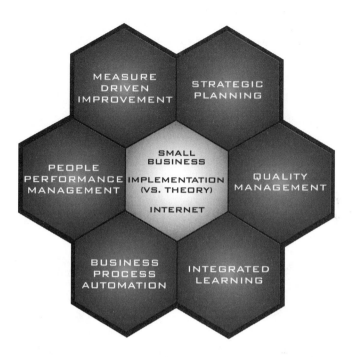

business process automation, people performance management and measure-driven improvement.

Continuing with the analogy, when learning golf, you start by learning one part of your swing at a time. Then gradually, as you master each piece, you get better and better at putting all the pieces together into an integrated swing that works.

In the following chapters, we're going to explain the individual pieces of the Methodology. To start, there are six fundamental disciplines, with a chapter on each. Within each chapter, we break that discipline down into a series of "steps." Each step has a brief explanation of its purpose, some hints and tips for using that step, the process for executing the step, and some examples to help understand what the step produces.

Be aware that reading about each discipline separately doesn't make you good at using the Methodology, any more than taking five golf lessons on different fundamentals of the game makes you a good golfer. In the end, you have to learn how to use all the disciplines *together*, and the only way to truly learn this is by doing.

You can think of the Six Disciplines Methodology as a series of annual, quarterly, weekly and daily repeatable cycles which, with each successive pass, helps your team learn how to better root out the barriers to lasting excellence.

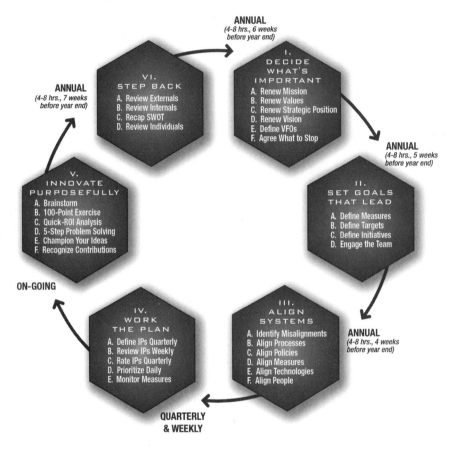

The *Six Disciplines for Excellence* are:

## I. Decide What's Important

The foundation of all strategy formulation is deciding what is most important to your organization (and by implication what's not important) so that the allocation of resources—time, money and creativity—can all be aimed toward this end. In this discipline, organizations systematically and regularly review and renew their mission, values, strategic position, vision, their most vital few objectives (VFOs), as well as agreeing what to stop doing.

## II. Set Goals That Lead

Well-defined goals are among the most effective communications tools available to any leader—yet most leaders don't know how to set goals that *lead their people in the right direction*. The purpose of this discipline is to produce annual goals that are clear and measurable. Pursuing these goals will lead the people in the organization to align their activities with the *VFOs* set in Discipline I. The result is a brief company goals statement that every team member should understand.

## III. Align Systems

One of the greatest barriers that any organization faces in pursuing its goals is itself. ("I have seen the enemy and he is us") For many businesses, the *systems* that make up the business—its policies, processes, technologies, measures, and people—are often at cross purposes with the priorities of the company. Why is this so? Because most organizations do not have an organized approach to keep their systems aligned with their strategy. Discipline III, purposefully sequenced after Disciplines I and II, taps the knowledge of the whole workforce to identify the areas where the company will get the greatest return on its investment in policies, processes, measures, technologies and people.

## IV. Work the Plan

One of the greatest organizational learning tools ever invented is the individual quarterly plan. In this discipline, every person in the company works with his/her team leader to develop *Individual Plans (IPs)* for the upcoming quarter. These goals are reviewed and checked for alignment with company goals. This quarterly plan serves as a timesaving template for a weekly *IP Status* report. The result is that every individual in the company learns how to set goals, understand company priorities, take responsibility for their own goals, report progress and use their innovative capability to solve problems.

## V. Innovate Purposefully

Innovation is just another name for *problem-solving,* and everyone in the company has the ability to solve problems. This discipline is unlike the rest in that it provides tools and principles that are used throughout the other disciplines to help people set clear goals. These goals will align with company priorities, and then employees will use their innate creativity to meet or beat those goals. Empowering principles, such as *Embracing Constraints* and *Taking Informed Risks,* plus tools like the *100-Point Exercise* and *5-Step Problem Solving,* are but a few examples of what's included in Discipline V. Like the yeast in bread, Discipline V is a small, but critical ingredient spread throughout the entire loaf.

## VI. Step Back

Sometimes we really "can't see the forest for the trees." This annual discipline helps the whole organization *Step Back* from the press of everyday business and gain perspective on business performance, and the factors that affect business performance. We do this through a series of "discovery exercises," exploring *Externals* (competitors, industry, economic) and *Internals* (goal performance, stakeholder feedback, measures, etc.).

In addition to the organization as a whole stepping back, all individual team members are encouraged to do the same by providing input on each other's performances. This is achieved by completing a *360°* and an annual performance appraisal for each team member.

## What Makes This Methodology Work?

Recall that a study referenced earlier showed that the reasons most businesses fail is not strategy, but its execution. Knowing what to do isn't the problem: doing it is! *The Six Disciplines Methodology has been specifically designed and optimized for execution.* Hence, when it's diligently and consistently applied, this Methodology will help organizations achieve lasting excellence.

So that you better understand how it's crafted to do this, we've included the design assumptions and requirements used in developing the Six Disciplines Methodology. Starting in succeeding chapters, we'll provide step-by-step examples of how the Methodology is used.

## Methodology Design Assumptions

1. **Those in the Business Know It Best**. The Methodology is optimized to draw priorities and decisions out of the people in the business, as opposed to suggesting what their priorities should be.

2. **A Commitment to Discipline Exists in the Organization.** Leadership, at a minimum, is committed to taking an orderly approach to learning how to plan and execute better. There's the willingness to pay the short-term price for long-term gains.

3. **People Trust Each Other**. People are sufficiently committed to the organization and each other, that they're willing to work through conflicts and challenges with openness and honesty. An authoritarian, high-control-based culture will not work with this Methodology.

4. **People Are Born to Innovate**. Innovation is just another name for problem-solving, and every worker has the innate ability and desire to solve problems.

5. **Principles for Excellence Transcend Type of Business.** Even though product and service businesses are very different, they're still made up of people. Setting priorities, and helping people learn to innovate and meet those priorities, involves basic disciplines that can be applied to all types of businesses.

## Methodology Design Requirements

1.  **Make It Easier.** Keep exercise time short, reduce paper and red tape. Assemble the practical parts of strategic planning, quality management, integrated learning, business process automation, people performance management, and measure-driven improvement into a single solution.

2.  **Think Holistically About the Business.** People must see the business as a whole and see how their roles relate to that whole. Their view must encompass both short- and long-term time horizons, as well as the perspectives of customer, employee, supplier and owner.

3.  **Be Process-Driven.** Organizations must learn how to build well-defined and measurable processes that are critical to the success of the business. Having key processes well-defined, managed, and measured stimulates innovation, helps offset organizational entropy and provides foundational support for lasting excellence.

4   **Establish Business Habits.** Establish a few key daily, weekly, quarterly and annual routines company-wide, to offset every individual's tendency to get distracted. Establishing habits at the individual and company level will make sustainability much higher.

5.  **Promote Life-Long Learning.** The Methodology must provide the structure and feedback that facilitates ongoing learning about how to improve individual and business performance. The Methodology itself must be adoptable in small increments to accommodate different learning rates and priorities.

6.  **Instill Constructive Accountability.** Expect people to be able to learn how to set goals and meet them. Constructive accountability is agreeing on what "winning" means and then helping each other do so. Destructive accountability is about fault-finding and catching someone doing something wrong.

7.  **Build a Measurement Culture.** Every person in the organization should eventually have meaningful measures that encourage innovation. It's true that what gets measured, gets managed and improved.

8. **Encourage Effective Communication.** Because communication challenges grow exponentially as the organization grows, the Methodology must help instill purposeful and systematic communication among the members of the organization as a by-product of its processes.

9. **Leverage the Internet.** Even though not every small business may "sell" over the Internet, the Methodology must help small businesses use the Internet for competitive advantage by improving their business processes, communications, learning, accountability and strategy execution.

10. **Proactively Pursue Alignment.** The forces of entropy will rapidly cause increasing amounts of time to be spent on low-priority activities, if not proactively addressed. The Methodology must be designed to continually refocus people on what's important, to offset the urgent forces that distract them.

## Reading tips for 'Six Disciplines for Excellence'

### Roles

We use the following roles when describing the Methodology. In your company, you may use different titles.

❑ **Facilitator:** Responsible for leading the meeting, encouraging participation and staying on the agenda. For major planning sessions involving the leadership team, it should be someone outside the company who's familiar with the Methodology. A good Facilitator significantly increases meeting effectiveness.

❑ **President:** The senior person in the organization who makes final decisions on strategy including mission, vision, values, etc. Some leaders are more "collaborative" than others. The Methodology can adjust to a wide range of leadership styles. However, in our examples, we've assumed a highly collaborative environment where people try to come to consensus as a group.

❑ **Leadership Team:** A small group of people who collaborate with the president to make key business decisions. This group should represent all the key business functional areas of the company. Typical size is three to five people, depending on organization size.

❑ **Extended Leadership Team:** As organizations grow, it makes sense to involve more people in the detailed planning steps. Such expanded involvement improves the quality and understanding of the plans, so they can be carried more effectively to the rest of the organization.

❑ **Human Resources (HR):** Typically manages payroll, benefits, employee records, recruiting, and may be involved in recognition and training processes as well. For smaller organizations, this is a part-time role that's supplemented by outsourcing or temporary help.

❑ **Cross-Functional Team:** A team assembled for a specific purpose that has representation from multiple functional areas. There are times in the Six Disciplines Methodology where "fleshing out the details" needs to be done outside of planning meetings, because of time constraints. Examples include drafting a mission statement for the first time or preparing a project plan.

In the next chapter, you'll see a wide variety of illustrations of *how* the Methodology works, using real-world examples.

## CHAPTER FOUR

## DISCIPLINE I
# *Decide What's Important*

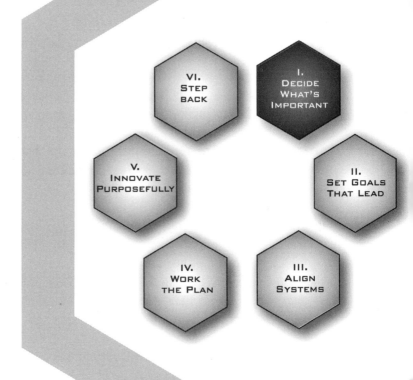

*The strategic agenda demands
discipline and continuity; its enemies
are distraction and compromise.*
        —MICHAEL E. PORTER

**I.**
**DECIDE**
**WHAT'S IMPORTANT**

I-A   Renew Mission
I-B   Renew Values
I-C   Renew Strategic Position
I-D   Renew Vision
I-E   Define VFOs
I-F   Agree What to Stop

# Overview

As you may recall from the research, one of the biggest differences between the highest- and lowest-performing small businesses was "*strength of leadership.*" This characteristic has two aspects. The first is the ability of leadership to define a clear direction for the company. This includes explaining that direction so people both understand it *and* connect with it. The second is identifying and delivering appropriate amounts of personal involvement in leading and supporting projects that are strategic to the company.

The purpose of this discipline is to get the leadership team to decide annually what its long-term priorities are and are not. This involves reviewing, renewing, revising and recommitting to its mission, values, vision and strategic position, and identifying clearly what the absolute "short list" of critical priorities of the business are.

We refer to these as *VFOs* (vital few objectives). To maximize the amount of resource and focus toward achieving the *VFOs*, the leadership team must also get agreement on what current activities or priorities can be stopped—the result, ultimately, being *greater success at every level of the business.*

Assuring that this discipline gets followed is one of the most important duties of company leadership. The foundational nature of this discipline is well illustrated by an example from air travel. Before a plane takes off, the pilot and navigator agree on where they're going in very specific terms, and the coordinates are entered into the navigation system. From that point forward, all activities of the crew and the plane are maximized around getting to that destination safely with the least amount of fuel consumed and the most comfortable ride.

Sometimes, the plane has to go "off course," or change altitude to avoid a storm or another plane, and then return to course later. 99% of both the crew's activity and the resources of the plane are dedicated to executing the strategy (getting to the destination), but none of that activity would be meaningful or successful if the one-percent effort of 'defining the destination' wasn't completed properly.

This example also reinforces our earlier observation about strategy *execution* being the bigger problem for most businesses than strategy formulation itself. 99% of the effort and energy goes to executing the strategy, and *this* is where most businesses fail. And yet, completely ill-defined strategy cannot be overcome by execution.

*All of a sudden, he woke up and felt overwhelmed and out of control, wondering, "How did I get here?"*

I want to share an illustrative story about another business I consulted with. "Tom" decided to start a contracting business. His initial idea was to focus on doing relatively small residential projects, and complete them promptly and on budget, as a way to differentiate himself from larger contractors. In our market, there are many contractors who build homes, but it's very hard to find someone to do small jobs promptly. In fact, it's even hard to get return calls from contractors for small jobs.

This idea, then, was the essence of his strategy. Tom started his business, and I became one of his first customers. The project was the remodeling of the basement of my home. Tom and another fellow did the work, and it was completed on time and within budget—a very good experience from the customer standpoint.

Over time, Tom hired a few more people, and he had to spend an increasing amount of his time both finding jobs to support his increasing payroll and managing his growing crew. This meant that less of his expertise was applied to the job. With payroll looming each week, he felt pressure to take on some jobs that were outside the scope of his original plan. He started building complete houses. Of course, in order to do that, he needed a bigger crew, a bigger payroll and a completely different set of business processes than a business optimized for small jobs. During this period, he had the opportunity to buy a masonry business, which he did.

A couple of years after his company completed our basement project, I contacted Tom about another small project. This job, once again, fit his company's original vision, but I didn't realize how his focus had drifted. He took my job, but my experience working with him was very different than the first job. He personally was much more harried. There were more schedule and quality challenges.

Tom's integrity caused him to make everything right, but the experience from my perspective (and apparently his) wasn't nearly as satisfying as the first project. The challenges and the frustrations Tom encountered with this approach continued to grow, as did mine as a customer.

Over time, Tom was able to see that what was happening to him happens to many other businesses. He started out with one idea in mind, but pressure to pay the bills and be "practical" led him all over the map, in terms of the jobs he was doing. He began to feel overwhelmed and out of control, wondering, "How did I get here?"

The good news is that regularly practicing the discipline of Deciding What's Important helps businesses sharpen their focus.

As shown in the chart on page 63, in Discipline I, the leadership team examines a summary of strengths, weaknesses, opportunities and threats (SWOT) that have come out of Discipline VI. Then, they review the mission, values, strategic position and vision, and update them if necessary. Next, they set the VFOs for each of four key views of the business: financial, customer, production and people. Finally, they decide what initiatives they can stop investing in to free up more resources to focus on the VFOs.

Typically, all these steps are completed in a half-day retreat held once a year. The first year may take a longer period, depending on whether some of the key strategy elements have to be built from scratch.

**Review & Renew**

- Mission
- Values
- Strategic Position
- Vision
- Goals Statement

**I. DECIDE WHAT'S IMPORTANT**

**Update**

- VFOs
- Stop List

**Consider Results from "Stepping Back"**

- SWOT Recap*
- External Trends
- Stakeholder Trends

* Strengths, Weaknesses, Opportunities, Threats

**STEP I-A**

# Renew Mission

## Introduction

A company's mission explains why an organization exists and what its purpose is. Purpose should be enduring—something the pursuit of which is limitless. Walt Disney thought of his purpose as "bringing happiness to millions."[1] He expressed the enduring nature of this purpose when he said, "Disneyland will never be completed, as long as there is imagination left in the world."[2]

The purpose of this step is to make sure that, before establishing long-term priorities, the leadership team has a clear understanding of what the mission of the organization is.

## Hints and Tips

❑ The most important attribute of purpose is *authenticity*. Purpose has to be something that comes from within; it should never be chosen based on what looks good to others.

❑ Ask yourself, "Will this purpose be valid in 20 or 30 years, or even longer?"

❑ The simpler the better. The most powerful ideas can be expressed simply with plain words and few of them, e.g., "bringing happiness to millions."

❑ Put your energy into communicating what the mission means and living it, as opposed to trying to get the perfect set of words or slogans.

❑ Focus on why, not how. "How" is strategy and will change over time.

❑ This is not about having posters. The best people aren't looking to work for a company that *has* a mission statement; they want to give their life to an organization that is *on* a mission.

## Process for Renewing Mission

| Process for Renewing Mission | | |
|---|---|---|
| **STEP** | **RESPONSIBILITY** | **DESCRIPTION** |
| 1 | Leadership Team | Review outputs from Discipline VI—SWOT*, Industry trends prior to meeting. |
| 2 | Facilitator | Brainstorm[†] on the question: In what ways are we not living up to our mission, from a customer's perspective? |
| 3 | Facilitator | Brainstorm on the question: In what ways are we not living up to our mission, from an employee's perspective? |
| 4 | Facilitator | Optionally brainstorm for suppliers, investors or other key stakeholder groups (using the same question) |
| 5 | Facilitator | Use the 100-Point Exercise[‡] to prioritize responses. |
| 6 | Facilitator | Lead discussion on the question: "Does the mission statement need to be changed?" If someone wants to change it, take time to figure out why. Sometimes, when new people join the organization, they have a desire to improve the mission. If there is no resistance to such changes, it may mean the current mission isn't really meaningful to people. People will resist changing something that's deeply meaningful. If there are frequent changes to the company's mission, it's a sure sign the organization is early in its journey on a path to excellence. |
| 7 | President | Make assignments for any follow-up actions (such as drafting updated statements). |

---

\* SWOT stands for a brief statement of Strengths, Weaknesses, Opportunities and Threats. It is an output of Discipline VI.

† See Chapter 8 for an explanation of how the Brainstorming exercise works.

‡ The 100-Point Exercise is a quick way to help participants tap their expertise to prioritize issues; In addition, people share their rationale, which is very informative to the rest of the group. See Chapter 8 for an explanation of how this exercise is conducted.

## Example Mission Statements

Please note that even though I've included the mission statement of Wal-Mart, a very large company, it wasn't large when it started!

---

**Wal-Mart**
To give ordinary folk the chance
to buy the same things as rich people.

---

**Business Consultant:**[3]
To provide strategic planning services
that improve the performance and efficiency
of start-up small businesses and increase their
chances of finding suitable financing.

---

**A New Restaurant/Diner:**[3]
To serve fresh, healthful home-cooked food
in a friendly, old-fashioned neighborhood café
to families, tourists, and business people in
thriving, downtown Smallville.

---

**An Educational Toy Maker:**[3]
To create, manufacture and market high-quality
educational toys and games that children will
find enjoyable and challenging, and will be a
good value for the purchaser.

---

## Example of 100-Point Exercise (for Mission Renewal)

Following is an example of the results of a *100-Point Exercise** related to a company's mission statement. Notice that a simple analysis of this form shows you *who* is most concerned about *what*. The Total column shows the priorities of the group as a whole.

| 100-Point Exercise for Mission Renewal | | | | | |
|---|---|---|---|---|---|
| | | | | | xx/xx/xx |
| | | POINTS AWARDED | | | |
| | JAN | SUE | STEVE | BRIAN | TOTAL |
| Ways not living up to mission from Customer's perspective: | | | | | |
| 1. Solutions too expensive to operate | | | 10 | | 10 |
| 2. Solutions too complex to learn | | 20 | | 40 | 60 |
| 3. Need better training to apply to strategic problems | 30 | 10 | 40 | | 80 |
| 4. Fraction of value of information is being used | 10 | | | | 10 |
| 5. Productivity would be greater if we could access information everywhere via the Internet | | | | | |
| From Employee's perspective | | | | | |
| 1. Growth rates are stressful to team members | | 30 | | 20 | 50 |
| 2. Growth rates create chaos—people feel like they can never catch up | 40 | 20 | 10 | 30 | 100 |
| 3. Inability to get time for training is a "Catch-22" | 10 | 20 | 20 | 10 | 60 |
| 4. Hiring too rapidly leads to mistakes in selection and too little time to understand our Values | 10 | | 20 | | 30 |
| **TOTAL** | **100** | **100** | **100** | **100** | **400** |

---

\* 100-Point Exercises are used in many places throughout this book, as shown above. To reduce your reading time, we're not going to include examples everywhere they're used. A complete description of the 100-Point Exercise and how it works is included in Chapter 8.

I.
DECIDE
WHAT'S IMPORTANT

I-A   Renew Mission
I-B   *Renew Values*
I-C   Renew Strategic Position
I-D   Renew Vision
I-E   Define VFOs
I-F   Agree What to Stop

## STEP I-B
# Renew Values

## Introduction

Peter Senge tells the following story about a team of business leaders grappling deeply with what they really meant by their *values:*

> The group had casually identified "honesty and forthrightness in all communications" as one of their operating ground rules. The management team had developed a vision they were beginning to get really excited about, when one of the senior salespeople commented offhandedly, "Of course, we don't mean that we'll be honest to our *customers.*"
>
> The entire process ground to a halt. The group reconsidered what they meant by "commitment to honesty and forthrightness in all communications." The president broke the silence by stating, "Yes. For me, this means being completely honest with our customers." The salesman responded, "If we do, we'll lose 30 percent of our bookings next month. In this business, *none* of our competitors are honest when they tell a customer when a new computer system will arrive. If we tell the truth, our delivery times will be 50 percent longer than what customers believe they get from our competitors."
>
> "I don't care," was the president's response. "I simply don't want to be a part of an organization that sanctions lying to our customers, our vendors or anyone else. Moreover, I believe that, over time, we'll establish a reputation for *reliability* with our customers that will win us more customers than we'll lose."

The exchange continued for more than an hour. At the end, the group was together in support of telling the truth. The salesperson knew that if the bookings dropped off in the next month or two, the other members of the team would not come screaming for his head. And he and the rest had begun to develop a vision of building a new reputation for honesty and reliability among their customers.[4]

Whereas mission answers the question of "why" an organization exists, values speak to the character or "personality" of the organization. Experience teaches that to cope with a rapidly changing world, organizations and individuals must decide on those things that won't change. These become the foundation upon which enduring success is built. Shared values should be just as enduring as the mission, and are just as important, if not more so.

The kind of leadership illustrated in the story above takes courage and conviction. It has to do with what kind of people we want to be and what kind of organization we want to spend our lives in. The purpose of this step is to renew and refresh the commitment of the leadership team to the core values of the organization *before* reviewing and updating its long-term priorities.

For those organizations that have already settled on what their core values are, the focus should be on reviewing how well the organization is doing in sticking to those values, and renewing their commitment to them. As shown in the example above, having integrity with your values will absolutely affect business strategy and priorities!

## Hints and Tips

☐ Values should be based upon that which is *already important* to you, not what you wish was important to you. They have to be built upon *passion and conviction.*

☐ They must be *enduring.* Ask yourselves questions like, "Will this be important 20 or 30 years from now?" or "Would I hold these values if I went to another organization?" or "Would I hold these values, even if it cost me my biggest customer?"

❑ Keep the list short and simple; three is ideal and five is a recommended maximum. People can't focus on a 10-point value system.

❑ Enduring success doesn't depend on a particular set of values—but it *does* depend on *having* clear values based on some enduring principles and sticking to them.

❑ Instilling values is a matter of both "talking the walk" and "walking the talk." People must both understand what the values are and mean, *and* see how they're applied in everyday decisions and interactions in the company.

❑ Give great emphasis on the values when recruiting people. Make sure new recruits are excited about the company's values before you hire. Doing this means that, as you grow, the entire team's commitment to your values will increase, instead of being diluted.

❑ Remember that every organization has values, whether you define them or not. The question is whether you're going to allow the character of your organization to be an accident or *intentional*.

## Process for Renewing Shared Values

| STEP | RESPONSIBILITY | DESCRIPTION |
|------|----------------|-------------|
| | **Process for Shared Values** | |
| 1 | Leadership Team | Review outputs from Discipline VI—SWOT, surveys, etc. prior to meeting. |
| 2 | Facilitator | Brainstorm on the question: In what ways are we not living up to our values, from a customer's perspective? |
| 3 | Facilitator | Brainstorm on the question: In what ways are we not living up to our values, from an employee's perspective? |
| 4 | Facilitator | Optionally brainstorm for suppliers, investors or other key stakeholder groups. |
| 5 | Facilitator | Use 100-Point Exercise to prioritize responses. |
| | Facilitator | Lead discussion on the question: "Does the values statement need to be changed?" If someone wants to change it, take time to figure out why. If there's no resistance to such changes, it may mean the current values statement isn't really meaningful to people. People will resist changing something that's deeply meaningful. Frequent changes are a sign the organization is still immature in its development. |
| 6 | President | Make assignments for any follow-up actions (such as drafting updated statements). |

## Example of Values Statements

---

### Branch-Smith Printing*

- To honor God in all that we do
- To pursue excellence with integrity and commitment
- To help people develop as individuals and as a team
- To grow profitably by committing ourselves to our customers' success

---

### Wal-Mart†

- Swim upstream, buck conventional wisdom
- Be in partnership with employees
- Work with passion, commitment and enthusiasm
- Run lean
- Pursue ever-higher goals

---

\* Small Business Baldrige Winner 2002
† Source: *Built to Last*

I.
DECIDE
WHAT'S IMPORTANT

I-A   Renew Mission
I-B   Review Values
I-C   *Review Strategic Position*
I-D   Review Vision
I-E   Define VFOs
I-F   Agree What to Stop

## STEP I-C
# Renew Strategic Position

## Introduction

Long-term business success is rooted in the ability to build and sustain a product or service offering that is different than that of rivals, and different in ways that are important to customers. The definition of this offering and how it relates to the customer and competitive offerings is a *Strategic Position*. For a strategic position to be sustainable, the detailed activities required to deliver it must be different. The offerings and activities must force competitors to choose between maintaining their current strategic position or attacking yours.

The purpose of this step is to renew commitment to the long-term strategic position the company is trying to build, before updating the organization's long-term goals. If you don't understand what strategic position is, I encourage you to read Michael Porter's article, "What is Strategy?"[*] It's the best piece on strategy I've ever read. In my experience, very few leaders really understand what "strategy" is. I know I didn't, for about 18 of my 23 years as a CEO.

Following is an illustration of how these principles work, using Dell Computers as an example. Remember that when it started, Dell was a tiny *one-person* operation. Dell began operations with a simple idea of selling computers *direct* to customers. At the time, almost *all* computers were sold through stores, dealers or a direct sales organization. Let's label this strategic position as "be direct" (a phrase Dell has used in its marketing). Since the beginning, every activity at Dell has

---

[*]  *Harvard Business Review* November 1996 reprint 96608

been optimized around the idea of "being direct." Dell started selling by phone, and then via the Internet. Dell then pioneered building product to order and optimizing inventory for build-to-order models, all taken *direct*. The way Dell markets, the way it supports, the way it manages materials and works with suppliers—thousands of activities back up Dell's strategic position of "being direct."

The focus on this strategy made for some interesting choices for Dell's competitors over the years. They could either *stay* with their existing strategies of selling through a channel, *abandon* those strategies, or *add* the direct model in addition to their channel strategy.

However their competitors would choose, Dell's well-conceived strategic position has put the competition in a situation where they had to make a trade-off between going after Dell's position and weakening their own current position, or maintaining their current position and letting Dell occupy their position unchallenged. The key in a strategy is using the strength of the competitors against them.

To illustrate: since Dell understood they were optimizing for being direct, they didn't make significant investments in opening stores, building a dealer channel, having inventory located in stores and warehouses, etc. This allowed Dell's cost structure to be much lower than alternate distribution strategies.

This put large, established competitors in a position where they could not have the economics of selling direct, *unless* they gave up their current business model—something that wasn't economically feasible for them to do. This is a classic example of a "trade-off." For this to work, company leadership has to do several things:

❑ They have to understand what the strategic position is that they're trying to build.

❑ They must be fanatical about aligning all the activities and resources of the company around building this position, and they must have the discipline to stay focused. This means having the courage to say "no" to the latest hot idea or competitive trend that doesn't support this position. If Michael Dell invests in building stores, that's a resource drain that weakens Dell's ability to be better at being direct. Falling into this trap makes it easier for competitors to catch up.

❑ They have to understand that a strategic position is a 10-year or more focus that transcends short-term strategies. For example, Dell has changed near-term strategies and tactics *many* times. They started with catalog sales, then went to telephone sales, then web sales, then web sales with make-to-order flexibility, then custom websites for corporate accounts, and so on. They're relentlessly innovating and changing, but what remains *constant* is the long-term strategic position: *be direct.*

As pointed out, Dell started small and has grown large. These principles apply to businesses of *all* sizes. Although many successful small business leaders may not use Porter's terminology, they still understand clearly what they stand for in the market and protect it dearly.

That's what a strategic position is all about. The purpose for this step isn't to teach you how to formulate strategy, but to make sure you document what your strategic position is, so it can be used to help the rest of the organization understand it and align their activities to it.

## Hints and Tips

❑ Keep the description of the strategic position simple. When you grasp it, it's usually straightforward to express: Dell's "be direct"; Southwest Airlines' "short flights"; Krispy Kreme's "freshest doughnuts"; and Federal Express's "overnight delivery."

❑ Although a strategic position is not forever, it should last 10 years or more. It provides a consistency to the annual planning and keeps the organization out of a constant reaction mode to competitors who have a different strategic position.

❑ Remind yourself and your organization that investing in activities *outside* the strategic position makes it easier for competitors to catch up.

❑ Understand that operational efficiency is about improving the processes and activities you have that support this strategic position.

As Michael Porter says, operational efficiency involves *"constant change, flexibility and best practices,"* but strategy, on the other hand, *"demands discipline, continuity; its enemies are distraction and compromise."*[5]

❑ The strategic position should fit on one page and contain the following elements:

❑ Short phrase that embodies the main idea, (e.g., Be Direct)

❑ Paragraph that explains what the short phrase means

❑ Bullet-pointed characteristics list of the target customer (geographics, age, income, occupation, industry, etc.—whatever it takes to clarify who's being targeted)

❑ 5-7 strategic themes that identify the broad focus/investment areas required to support the strategic position (see example)

## Process for Reviewing Strategic Position

### Process for Reviewing Strategic Position

| STEP | RESPONSIBILITY | DESCRIPTION |
|------|----------------|-------------|
| 1 | Leadership Team | Review outputs from Discipline VI—SWOT, surveys, etc. prior to meeting. |
| 2 | President | Be prepared to defend the current strategic position statement if necessary. One of the biggest temptations is to continually change long-term strategy. A well-conceived strategic position should last several years—maybe ten or more—unless there is some very unexpected event in the industry. Frequent changes to the strategic position means the company doesn't really have a long-term strategy, or at least hasn't written it down. |
| 3 | Facilitator | Brainstorm on the question: "Does the description portion of the strategic position statement need to be changed? If so, in what ways?" |
| 4 | Facilitator | Brainstorm on the question: "Does the description of the target market need to be changed?" If so, in what ways?" |
| 5 | Facilitator | Brainstorm on the question: "Do the strategic themes need to change? If so, in what ways?" |
| 6 | Facilitator | If there isn't agreement, use the 100-Point Exercise to help develop consensus. |
| 7 | President | Assign someone responsibility for drafting any changes. |

## Example of Strategic Position Statement

### Solomon Software Strategic Position Statement

Brief Strategic Position:

**Flexibility leader for business systems**

Description

The ultimate measure of flexibility from a business perspective is *time*. How quickly can the business get done what it needs to do? What's the time from problem to solution? *We will focus on providing the best set of products and services to help businesses respond to their business challenges in the shortest amount of time.*

Target Customer
- Businesses
- Small- to medium-sized locations
- U.S., selected international regions
- Strong IT staff
- Selected SIC

Strategic Themes (all focused on time to solution)
- Technological innovation
- Applications breadth, so business can work with single integrated solution
- Full-service local implementation & support partners
- Regional technology centers
- Real-time support

I.
DECIDE
WHAT'S IMPORTANT

I-A   Renew Mission
I-B   Renew Values
I-C   Renew Strategic Position
*I-D   Renew Vision*
I-E   Define VFOs
I-F   Agree What to Stop

## STEP I-D

# Renew Vision

## Introduction

This step helps leadership prepare to establish company goals, by reviewing and renewing its commitment to the company vision. Many planning experts recommend that the vision statement be used to cast a very general and long-term view of where the company is headed, like Microsoft's frequent statement in the '80s and '90s about "a computer on every desktop."

The Six Disciplines approach is different, in that we use the organization's mission and values to paint the longest-term picture of the company—its purpose and character. Then we use the strategic position statement to define the longest-term view of where strategy is to lead. The purpose of the vision statement is to help develop a more *concrete* picture of what the company will look like in *ten years*, in pursuit of the mission and strategic position.

To do this, we tap the unique human ability to imagine what yet doesn't exist, by asking leaders to answer three questions: 1) What do you want the organization to *be* in 10 years? 2) What do you want the organization to *have* in ten years? and 3) What do you want the organization to *do* in ten years?* Even though the resulting vision statement is more detailed than some experts recommend, it's my experience in working with small businesses that a more tangible vision increases understanding and motivation. It's one more step in the process of moving people from *"good intentions to concrete reality."* [6]

---

\* I learned a similar approach from *The 7 Habits of Highly Effective People*, by Stephen Covey, which was focused on helping an individual discover his/her purpose. The Six Disciplines approach is designed to work with small businesses, instead of individuals.

## Hints and Tips

❑ A vision is not a plan. Don't let the idea that you don't know whether you can achieve your vision get in the way. The purpose of a vision statement is to stimulate and guide strategy formulation over the years.

❑ Don't revise it every year just because you think you might not make it. Give your organization several years to work and pursue the vision. The vision should serve to stretch and challenge the organization.

❑ Consider changing the vision only if there's something fundamentally wrong with it in terms of "direction" (in other words, it no longer leads you where you want to go).

❑ Keep the vision statement short and to the point. Most vision statements should be less than one page. Use bullet points and an outline format.

❑ In day-to-day interactions and group meetings, look for ways to elaborate on the vision and help people connect what they're doing with that vision.

## Process for Renewing Vision

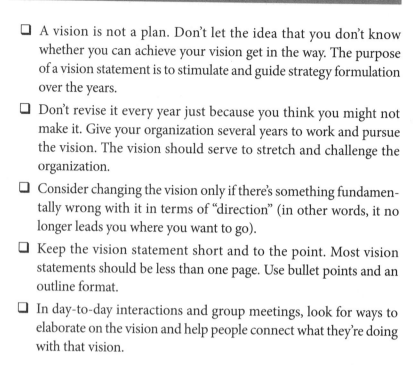

| | **Process for Renewing Vision** | |
|---|---|---|
| **STEP** | **RESPONSIBILITY** | **DESCRIPTION** |
| 1 | Leadership Team | Review vision statement prior to meeting. |
| 2 | President | Be prepared to defend the current statement, if necessary. One of the biggest temptations is to continually change long-term strategy. A well-conceived vision should last several years—we suggest ten—unless there is some very unexpected event in the industry. Frequent changes to the vision means the company doesn't really have a long-term strategy, or at least hasn't written it down. |
| 3 | Facilitator | Lead a discussion on the question: "Does the vision statement need to change? If so, in what ways?" |
| 4 | Facilitator | If there isn't agreement, use the 100-Point Exercise to help develop consensus. |
| 5 | President | Assign someone responsibility for drafting any changes. |

## Example Vision Statement

### Vision Statement—Solomon Software

19xx

**Be**

1. The flexibility leader for small- to mid-sized business solutions.
2. A place that attracts the best regional or local talent and a place where people want to make a career.
3. The kind of organization that sets reasonable targets and meets them, as opposed to setting stretch targets and falling short.

**Do**

1. Roll out regional consulting offices to provide high-quality implementation support, project management and technical expertise to complete the channel.
2. Roll out a complete next-generation product, fully optimized to leverage the Internet to further our strategic position as flexibility leader.
3. Pay off all debt and have cash equal to four months' sales.

**Have**

1. A market share in the 'top three' in terms of units shipped in the U.S.
2. At least two business partners doing more than $500K purchases from us in the top 25 SMSAs.
3. Have sales per employee of $200,000.

I.
DECIDE
WHAT'S IMPORTANT

I-A   Renew Mission
I-B   Renew Values
I-C   Renew Strategic Position
I-D   Renew Vision
*I-E   Define VFOs*
I-F   Agree What to Stop

**STEP I-E**

# Define VFOs

## Introduction

Someone told me many years ago that "making things simple is hard." There's tremendous power in simplicity, but sorting through the myriad options and conflicting priorities to agree on the absolute most vital few objectives (VFOs) for the company is one of the fundamentals of leadership. The purpose of this step is to define the VFOs that over the next three to five years will best move the company toward its vision. These VFOs are recorded on the Company Goals Statement.

*VFOs* as defined in this Methodology are general statements that are not measurable. Quantified goals come later in Discipline II. In the *Balanced Scorecard,* Kaplan and Norton provide a great explanation of how to compensate for the tendency of goals to be overly weighted to financial topics and underweighted to other areas of strategic importance. They propose developing a "balanced scorecard" that consists of four different perspectives of the business. In a similar manner, to assure complete coverage and systematic treatment of priorities, goals are developed for each of four *views* of the company. Each view represents a major category of asset every company has and must manage successfully. These views are:

❑ *Financial.* Refers to assets that appear on the financial statements of a company: cash, receivables, inventory, property, etc. The condition of the financial assets represents a lagging (trailing) indicator of the success of company strategy.

❑ *Customer.* Represents the most important asset of any business, and yet it doesn't directly appear on the balance sheet of the company. Current and future customers are the future of the business.

❑ *Production.* Refers to the production capability used to create and deliver the promises made to the customer. The content of this asset group varies widely, depending upon the type of business. For example, in an engineering firm, the Production capability includes the ability to estimate a job and the expertise to design work and manage projects. In a distributorship, the Production capability includes the ability to take an order quickly and accurately, to manage inventory effectively, and to deliver goods on time.

❑ *People.* Represents the human resources that operate the business. When considering the People view, questions arise: How and what type of people are needed? How are they trained? How are they empowered to reach their potential in ways that align with the business? No business can thrive if its plans don't consider the impact on its people resources.

These views are interrelated and provide a structured way to think through priority development in the following sequence: 1) Financial 2) Customer 3) Production and 4) People. The *Financial* view is the most basic. The most fundamental requirement is to protect the financial health of the organization. If this is sufficiently ignored or neglected, the organization will die.

The way the organization is kept healthy is to understand who its *Customers* are, what their needs are, and which of those needs this organization is going to meet. Once that has been decided, *Production* capability has to be developed to deliver on those promises. Last of all, a motivated team of the right kinds and number of *People* has to be in place to deliver on the goals for the *Financial, Customer* and *Production* views of the business.

## Hints and Tips

❑ Keep the total number of VFOs small. Remember, you're looking for the vital *few*. As a general guideline, one to three VFOs per view—for a total of somewhere between six to ten—is reasonable. Frequently, the Production view has the most VFOs.

❑ Define the VFO in simple terms; for example: *grow sales rapidly* or *increase profit margins.*

❑ Be relentless in eliminating conflicting VFOs. For example, in most industries, *grow sales rapidly* is in conflict with *increase profit margin rapidly.* Conflicting VFOs set up the organization for failure.

❑ The VFOs have to support each other. For example, if there's a VFO in the Financial view to grow sales rapidly, then in the Customer view, you should set a VFO that shows how you're going to grow sales; such as, *grow number of new customers* and/or *grow revenue to existing customers* (after market sales).

❑ Defer questions about how you're going to measure these VFOs and what the actual targets are until later.

❑ In the end, the VFOs should allow anyone in the company to tell a story (see Example section).

❑ Because the planning period for VFOs is three to five years, they shouldn't change every year. Rapid changes in the VFOs means the company doesn't have a stable long-term strategy and produces less-than-optimal performance.

❑ Resist the temptation to be all things to all people. Be very focused on a few things, and do them well.

## Process for Developing the Vital Few Objectives

### Process for Developing the VFOs

| STEP | RESPONSIBILITY | DESCRIPTION |
|---|---|---|
| 1 | Leadership Team | Has completed reviews of strengths, weaknesses, opportunities, threats (SWOT), mission, vision and strategic position before this meeting. |
| 2 | Facilitator | Make sure there is agreement on the planning horizon being discussed. Three to five years is recommended. |
| 3 | Facilitator | Brainstorm on the question: "To reach our vision, what are the most important Financial VFOs for the company to achieve over the next three-year period?" Example responses might be: "Sales growth" (growth strategy), "Increase return on capital" (sustain strategy), and "Maximize operating income." |
| 4 | Facilitator | Use the 100-Point Exercise to firm up the top Financial VFOs identified above. |
| 5 | Facilitator | Brainstorm on the question: "To reach our vision and Financial VFOs, what are the most important VFOs related to new or existing Customer (market) segments to achieve over the next three-year period?" Examples might be: "Grow number of new customers," "Grow sales from existing customers in market X" and "Enter market Y." |
| 6 | Facilitator | Complete a 100-Point Exercise on the Customer question (above) to firm up the top VFOs for the Customer View. |
| 7 | Facilitator | Brainstorm on the question: "To achieve our vision, Financial VFOs, and Customer VFOs, what are our most important VFOs—in terms of Production capability—to achieve over the next three years?" Example responses might be: "Re-engineer service delivery process," "Add Internet order-taking capability," "Reduce order to ship time," and "Reduce defect levels." |
| 8 | Facilitator | Complete a 100-Point Exercise to firm up the top VFOs for this Production View. |
| 9 | Facilitator | Brainstorm on the question: "To achieve our vision, Financial VFOs, Customer VFOs and Production VFOs, what are the most important VFOs to achieve, with regard to our People over the next three years?" Example responses might be: "Train everyone on technology X," "Implement quarterly incentive system to align people with corporate VFOs," or "Implement 360° feedback system," etc. |
| 10 | Facilitator | Complete a 100-Point Exercise on the people question (above) to firm up the top VFO for this People View. |
| 11 | Facilitator or President | Prepare a draft of the VFOs portion of the Company Goals statement compass by selecting the top two to three items from each of the asset categories and recording those VFOs on the form (this may be completed by the President as well). |
| 12 | President | This Goals statement is finalized by the president or leadership team, after they've reviewed this draft and agree on it. |

Note: Unlike previous exercises, this one was written assuming that the leadership team was developing a set of VFOs for the first time. Once the VFOs are identified, they should be reviewed each year. However, just like vision, they shouldn't change a great deal every year; perhaps every three to four years they are renewed.

## Example of VFOs on Goals Statement

Following is an example of the Vital Few Objectives recorded on a Company Goals statement form. At this stage of the Six Disciplines, only the VFOs column is completed; the remaining columns will be filled out as we progress through Discipline II.

| | | | | TARGET | | | | |
|---|---|---|---|---|---|---|---|---|
| **Company Goals Statement** **Solomon Software** Plan Year 2xxx | | | | | | | Last Revised xx/xx/xx | |
| **VFOs** | **RESP** | **DUE DATE** | **MEASURE/ INITIATIVE** | 2004 | 2005 | 2006 | 2007 | 2008 |
| FINANCIAL VIEW | | | | | | | | |
| 1. Grow profitability | | | | | | | | |
| 2. Sustain industry growth rate | | | | | | | | |
| CUSTOMER VIEW | | | | | | | | |
| 3. Grow client satisfaction | | | | | | | | |
| 4. Grow sales per customer | | | | | | | | |
| 5. Grow sales per partner | | | | | | | | |
| PRODUCTION VIEW | | | | | | | | |
| 6. Improve quality | | | | | | | | |
| 7. Broaden functionality | | | | | | | | |
| 8. Grow field consultants | | | | | | | | |
| 9. Roll-out Internet product | | | | | | | | |
| PEOPLE VIEW | | | | | | | | |
| 10. Grow team member satisfaction | | | | | | | | |
| 11. Increase productivity | | | | | | | | |

A well-crafted Company Goals Statement should serve as the outline for a story. The statement above tells this story:

> "Over the next few years, we want to grow profitability, instead of concentrating on increasing market share. We want to maintain the same growth rate as the market. We will focus on increasing customer satisfaction, growing sales per customer and growing sales per partner, balancing our focus on new customer capture. To achieve these customer

VFOs, we will work on improving quality of products and services, broaden the functionality of product line, focus on expanding the amount of consulting resources available to assist clients, and we will begin the work to complete a new Internet-optimized product. We want to slow down and increase team member satisfaction and let them 'catch-up' from our rapid growth. We also want to invest to improve their productivity."

I.
DECIDE
WHAT'S IMPORTANT

I-A  Renew Mission
I-B  Renew Values
I-C  Renew Strategic Position
I-D  Renew Vision
I-E  Define VFOs
*I-F  Agree What to Stop*

# STEP I-F
# Agree What to Stop

## Introduction

"The essence of strategy is deciding what *not* to do."[7] Unless your priorities are clear enough that you know what not to do or what not to allocate resources to, you don't yet have "strategy." One way to test how committed the organization is to the VFOs is to get agreement on the projects and priorities in the organization that can be *stopped. That is the purpose of this step.*

Effective strategy execution requires that the resources of the organization are aligned to its purposes. There are many internal and external forces that fight against alignment. I learned this lesson in a way I'll never forget.

After Solomon Software was in business for about 10 years, cash flow was unacceptable for the future survival of the company. As its leader, I'd been aggressively funding projects for future growth, yet under-investing in taking care of current business. Faced with drastic action, I called another CEO (one who had successfully restructured) to ask for advice. The advice surprised me:

> There's a lot more wasted activity in your organization than you imagine. Many of the things you think are critical to your business really are *not*. Get over the emotion of the mistakes that got you here! Your first priority has to be to get the organization viable and going forward. Scrutinize every expense, position and project, and free up resources for redevelopment of the company. Whatever amount of resource you *think* is critical—I guarantee you, it's significantly less than you think.

We took this counsel to heart. We analyzed our expenses and concluded we could cut about 25%. However, based on the input of this other CEO, we also assumed we were probably underestimating; so we set our target at 40% reduction. We prepared for a 10 to 15% drop in sales and implemented the reductions.

The results stunned me! Sales didn't decline; they increased! Our performance went up, not down! We were actually getting *more* of the important things in the organization completed faster *and* easier. The reason for all this startling success? *We were finally willing to stop the activities that were not important.*

I couldn't *believe* how much waste we had built into the organization over time. As a result, we had the cash and the people available to work on developing new products and *still* have competitive profitability. Over the next 10 years, the company grew to six times the size it was, as a result of getting our resources aligned with our priorities.

At great expense to my co-workers, partners and me, I learned the most difficult business lesson of my life: the forces of business and human nature cause programs and projects to *expand*, resulting in an ever-increasing misalignment of resources. An organization must have the self-discipline to free up resources and reallocate them to higher-value projects *and* to deliver competitive profitability at the same time. If an organization doesn't discipline itself to do this, our wonderful free market will. Leaders who've been through this know *exactly* the lessons I'm talking about.

## Hints and Tips

❑ Think of the company resources as being divided among three categories: "critical", "discretionary", and "available for reassignment." The job of leadership is to *stop* doing that which is of a discretionary nature, and reallocate as much resource as possible to "critical" priorities.

❑ If you say that A, B and C are the most important aspects of your company, but you're unwilling to stop allocating resources to D,

E and F, you've deluded yourself and set your organization up for failure.

❑ Not all items on the "stop list" are phased out immediately. Many are phased out over time. Sometimes *stop* just means "invest no more and maximize cash flow for the remaining life."

❑ Other kinds of projects should be killed immediately and put behind you. I know from experience it's difficult to "throw in the towel" on a project. We're taught from birth to "never give up." Sometimes, we must take courage, move on and learn from that project.

❑ Teach everyone in your organization that stopping projects or activities is not "failure;" it's the mark of a disciplined organization. People should be encouraged and rewarded for identifying projects, processes, procedures, etc. to stop.

## Process for Agreeing on What to Stop

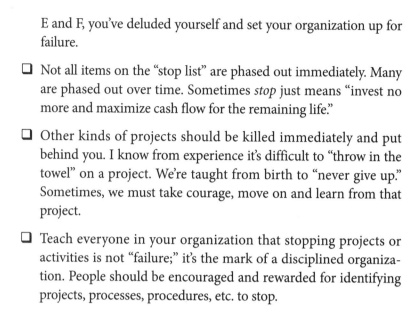

| \multicolumn{3}{c}{**Process for Agreeing on What to Stop**} | | |
|------|------|------|
| **STEP** | **RESPONSIBILITY** | **DESCRIPTION** |
| 1 | Facilitator | Lead the team through a Brainstorming exercise for the question: "Are there any projects, policies, product lines or other activities that are not aligned with our vision and VFOs and could we therefore stop those activities?" |
| 2 | Facilitator | Develop consensus by using the 100-Point Exercise and the related discussions. |
| 3 | Facilitator | Assign someone responsibility for drafting the Stop List. Remember in drafting this list that it should be published to the team members. There may be some sensitive items that need to be managed separately from the public list. |
| 4 | President | Assign someone responsibility for any item on the Stop List that requires further research or a plan to withdraw from that activity over a period of time. |

## Examples

### Stop List Solomon Software

19xx

1. Stop targeting low-end market—put ProfitWise product line in "milk" mode—maintenance releases for critical items only.
2. Eliminate Unix as a target platform. Development should optimize architecture for Windows platform.
3. Eliminate support of multiple databases. Optimize architecture for SQL Server.
4. Remove from our target market list foreign markets that require double-byte language sets. Cease all investments related to supporting this ASAP.
5. Phase out OEM program, sign no more new relationships and put existing relationships into maintenance mode.

**I.**
**DECIDE**
**WHAT'S IMPORTANT**

I-A   Renew Mission
I-B   Renew Values
I-C   Renew Strategic Position
I-D   Renew Vision
I-E   Define VFOs
I-F   Agree What to Stop

## RECAP OF DISCIPLINE I
# Decide What's Important

To be effective, leaders cannot "blow an uncertain trumpet." Of the many options available, choosing exactly what the company is going to focus on is one of the most important roles of leadership. Deciding annually what the organization's long-term priorities are—and are not—is essential.

Selecting your VFOs (vital few objectives) will help you define your destination, and avoid becoming sidetracked and bogged down in activities that can and should be stopped.

The following steps covered in this chapter help get that done in a systematic way:

- ❑ I-B   Renew Mission
- ❑ I-C   Renew Values
- ❑ I-D   Renew Strategic Position
- ❑ I-E   Renew Vision
- ❑ I-F   Define VFOs
- ❑ I-G   Agree What to Stop

Building on the foundation produced by *Discipline* I, the next chapter transforms *VFOs* from very broad statements of priority to specific, well-defined measures and targets. This transformation is necessary to help every worker connect what they're doing with the purposes of the company.

## CHAPTER FIVE

# DISCIPLINE II
# *Set Goals That Lead*

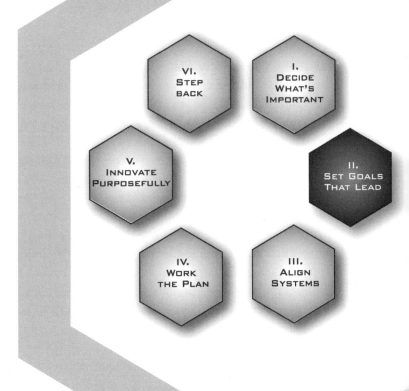

*Poorly designed goals don't provide adequate direction to the team—in fact they actually mislead them.*

**II.**
**SET GOALS**
**THAT LEAD**

II-A   Define Measures
II-B   Define Targets
II-C   Define Initiatives
II-D   Engage the Team

# Overview

Imagine you're the president of Grand Slam, Ltd., a $7 million sports facilities consulting company with three major divisions: Facilities Design, Equipment Sales and Construction Management. You gather your three division heads and tell them, "Our top priority over the next three years is to increase sales by 35 percent. This is a great team and I know you can do it." Then, you dismiss the group. What do you think will happen?

Without further input, the response could easily proceed like this: Facilities Design starts looking for bigger customers to increase the size of engagements. Equipment Sales increases the advertising budget and starts running new promotions. Construction Management develops a plan aimed at expanding services to include "outsourced facilities maintenance," because that would generate significant revenue from the 200 past customers of Grand Slam.

All these ideas individually may be great, but doing them all at once could be a *disaster*. For example, moving up-market in terms of size of customer could change the types of products Equipment Sales needs to carry, adding inventory costs. It could also dramatically increase demand for Construction Management resources that are now being consumed by the expansion into 'facilities maintenance.' The point is, no organization has the resources to do *all* things at once. Therefore poorly designed goals don't provide adequate direction to the team—in fact they actually mislead them.

Now let's imagine a different scenario. You walk into the same room and say, "Our top priority over the next three years is to increase sales by 35 percent. To do that, we want to *sustain* the same rate of new customer adds, *sustain* the average revenue per new customer add, and *increase* the average revenue for our existing customer base by 10 percent next year, 15 percent the following year, and 25 percent in the third year.*

"Sally, by November 1, I'd like you to take responsibility for putting together a cross-functional team from all divisions, a quarterly plan, a budget for reaching next year's goal, and annual plans for the following two years."

> No organization has the resources to do all things at once; goal setting, by itself, is not enough.

You can easily *feel* the difference. The first approach creates confusion, frustration and failure. The second approach identifies VFOs, *measures, targets* and responsibility. These two vignettes illustrate the difference between just defining goals and defining *goals that lead the team to move in the right direction.*

The purpose of *Discipline II—Set Goals That Lead*—is to help organizations formulate goals and initiatives that lead people to take action that's aligned with what's most important to the organization. To be complete, a goal must include:

- ❑ A VFO (for example, grow *sales*)

- ❑ a measure that indicates how to track progress relative to the VFO (for example, *revenue growth per existing customer*)

- ❑ a target that quantifies the measure (for example, 10%)

- ❑ a target date that indicates the deadline for achieving the target

The process of setting goals starts by working through the VFOs that have come out of Discipline I. The leadership team needs to work through each VFO, identifying the measure or two that best represents the intent of the VFO. Once the measures are agreed upon, three- to five-year targets are proposed for each measure.

These long-term targets quantify how far and how fast the organization needs to go in pursuit of its vision. After targets are agreed upon, broad initiatives are identified for achieving the near-term targets.

---

* To keep this example simple, assume that the stated increases in existing customer revenue results in total revenue increasing 35 percent over three years.

Then, someone is assigned to take responsibility for these initiatives, so that more detailed plans can be developed in Discipline IV.

Typically, all these are completed in a half-day retreat once a year. This meeting can be combined with Discipline I in a single-day retreat, once the leadership team is used to going through these steps.

There's no greater tool for improving the performance of an organization than setting well-thought-out goals—it's one of the most effective communication tools of leadership. But it takes a long-term, disciplined approach for an organization to learn how to do that.

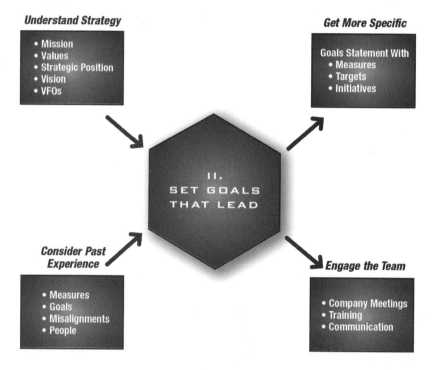

Setting appropriate goals requires preparation back in Discipline VI and Discipline I. It then takes multiple planning cycles to learn the consequences of the goals you set. However, by thoroughly following through with this process each year, *your team will get better* at defining well-thought-out goals that lead to better performance.

II.
SET GOALS
THAT LEAD

II-A *Define Measures*
II-B Define Targets
II-C Define Initiatives
II-D Engage the Team

## STEP II-A
# Define Measures

## Introduction

The first step in translating a VFO into a *goal that leads* is identifying how progress against that VFO is to be measured. Picking the right measure is a critical responsibility because of how much the measure communicates about how to reach the VFO. To illustrate, let's assume the VFO is "Increase Market Share." That VFO provides no guidance as to how it should be reached.

Following are different ways to increase market share:

❑ increase number of customers

❑ increase average sales to new customers by selling more products and services

❑ increase sales to new customers by increasing price

❑ increase *unit* sales to existing customers by lowering price

❑ increase sales to existing customers by marketing other products

There are many different ways to think about market share. However, picking the measure forces the *leadership team* to clarify strategy. For example, if the measure chosen for "Increasing Market Share" is "Percent Increase in Number of New Sites," the organization has a much clearer idea of what leadership is trying to accomplish. Kaplan and Norton, in *The Balanced Scorecard* state it this way: "[The purpose in] . . . selecting specific measures . . . is to identify the measure that best communicates the meaning of the strategy."[1]

One time at Solomon, we focused on capturing as many new customers as we could, because we had a short-lived competitive advantage that would allow us to capture new customers more easily. Once we had a relationship with a client, the lifetime value of that customer was worth multiples of the initial purchase. During this period, we were willing to invest heavily to capture new customers, so a good measure for increasing market share was "percentage of growth in number of new sites in our target market."

Sometimes, the strategy might be to take two approaches simultaneously, e.g., grow both "new sites" and "average revenue per site" for existing sites. In that case, you would probably establish two different measures—one to get the sales organization to focus on new site sales and another to get the services organization to focus on aftermarket sales.

The bottom line is that through the process of carefully selecting measures, leadership is firming up what they want and why, significantly increasing the likelihood that others in the organization will understand as well.

## Hints and Tips

- ❑ Keep the number of measures small, with one or two per VFO.

- ❑ Make sure measures are of long-term strategic value, not short-term or simply related to diagnostics. The company can have any number of detailed measures it needs, but such detail doesn't belong on the company goals statement.

- ❑ Try to have a balance of leading and lagging measures. For example, the number of complaints might be a leading indicator of sales. In this case, sales are a lagging indicator.

- ❑ Avoid the temptation to load up on financial measures, which tend to be lagging indicators.

- ❑ Be specific about how the measure is computed. Try to keep it simple (see examples).

❑ It's better to pick a measure of average quality than a superb measure for which no data is readily available. Pick something practical for the short-term and work on improving your data-tracking capability over the long-term. For example, it may not be practical to survey every customer for satisfaction, but you could do a sample of every tenth customer.

## Process for Defining Measures

| STEP | RESPONSIBILITY | DESCRIPTION |
|------|----------------|-------------|
| | | **Process for Defining Measures** |
| 1 | Leadership Team | Read last year's goals statement in preparation for meeting. |
| 2 | Facilitator | Read each VFO and measure, and identify any the Leadership Team wants changed. |
| 3 | Facilitator | If the VFO is new or needs to be changed, the group discusses and decides on what measure(s) would best reflect the intent of the VFO (keep the number of measures as few as possible). |
| 4 | Facilitator | Discuss how the measure is to be calculated. Prepare an actual example, such as "number of customers added/customers added by top five competitors." Identify sources of data, especially for external sources, like market research firms. If the way to calculate can't be agreed on quickly, it should be assigned to someone for follow-up. The meeting should not get bogged down, but specific details—like whether the measure is based on units or dollars derived from new or existing customers—should be clarified, at a minimum. |
| 5 | Facilitator | Continue until all the measures are agreed upon for each VFO. If the total number of measures is excessive (beyond 10-12), the group should consider shortening the list. |

## Example Goals Statements (with Measures added)

### Company Goals Statement

Plan Year 2xxx                                                                    Last Revised xx/xx/xx

| VFOs | RESP | DUE DATE | MEASURE/ INITIATIVE | 2004 | 2005 | TARGET 2006 | 2007 | 2008 |
|------|------|----------|---------------------|------|------|------|------|------|
| **FINANCIAL VIEW** | | | | | | | | |
| 1. Grow profitability | | | Operating margin % | | | | | |
| 2. Sustain industry growth rate | | | $ Sales growth % | | | | | |
| **CUSTOMER VIEW** | | | | | | | | |
| 3. Grow client satisfaction | | | Overall satisfaction rating | | | | | |
| 4. Grow sales per customer | | | Average sales per post-implementation customer | | | | | |
| 5. Grow sales per partner | | | Average of % of partner business for the top 100 partners | | | | | |
| **PRODUCTION VIEW** | | | | | | | | |
| 6. Improve quality | | | # post-release errors with severity of less than 4 | | | | | |
| 7. Broaden functionality | | | Distribution suite sales ($k) | | | | | |
| 8. Improve lead qualification | | | Close rate of qualified leads | | | | | |
| **PEOPLE VIEW** | | | | | | | | |
| 9. Grow team member satisfaction | | | Overall satisfaction rating | | | | | |
| 10. Increase productivity | | | Trailing 12-month sales per employee | | | | | |
| 11. Roll-out Internet product | | | Sales as % of Total | | | | | |

II.
SET GOALS
THAT LEAD

II-A Define Measures
*II-B Define Targets*
II-C Define Initiatives
II-D Engage the Team

# STEP II-B
# Define Targets

## Introduction

Big stakes are involved when you set targets for your organization. What really brought this home to me was an article I read several years ago by Michael Hammer called "Reengineering Work: Don't Automate, Obliterate."[2] This article was a case study of Ford Motor Company undertaking a project to streamline its accounts payable operations. (Even though this is a big company, bear with me; the principles apply to us all.)

At the time, Ford had about 500 people handling payables processing. It had set a goal to improve efficiency by 20%, so the same work could be done by 400 people. However, someone on this project wisely asked the question, "Do we have the right target?"

So, Ford benchmarked its performance in accounts payable with Mazda Corporation. After adjusting for the size difference between the two companies, Ford officials discovered that their payables operation was 500 percent larger (less efficient) than Mazda's. It challenged them to ask themselves, "Why can't we do that?" And to make a long story short, they did.

For Ford, setting the right target led to a completely different approach in implementation. The 20% reduction approach would have involved minor changes, and tuning of the existing approach. Closing the 500 percent gap required a whole different level of innovation, which paid off *big-time* for the company.

Setting long-term targets for a small business has the same kind of power as this example. Set them too low and you stifle creativity and under-perform. Set them too high and your people are frustrated and set up for failure. Admittedly, this isn't easy. There are many unknowns in any given "next five years," and developing *detailed* five-year plans is usually not practical.

Asking the team to estimate annual targets, however, forces people to drill down and think about the broad steps required to get there, and to identify possible conflicts among the targets. By looking out five years, the collective wisdom of the leadership team is used to reflect the pace at which the organization should move toward its VFOs.

It's best to think of this process as a combination of top-down goal setting with bottom-up planning to confirm the top-down targets. There's interplay between these two extremes until they converge. For example, in the software business, when it was time to invest in building a "next generation" technology, we preferred that such an investment take place gradually over a period of three to four years, instead of rushing to do it in two.

This pace allowed for a higher quality job, allowed technology to settle down, and balanced our investments between next generation and current generation. The *targets* we set provide some context or framework around which staffing plans and budgets can be built to verify the validity of the top-down goals.

## Hints and Tips

- ❑ View the first version of the targets as a "draft" until teams have had the chance to define the initiatives associated with each of the targets. (This occurs next). The insights gained from defining the initiatives may justify revisions of the targets.

- ❑ Get the people who are responsible for delivering the results involved. They'll better understand the hurdles to be overcome, and will have more buy-in if they can have input in developing the annual targets.

- ❑ Wisdom is required to know how aggressive to make these targets. Lofty goals can challenge the organization to be creative and achieve greater things, but goals that are unrealistic can become discouraging. The best protection from being too aggressive is to ask highly motivated and qualified people whether these are achievable targets.

❑ Remember that these targets are set to guide the development of detailed plans, not the other way around. This means the goals have to be set by relying on the judgment of the team, rather than by the process of building detailed supporting plans first.

❑ While the vision statement should remain unchanged for several years and serve as a constant toward which the company is aiming, the five-year targets should be updated each year to reflect the most current thinking.

❑ The greatest attention needs to be given to the upcoming year's targets, because they will be used to build more detailed plans for the next quarter and year.

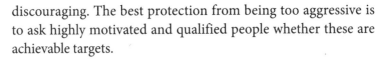

## Process for Defining Targets

| STEP | RESPONSIBILITY | DESCRIPTION |
|---|---|---|
| 1 | Leadership Team | Attendees should have a copy of the latest goals statement with VFOs and measures identified. |
| 2 | Facilitator | Walk through each measure in the order presented on the goals statement, and set three- to five-year draft targets for each of them. Factors to be considered in setting the targets are the vision for the company, the history of what has been achievable in the past, and what seems reasonable for the future. |
| 3 | Facilitator | Sometimes, there are items that require "off-line" work; e.g., perhaps some additional information needs to be gathered, some calculations performed, etc. If this is the case, the group should assign someone to do that after the meeting and update the results. |
| 4 | Leadership Team | Provides the goals statement, which now includes the draft targets, to other team leaders in the organization to get more people thinking about these goals and how to achieve them. |
| 5 | President | If there are debates and indecision as to how aggressive to be with targets, be prepared to make the final decision. |

The drafted goals statement is finalized after the initiatives are identified in a subsequent step.

## Example of Goals Statement (With Targets Added)

### Company Goals Statement

Plan Year 2xxx                                                                 Last Revised xx/xx/xx

| VFOs | RESP | DUE DATE | MEASURE/ INITIATIVE | TARGET 2004 | 2005 | 2006 | 2007 | 2008 |
|---|---|---|---|---|---|---|---|---|
| **FINANCIAL VIEW** | | | | | | | | |
| 1. Grow profitability | | | Operating margin % | 8% | 9% | 11% | 13% | 13% |
| 2. Sustain industry growth rate | | | $ Sales growth % | 7% | 7% | 6% | 6% | 6% |
| | | | Sales (m) | $8 | $8.6 | $9.1 | $9.6 | $10.2 |
| **CUSTOMER VIEW** | | | | | | | | |
| 3. Grow client satisfaction | | | Overall satisfaction rating | 77% | 80% | 82% | 84% | 86% |
| 4. Grow sales per customer | | | Average sales per post-implementation customer | $7.5k | $7.9k | $8.2k | $8.7k | $9.1k |
| 5. Grow sales per partner | | | Average of % of partner business for the top 100 partners | 40% | 42% | 45% | $48% | 51% |
| **PRODUCTION VIEW** | | | | | | | | |
| 6. Improve quality | | | # post-release errors with severity of less than 4 | 900 | 810 | 740 | 665 | 600 |
| 7. Broaden functionality | | | Distribution suite sales A ($k) | | | $200 | $300 | $400 |
| 8. Improve lead qualification | | | Close rate of qualified leads | 20% | 25% | 30% | 33% | 35% |
| 9. Roll-out Internet product | | | Sales as % of total | | | | 3% | 15% |
| **PEOPLE VIEW** | | | | | | | | |
| 10. Grow team member satisfaction | | | Overall satisfaction rating | 85% | 86% | 87% | 87% | 88% |
| 11. Increase productivity | | | Trailing 12-month sales per employee | 125k | 129k | 133k | 137k | 141k |

II.
SET GOALS
THAT LEAD

II-A Define Measures
II-B Define Targets
*II-c Define Initiatives*
II-D Engage the Team

# STEP II-C
# Define Initiatives

## Introduction

Identifying the *initiatives* required to achieve each target is the final piece in the company's strategy. We've been on a journey which starts from our vision of the company 10 years into the future, yet eventually leads us directly to the here and now. With the addition of initiatives, the goals statement tells a story of what the vital few priorities of the company are, how we're going to measure our progress toward those priorities, how far and how fast we'll try to go, and how we're going to get there.

An initiative is another name for a program or project. A well-defined initiative is associated with a VFO, has someone responsible for it, and includes a due date. Depending on scope, an initiative may stand alone or be broken into smaller projects and assignments over a period of several quarters. Following are some examples of initiatives you might use (depending upon the type of business) if you're trying to "increase the new customer growth rate percentage":

❑ Design a major new direct-mail campaign

❑ Run a Fourth of July Sale

❑ Hire an additional sales person

❑ Introduce a new type of service

Picking the right initiatives requires understanding the intent of the VFOs, measures and targets. For example, changing the long-term growth rate of the company may require some short-term initiatives that produce near-term results, and some long-term initiatives that won't have an effect for two or three years.

The main reason for placing the initiatives on the goals statement is to help everyone in the organization understand what the overall strategy is, and how a given target is going to be met. This understanding helps people make better decisions, channeling their creativity and energy toward the purposes of the company.

## Hints and Tips

❑ The purpose of an initiative is to bring about change. For example, if the goal is to increase sales growth from 5% to 8%, the initiatives tell how.

❑ Large initiatives should be broken into smaller phases or projects. For example, in a consulting organization, the decision to open a new office in another geographical area might be a multi-year initiative. Different stages might include: doing the research to size the potential market, evaluating real estate opportunities, recruiting and training staff, *then* launching the office.

❑ When forming a team to work on an initiative, make sure one person is responsible for the team and the results of the initiative. That person should develop supporting schedules, budgets, staffing and other resource requirements.

❑ Keep the number of overall company-wide initiatives that are underway at the same time to a small and manageable number. Such focus improves the predictability and quality of execution.

❑ Remember that change initiatives do *not* represent 100% of the activities of the company. Every company has the ongoing routines and processes that must be done every day to stay in business, such as consulting, supporting customers, accounting, etc. These *sustaining activities* consume a large percentage of all resources. The initiatives are those few, most important things that guide how to deploy discretionary resources that are available each year to bring about changes that position the company for future success.

## Process for Defining Initiatives

| | Process for Defining Initiatives | |
|---|---|---|
| **STEP** | **RESPONSIBILITY** | **DESCRIPTION** |
| 1 | Leadership Team | Review the goals statement and vision statement prior to the meeting. |
| 2 | Facilitator | Read the VFO, measure and target and lead a brainstorming session on ideas for initiatives to achieve the target. The results are written on an easel (post-it paper) so everyone can see them. Repeat this for each measure. Note that some ideas may appear again, but for different measures. |
| 3 | Facilitator | Use the 100-Point Exercise to narrow the list to the top two or three initiatives for each target. |
| 4 | President | Assign someone to be responsible for each initiative and to evaluate feasibility (cost, resources required, schedule) for approval at a later date. |
| 5 | President | After these plans are prepared, reconcile budgets and finalize which initiatives will be implemented in the upcoming year. Record them on the goals statement. As a result of these work plans, it may be necessary to revise some of the targets, now that better information is available. |

## Example of the Goals Statement (with Initiatives added)

### Company Goals Statement

Plan Year 2xxx                                                            Last Revised xx/xx/xx

| VFOs | RESP | DUE DATE | MEASURE/ INITIATIVE | TARGET 2004 | 2005 | 2006 | 2007 | 2008 |
|---|---|---|---|---|---|---|---|---|
| **FINANCIAL VIEW** | | | | | | | | |
| 1. Grow profitability | | | Operating margin % | 8% | 9% | 11% | 13% | 13% |
| 2. Sustain industry growth rate | | | $ Sales growth % | 7% | 7% | 6% | 6% | 6% |
| | | | Sales (m) | $8 | $8.6 | $9.1 | $9.6 | $10.2 |
| **CUSTOMER VIEW** | | | | | | | | |
| 3. Grow client satisfaction | | | Overall satisfaction rating | 77% | 80% | 82% | 84% | 86% |
| 4. Grow sales per customer | | | Average sales per post-implementation customer | $7.5k | $7.9k | $8.2k | $8.7k | $9.1k |
| | Susan | Q2-YY | Existing customer promo #1 | | | | | |
| | Susan | Q4-YY | Existing customer promo #2 | | | | | |
| 5. Grow sales per partner | | | Average of % of partner business for the top 100 partners | 40% | 42% | 45% | $48% | 51% |
| | David | Q2-YY | Implement Mindshare program | | | | | |
| | David | Q2-YY | Change sales incentive systems | | | | | |
| **PRODUCTION VIEW** | | | | | | | | |
| 6. Improve quality | | | # errors severity less than 4 | 900 | 810 | 740 | 665 | 600 |
| | John | Q4 | New development model selected | | | | | |
| | John | Q2 | Implement release control group | | | | | |
| | John | Q1 | Implement code inspections | | | | | |
| 7. Broaden functionality | | | Distribution suite sales A ($k) | | | $200 | $300 | $400 |
| | John | Q3 | Implementation plan completed | | | | | |
| 8. Improve lead qualification | | | Close rate of qualified leads | 20% | 25% | 30% | 33% | 35% |
| | Susan | Q4 | Revamp lead process & automate | | | | | |
| | David | Q4 | Train partners of new lead process | | | | | |
| 9. Roll-out Internet product | | | Sales as % of total | | | | 3% | 15% |
| | John | Q2 | Requirements approved | | | | | |
| | John | Q4 | General design approved | | | | | |
| **PEOPLE VIEW** | | | | | | | | |
| 10. Grow employee satisfaction | | | Overall satisfaction rating | 85% | 86% | 87% | 87% | 88% |
| | Mary | Q1 | Implement monthly meetings to communicate progress | | | | | |
| | Mary | Q2 | Implement written quarterly plans | | | | | |
| 11. Increase productivity | | | Trailing year sales per employee | 125k | 129k | 133k | 137k | 141k |
| | Mary | Q2 | Implement training program requiring 16 hours per quarter | | | | | |
| | Mary | Q4 | Revamp hiring process | | | | | |

II.
SET GOALS
THAT LEAD

II-A   Define Measures
II-B   Define Targets
II-C   Define Initiatives
*II-D Engage the Team*

# STEP II-D

# Engage the Team

## Introduction

We said in Chapter 1 that the number one difference between the highest- and lowest-performing organizations was strength of leadership. On the average, the top performers were 155% stronger than the bottom performers. However, what we didn't say was that the 155% rating was an *average* of several factors.

One of those factors was *the ability to motivate or engage the people in the company in pursuing its goals.* For this isolated factor of *motivation,* top performers rated *281% higher*! Obviously, one of the top priorities of leadership is learning how to *engage* their team to strive for the company's goals.

Given that execution is a far greater challenge than strategy formulation, the ultimate core competency for any organization is realized when "all individuals make strategy *(execution)* their everyday job."[3] To achieve this kind of engagement *first* requires overcoming any lack of understanding. Research shows that "less than 5% of the typical workforce understands their organization's strategy."[4]

The existence of a well-thought-out mission, strategic position, and values and goals statement provides an essential foundation for building this understanding. Because of the size of their organizations, small business leaders have an enormous advantage in being able to get in at the "ground level" to build the kind of understanding that really unleashes the innovative potential of their team.

However, even though *understanding* is critical, it's only the first step. The next stage for the team is that of being fully *committed* to using their energy and capability in the pursuit of these goals. This cannot be achieved just by words; it has to be achieved by *action*. Recall that "people go in the direction leadership is walking, not pointing" (Chapter 1).

If leaders want others to be engaged, they must be visibly engaged as well. People need to see the leaders working hard to make sure the rest of the team members achieve the goals of the company.

One of the greatest examples of leadership for engaging people was demonstrated to me by an individual at Solomon Software, someone who had *no* management responsibility at all. This took place during a meeting when we were announcing the layoffs of a significant number of our long-term employees (and friends) in 1991. The meeting was for the people who were offered continued employment.

> The ultimate core competency for any organization is realized when "all individuals make strategy (execution) their everyday job."

The atmosphere was understandably very somber, with lots of questions, concerns, fears and doubts. However, toward the end of the meeting, one young woman stood and quietly said something to the effect that she was glad to have a job and was committed to doing her part to make this company work. It was a turning point for our company. Single-handedly, she stemmed the tide of fear, took a stand, and helped us all start the process of reengaging in what turned out to be a decade of 500% growth!

Following are some specific suggestions for getting the "engage" process started; please realize, however, that all six of the disciplines are designed to help people connect with the priorities of the company.

## Hints and Tips

❑ Ask yourself whether you're getting compliance or commitment to the goals of the company.

❑ Helping people become engaged is the role of every leader in the company, regardless of whether you're president or an individual with no formal management responsibilities. Remember that people are given more responsibility because they first demonstrate they can lead themselves.

❑ Leaders have to live the goals of the company. Goals have to be a part of everything they say and do. They need to consistently focus attention on these goals and hold people accountable for them.

❑ Think of the goals statement as the outline of a story. You're teaching each person in your organization how to tell the story contained in the outline.

❑ Rely on a mixture of group presentations and one-on-one reinforcement. Talking about the goals one-on-one shows respect for the individual; it allows interaction with less intimidation. Interaction moves people from compliance to enrollment, and from enrollment to *commitment*.

❑ Make sure all the key company statements—such as mission, vision, values, strategic position, and goals—are available and visible to every team member and are talked about regularly.

## Process for Engaging the Team

The following steps are just an illustration of suggested approaches, based on my own experience. In the end, the president of the company has to devise a strategy that fits his or her own style.

| Process for Engaging the Team | | |
|---|---|---|
| **STEP** | **RESPONSIBILITY** | **DESCRIPTION** |
| 1 | President | When the goals statement is approved, schedule a company meeting. At that meeting, make sure everyone has a copy of all the key company statements. Review mission, values, strategic position and vision as a background to the goals statement |
| 2 | President | Explain that the goals statement is the script for a story that everyone in the room should be able to tell. Then, illustrate that by telling the story. |
| 3 | President | Have people break into small groups to discuss what the strategy means and to come up with questions. You can then field the questions or ask other people on the leadership team to answer them (which gets more people involved). |
| 4 | Volunteer | You could have some fun and offer a free lunch to any volunteer who'll come up and tell the goals statement story using his or her own words. The idea is to help people realize they don't have to use your words to tell this story. |
| 5 | President | In status meetings, continue to follow progress of initiatives and be engaged in helping the group resolve problems. People will assign the importance of these projects to the priority you place on them. |
| 6 | President | When interacting with people one-on-one, ask what they are working on and comment on how important their efforts are to the strategy. Continue to help them tie their work to the strategy. |
| 7 | President | In subsequent quarterly meetings, retell the goals statement story. Better yet, ask someone else to tell the story. Report on progress toward the goals. |
| 8 | President | Set the expectation that team leaders will incorporate into their meetings discussion of strategy, goals, mission, etc., thereby modeling the same things you model to them. |
| 9 | President | Survey your people annually and ask them how well they understand the strategy. Keep trended history of the responses, to see if you're improving in your ability to engage the team. |

II.
SET GOALS
THAT LEAD

II-A Define Measures
II-B Define Targets
II-C Define Initiatives
II-D Engage the Team

RECAP OF DISCIPLINE II

# Set Goals That Lead

The goal-setting process starts with the leadership team working through each of the VFOs that were established in Discipline I. Well-crafted goals that are specific and measurable help people in the organization understand *how* to pursue these VFOs. Properly defined, these goals keep people focused on doing the right things, by following the steps that lead to successful achievement of the organization's objectives.

However, like any useful tool, they take lots of practice to learn to use. The following steps describe how to *set goals that lead*:

- ❏ II-B  Define Measures
- ❏ II-C  Define Targets
- ❏ II-D  Define Initiatives
- ❏ II-E  Engage the Team

With a clear understanding of company goals, the next challenge is to identify and prioritize any barriers that might exist in the *systems* of the company. The elimination of these barriers will unleash company performance over time.

CHAPTER SIX

## DISCIPLINE III

# *Align Systems*

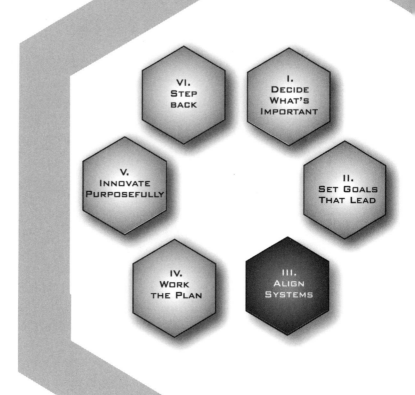

*Unfortunately, many of us are caught trying harder and harder to "whistle a symphony" when we should really be building an orchestra.*

III.
ALIGN
SYSTEMS

III-A Identify Misalignments
III-B Align Processes
III-C Align Policies
III-D Align Measures
III-E Align Technology
III-F Align People

## Overview

Now comes the hard part! Although critical, deciding what's important and setting meaningful goals are *not* where most organizations fail. Remember that in Chapter 1, we referenced that up to 90% of effectively formulated strategies fail due to *execution*. It's after goals are set that companies run into one of their most challenging foes—their own internal systems and processes!

The challenge of executing strategy sneaks up on us. In some ways, when we first start a business, there's a kind of simplicity. It's sort of like an individual whistling a simple tune he's made up in his own head. As the business grows bigger and more complex, however, this person's simple tune gradually transforms into a "symphony," requiring an orchestra to play it and a conductor to lead it. Unfortunately, many of us are caught trying harder and harder to "whistle a symphony" when we should really be building an orchestra.

An orchestra is a complex *system* made up of many different parts, all of which have to be *aligned* so their tempo, mix and volume all synchronize around the composer's music and the conductor's leadership. A business is an even *more* complex system.[*]

Continuing the analogy of a symphony, in Disciplines I and II we've written the composition we want to play (goals statement). *Discipline IV—Work the Plan* (coming up in the next chapter) focuses on actually *playing* the music. However, the purpose of *this* chapter's Discipline *(Discipline III—Align Systems)* is to make sure we have the

---

[*] The term "system" is used in a general sense. The business as a whole can be thought of as one big system made up of many smaller systems (similar to the human body being one system made up of circulatory system, nervous system, etc.).

right "types" and number of instruments, the right musicians, the correct floor layout, sound systems, electrical services, music stands and copies of the music before rehearsal starts.

The typical business is made up of combinations of many of the following types of components:

❑ *Processes*—the steps for getting something done, such as how you recruit and train a new employee or estimate a project.

❑ *Policies*—the business rules used to guide decisions in the process steps, such as credit terms, commission amounts, customer returns, borrowing limits and compensation levels.

❑ *Technologies*—the software, machines and instruments that help automate the implementation of processes and policies. Printing presses, billing software, copiers, phone systems, leads management software and computer networks are all examples of "technologies."

❑ *Measures*—quantified indicators used to track the effectiveness of processes and policies, such as average time to close a lead, customer satisfaction trends, repeat sales per customer per year and average days to receivables collection.

❑ *People*—the source of imagination and energy that drives the definition, execution and improvement of all the above.

A small business is a system with many dozens of smaller systems that determine the performance of the company. Processes, policies, measures, technologies and people all work together to develop formal or informal systems. These systems could, for example, determine how leads are generated and qualified, how services are delivered, how orders are taken or collections managed, etc.

Answering the phone can serve as a simple illustration. It involves a process (what buttons to push in what order, how to transfer calls, etc.); policy (how many rings, how long on hold); technology (the phone system itself); measures (what it costs to operate the phone, minutes on the phone, number of calls, etc.); and people (to answer the call).

One thorny problem is that many of the "systems" that exist in a business were not formally designed or, if they were, business priorities have changed and the systems haven't. That's why *having an organized effort for aligning systems is so important.* The term *alignment* means "close cooperation." So the discipline of "aligning systems" means getting all the components of the organization working in *close cooperation* to meet the goals of the company.

Anyone who has run a growing business for any length of time knows this can sometimes feel like you're "pushing a rope uphill." In thinking about this battle, it's useful to think about two different types of misalignment.

## Creeping Misalignment

*Creeping misalignment* occurs every day, often in very small ways, as the organization changes. Again, phone answering is an example. When a business gets started, the phone-answering approach is typically pretty simple. First, whoever's available answers the phone and can easily tell who's in and who's not. Phone messages are stuck on the appropriate person's desk somewhere. At this stage the person calling never knows who's going to answer the phone.

> One thorny problem is that many of the "systems" that exist in a business were not formally designed.

As the business grows, call volume increases. More mistakes get made in message handling and people get tired of being interrupted to answer other peoples' calls. Eventually, the pain gets so great that an administrator is hired and given responsibility to answer the phone. Since the office is still fairly small, the administrator knows who's in and who's not, approximately when they'll return, etc. This approach provides a consistent voice and some friendly, personal service and attention to the caller.

As the business keeps growing, however, the administrator can't handle the call volume. An automated system is installed with voice mail. It works okay, *if* callers know who they want to talk to. The caller gets a standardized experience, but it's less personal and a little discomforting if there's an urgent issue.

This example illustrates *creeping misalignment*. As the business changes, the "current" approach slowly becomes less aligned with other goals of the company. As a result, it becomes an increasing drag on the success of the company until corrected.

## Strategic Misalignment

A second kind of misalignment is *strategic misalignment*. This occurs suddenly, when the organization sets a strategic VFO and the systems and resources of the organization are *not* deployed to support that VFO. I experienced the frustration of strategic misalignment once after our annual planning cycle at Solomon Software. In this meeting, we concluded that we wanted to target a certain segment of our market based on the profitability of customer relationships. We worked out a general strategy for marketing using a new segmentation approach, and allocated funds for doing so.

Executing this strategy required having more complete market segmentation data by level of profitability within sales territory. When this information was requested, we discovered our systems were significantly misaligned with our new priorities. It turns out the information we needed wasn't easily available, because portions were stored in three different databases using different technology.

With a backlog of other high-priority projects to work on, our overcommitted IT staff wouldn't be able to get our information without disrupting many other projects and with a much larger investment than we would have liked. This type of misalignment typically surfaces *suddenly* as a barrier to implementing new strategies.

## What to Do?

The first thing to do is realize that the cumulative effect of dozens of creeping and strategic misalignments is a significant constraint on the ability of an organization to execute its plan. One source[1] estimates that *up to 50% of the resources of the typical organization are not being effectively applied to the mission and vision of the company.* As mentioned earlier, my own experience with reducing the workforce at Solomon and seeing performance go up was a painful reminder that if leaders don't learn how to align resources with goals, the free market will.

Second, you need to realize that achieving alignment is *not* an "event;" it's an ongoing battle that's part of what it means to work *on* your business. *Successfully waging this battle is key to achieving excellence that lasts.* Remember that 96% of all business start-ups in the U.S. fail within 10 years, but the failure rate of franchises is less than one third of the rate of regular businesses.[2]

Why is this so? A significant part of franchises' greater general success is because of alignment. The best franchises have thought through very carefully who their target customer is and what the promise is that they want to make to that customer. *And* they've thought through all the internal systems and processes to deliver on that promise in the most efficient and effective way. Franchises have learned to invest in developing and maintaining alignment of resources to mission.

Third, as the old proverb goes, "Eat the elephant one bite at a time." When you take the broad view that everything that goes on in a company is a system or part of a system, it can become overwhelming trying to improve it all. As shown on the next page, Discipline III can be used once a year as a part of annual planning. It is used to help evaluate all major systems quickly, and decide which processes, policies, technologies, measures and people investments offer the greatest opportunity for improving business performance.

The best approach is to focus on one or two key opportunities at a time. Next, a prioritized list of alignment projects is produced, which includes team member development focus. And finally, team member development opportunities and organizational changes are identified to better align the team with company priorities. These are folded into the quarterly plans described in *Discipline IV—Work the Plan*.

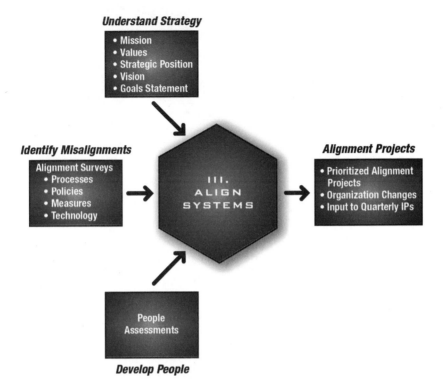

III.
ALIGN
SYSTEMS

*III-A Identify Misalignments*
III-B Align Processes
III-C Align Policies
III-D Align Measures
III-E Align Technology
III-F Align People

## STEP III-A
# Identify Misalignments

The first step in attacking what seems like a myriad of processes, policies, measures, technologies and people is to figure out which one or two opportunities will provide the best return on investment to the company. For example, in your particular business, is it more important that you improve your *leads-generation process* or improve your *job-estimating process?*

Because we believe that those *in* the business know it best, this step focuses on drawing out the knowledge about the business that exists in your team. In other words, if you follow the Methodology and make sure everyone is trained and engaged on the strategy and goals of the company, then *the best people to identify misalignments with that strategy are the people who work in the business every day at all levels in the company.* These people understand first-hand how things *really* work, and are a great resource for identifying areas that aren't working well and will need to change to meet new strategies.

This step leads you through the process of preparing and conducting a survey that provides a company-wide view of the suitability of current business processes, policies, measures and technologies, when compared to the priorities of the company. The leadership team collects all that input and then sets final priorities for alignment investments in the context of all the other priorities in the company.

One landscaping design company I worked with illustrates the entire process. This company was considering changing its strategy to expand its services to include landscape maintenance, in addition to its design services. The design business was very project driven, so once a project was completed, they moved on to another customer.

In contrast, being in the landscape maintenance business would require completely new business processes: scheduling people and supplies (for fertilizing, feeding, weeding, trimming, etc.) multiple times per year, in a very timely fashion, working with the *same* clients. To make good business decisions on adding this new business focus meant walking through all the key processes and policies required to satisfy the client *and* identifying where they didn't align with current processes.

Failure to think these things through would have resulted in enormous waste, inefficiency, upset customers and overall reduction in profitability. After thinking it through, the owner concluded this would not be a good decision for his company.

## Hints and Tips

❑ Don't be concerned about the completeness of the survey responses the first time you administer it. Many people in small organizations don't realize that much of the activity they do each day is really part of a "system." By simply administering the survey, you'll gradually raise the awareness of what systems are and the need to improve them.

❑ When preparing questions for the survey, start with general questions, progressively gathering more detailed information in areas that are identified as "high priority." For example, on the survey, you *could* break accounts payable processing into several more detailed processes: requisitioning supplies, approving invoices for payment, entering invoices, writing and mailing checks, processing refunds, etc. However, if this isn't a critical area in your company, you're better off just treating it as the "Accounts Payable Process" for rating purposes. If it continues to be a low priority, then don't invest any more in it.

❑ Be alert for processes that are "missing." These are the toughest to identify. People can rate processes if you put a list in front of them, but they may not think of identifying a process that's missing altogether. All you can do is keep asking people to consider "what's missing." This is especially relevant when there's a significant change in strategy, such as when the landscaping company considered a new service offering.

❑ Focus. Resist the temptation to try to tackle too many items at once. Pick one or two items, and work on them. Don't move on until they're functioning well. A correctly-designed system will continue to improve and be self-sustaining because of the focus that measures bring to improvement.

## Process for Identifying Misalignments

| | Process for Identifying Misalignments | |
|---|---|---|
| **STEP** | **RESPONSIBILITY** | **DESCRIPTION** |
| 1. | President | Designate someone to review the template survey provided in this book and revise, as necessary, to reflect the systems and processes in your own organization. |
| 2. | Responsible Person | Send out the System Alignment Survey to all your team members and ask them to complete it, including their name. They should have had a briefing on the goals statement first, and have a copy on hand. This survey could be completed in the meeting when the goals statement is reviewed. |
| 3. | Responsible Person | Summarize the results of the survey with average ratings for each item. |
| 4. | Facilitator | Gather the leadership team and review the lowest-rated items; then make a list of potential projects. Other items can be added to this list, such as improving the measures that appear on the goals statement. |
| 5. | Facilitator | Conduct a Quick-ROI Analysis (Discipline V) to evaluate what the top 2-3 priority projects are. |
| 6. | Leadership Team | As projects and plans are identified, incorporate them into quarterly IPs, which are discussed in Discipline IV—Work the Plan. Policy issues can sometimes be resolved very quickly. If the process itself has to be redesigned, such work can range from being simple to being a major effort, depending on how many people use it, the amount of change to be made, and the dependence upon technology. |
| 7. | President | If you need expertise or resources you don't have, you should work to establish a long-term partnership with someone who does. High-performing organizations (Chapter 3) learn how to make effective use of trusted relationships. |

## Example of Alignment Survey

| Alignment Survey | | | | |
|---|---|---|---|---|
| PROCESS | OVERALL ALIGNMENT OF PROCESS WITH GOALS | ALIGNMENT OF POLICIES USED BY THE PROCESS | TECHNOLOGY SUPPORT FOR PROCESS | ADEQUACY OF MEASURES FOR MANAGING PROCESS |
| RATE THE ITEM IN EACH COLUMN AS: 1-POOR, 2-FAIR, 3-GOOD, 4- VERY GOOD, 5-EXCELLENT | | | | |
| FINANCIAL PROCESSES | | | | |
| Budgeting/capital allocation | | | | |
| Company debt management | | | | |
| Financial reporting | | | | |
| Payables | | | | |
| Reimbursable expenses (travel, etc.) | | | | |
| Receivables | | | | |
| Credit management | | | | |
| Cash management | | | | |
| Fixed asset management | | | | |
| Long-term planning | | | | |
| Billing | | | | |
| Shareholder relations | | | | |
| CUSTOMER PROCESSES | | | | |
| Relationship management | | | | |
| Leads management | | | | |
| Marketing | | | | |
| Public relations | | | | |
| Customer service (requests, complaints, returns) | | | | |
| Order-taking | | | | |
| Sales | | | | |
| Consulting | | | | |
| Pricing/quoting | | | | |
| Satisfaction/retention tracking | | | | |

## Alignment Survey (cont'd)

| PROCESS | OVERALL ALIGNMENT OF PROCESS WITH GOALS | ALIGNMENT OF POLICIES USED BY THE PROCESS | TECHNOLOGY SUPPORT FOR PROCESS | ADEQUACY OF MEASURES FOR MANAGING PROCESS |
|---|---|---|---|---|
| RATE THE ITEM IN EACH COLUMN AS: 1-POOR, 2-FAIR, 3-GOOD, 4- VERY GOOD, 5-EXCELLENT | | | | |
| **PRODUCTION PROCESSES** | | | | |
| Project accounting | | | | |
| Scheduling | | | | |
| Time accounting | | | | |
| Shipping | | | | |
| Inventory management | | | | |
| Purchasing | | | | |
| Work order management | | | | |
| Receiving | | | | |
| Workflow/alerting management | | | | |
| Facilities management | | | | |
| Phone call management | | | | |
| E-mail management | | | | |
| Website management | | | | |
| IT infrastructure management | | | | |
| Remote access management | | | | |
| Disaster recovery (includes data backup) | | | | |
| Information security management | | | | |
| Quality tracking | | | | |
| **PEOPLE PROCESSES** | | | | |
| Recruiting & selection | | | | |
| Payroll | | | | |
| Compensation management | | | | |
| Commission | | | | |
| Incentive | | | | |
| Benefits | | | | |
| Performance management | | | | |
| Development | | | | |
| Recognition | | | | |
| Separation | | | | |
| Headcount budgeting | | | | |

**III.**
**ALIGN**
**SYSTEMS**

III-A  Identify Misalignments
*III-B Align Processes*
III-C  Align Policies
III-D  Align Measures
III-E  Align Technology
III-F  Align People

# STEP III-B
# Align Processes

If your business isn't running right, it's likely you have a process problem. Either you have a missing process, or a poorly-defined process, or you're not properly executing the processes you have. Many business leaders can't even identify their core processes, let alone tell you how well they're working, based on measurable data. Yet businesses rise or fall based on the effectiveness of their processes.

Simply put, a process is a sequenced set of activities that produce an end result. Generating and qualifying sales leads is an example of a process. Collectively, processes are like the blueprints that describe how the business works and keeps its promises to all its stakeholders.

But don't confuse simplicity with significance. As one expert put it, "For thousands of years, organizations have depended on their business processes for survival and growth. Business processes are responsible for all profits and losses. Obviously people have been trying for centuries to get the processes right."[2] And we're *still* trying, and it *isn't* easy.

The difficulty of defining and managing processes is magnified because we're attempting to deal with what happens in the ever-changing real world, not in some textbook. Figuring out what all the exceptions are and what to do about them can sometimes feel like "herding cats." Sometimes it feels like all these *circumstances* have a mind of their own.

This is why we recommend strongly that an organization pick one important process and build or rebuild it *right*, before moving on to the next. Make it solid, so it becomes a firm foundation you can depend upon working really well. You'll find that each time you do a process *right,* the next process gets a little easier to do right, because it's built upon and surrounded by other sound processes.

Well-designed processes have certain characteristics that make them robust and effective. Good processes, as a rule, are:

- ❑ *Defined*—The steps, sequence of steps that make up the process, and the responsibility for executing the steps are *explicitly* known and understood. This usually contrasts with processes that come into being in ad hoc ways over time, where different individuals understand pieces of the process, but no one understands how the pieces fit together.

- ❑ *Transferable*—Others can be trained to execute the process. A good definition is a prerequisite to teaching others how to carry out the process.

- ❑ *Repeatable*—The steps are defined clearly enough that if you follow them, you'll get the same result. Quality results depend on repeatability—the ability to control what results you get *every* time. Another benefit of repeatability is that it enables process changes to be tested for improvement. In other words, if you make a change to a repeatable process and you get better results, the change is probably a good one. If results are not repeatable, either before or after the change, you have no idea whether the change was beneficial.

- ❑ *Flexible*—The process should be designed to allow for future changes. With technologies changing, people changing and new innovative ideas flowing, it's important that key processes contribute to ongoing improvement.

- ❑ *Aligned*—The purpose of the process (its result) aligns with the strategy of the organization. Over time, as strategies change, processes must have a thorough and abiding congruence with organizational priorities.

- ❑ *Measurable*—The output of the process has some way of being measured to ensure proper execution and to test innovations and process improvements for effectiveness. Clearly identifying the measure and making sure it aligns with company priorities provides the "goal" around which the process is designed.

## Hints and Tips

❏ In designing or improving a process, it's *critical* that you get the actual people who execute the process involved in defining and changing it. These are the only people who *really* understand all the exceptions and how things actually work.

❏ Start by getting the critical process defined. Just defining the way a process currently works often identifies significant improvement opportunities.

❏ Process improvement depends on a very simple cycle: make a change; measure the results to see if the change worked; if it does, then formally adopt the change and start all over again with the next change. Note that this cycle breaks down if the process isn't defined, repeatable or measurable.

❏ Keep documentation simple. This book is filled with examples of four- and five-step processes. Clearly, there are some processes that are more complex and need much more detail to diagnose; but *start at a summary level and only drill down where necessary.* Also, remember that you're not documenting *every* process—just the critical few you've decided to focus on.

❏ You don't need outside "experts" to document a process. The experts on the way your business really works are inside your company—your own team members.

❏ If you don't invest the time to maintain a process and keep it aligned with the business priorities, it *will* get more and more out of date over time.

## Process for Aligning Processes

| Process for Aligning Processes | | |

| | RESPONSIBILITY | DESCRIPTION |
|---|---|---|
| 1. | Team Leader | Assemble a small cross-functional team of people who are involved in executing the process or using the output of the process. |
| 2. | Team Leader | Lead the team through exercises to get agreement on the result(s) the process is currently producing and how it's measured. |
| 3. | Team Leader | Lead the team through exercises to get agreement on what the steps in the current process are, the results/outputs of these steps, and who's responsible for each step. This may require off-line work assignments to gather information. |
| 4 | Team Leader | Lead the team to decide what the process should be producing, given the goals of the company, and how it should be measured. (More about how to define good measures in Step III-D Align Key Measures) |
| 5 | Team Leader | Lead the team to decide which baseline measure will be used to benchmark future improvements (if different than the current measure). For example, if the current process is resulting in 100 qualified leads a month, that is the baseline against which to measure revisions. If there is no baseline, then establish one when the first revisions are tested. |
| 6 | Team Leader | Make revisions to the process one at a time and measure the results produced to verify that they are, indeed, improvements. Note: some processes may be so poorly defined or inadequate that the team may want to redesign the process before even starting the benchmarking. |
| 7 | Team Leader | If the results improve, establish the revised process as the production process and use it as the baseline. Then go back to process step "x" and make another improvement. This process of improvement should continue as long as you're getting a return from the improvement efforts, or perhaps until another higher priority improvement effort is chosen to focus upon. |

## Example of a Process Definition

Following is an example of some things you might consider when thinking through a process that needs to align with your company priorities. The sample Systems Alignment Survey provides a much longer list of items that may be considered.

### Complaint Resolution Process

Updated by: J. Thomas                              Date Revised: xx/xx/xx

Purpose:
Describe process for resolving a complaint received from a customer. This process applies regardless of whether it's reported in writing, by phone, e-mail or any other method.

Measures: Elapsed time to close. Successful resolution %

| STEP | RESPONSIBLE | DESCRIPTION |
|---|---|---|
| 1 | Recipient | Whoever receives the complaint from any source is responsible for documenting it on a complaint form (computer) and forwarding it to Customer Service within one business hour of receipt. |
| 2 | Service Rep | Contacts the customer and gets all the background on the issues; then describes the process for resolution. This contact is to be completed within four business hours of receipt. |
| 3 | Service Rep | If the complaint is routine, the Rep addresses/provides a solution to the client and proceeds to Step 5. If the complaint is non-routine, the Rep forwards it to the responsible person (subject matter expert). |
| 4 | Responsible Person | Decides what the options are for resolving the problem and the timeframes required. Provides that information back to the Rep within 24 hours. |
| 5 | Service Rep | The Service Rep re-contacts the customer and offers the solutions and timeframes or a refund. |
| 6 | Customer | Makes a decision as to what option to take. |
| 7 | Service Rep | Manages this complaint, keeping the client informed until the complaint is closed. Asks for a rating on the resolution of this complaint, and the final result is logged in the computer. |

III.
ALIGN
SYSTEMS

III-A Identify Misalignments
III-B Align Processes
III-c *Align Policies*
III-D Align Measures
III-E Align Technology
III-F Align People

**STEP III-C**
# Align Policies

One time, I returned from a trip and landed at the Detroit airport. When I got to the tollbooth to pay my parking fees and realized I didn't have enough cash, I gave the attendant a credit card. She said they didn't accept credit cards (a policy), but I was relieved to hear that I could fill out a credit application (another policy). I hurriedly completed the one-page application, while glancing at the line that was growing behind me.

When I handed it to her, she took one look at it, reached out the window, tore it into little pieces and handed it back to me. I asked what was wrong and she said, "We don't take credit from people in Ohio!" (A third policy). Now the line was *really* long behind me, but I asked, "What am I supposed to do?" She said, "Sweetheart, I don't know, but I can tell you this: you are *not* leaving until you come up with $33." She got out of the booth, backed up the line and made me turn around.

Stunned, I went back into the airport. I walked into a store and asked if I could buy something with a credit card and add on $35 to the bill, so I could get some change. "No" was the answer (another policy). I went to ten different stores and got the same answer. An hour later, in desperation, I went up to an airline counter and asked if they could help. A woman behind the counter said there was nothing they could do, either.

But then she reached under the counter, got out her purse, and handed me $40. She wrote down her name and address and gave it to me (a "love your neighbor" policy). It was hard to believe this woman was giving a complete stranger $40 and trusted me to return it. (By the way, I sent her a "thank you" note and paid her back double for restoring my faith in people!)

Policies and the way they're handled determine what people think of you and your business. I imagine everyone could cite many examples of policies that offend customers, rather than win them.*
The purpose of this step is to help identify policies that are fighting against the priorities of the company, so that they may be fixed!

*A* policy *is a decision rule that guides the operation of the business.* Policies are separate from, but related to, processes. For example, a step in a credit process might be to check credit history, whereas the credit policy would indicate what decision to make for a customer with a below-average rating. The very word "policy" can bring to one's mind the image of bureaucracy, poor customer service and barriers to getting things done.

The concept of a "policy" is good, but our implementation often is not. A well-crafted policy helps organizations function efficiently and deliver quality in a predictable, repeatable way. However, a poorly designed or outdated policy does the opposite—it hampers quality and efficiency. By establishing a discipline that reviews policies on a regular basis, those policies that are no longer contributing to the goals of the organization are identified and improved, or eliminated.

An organization can have aligned processes and misaligned policies, or vice versa. For example, at one point in our history at Solomon, our credit management process was well defined and executed, but our credit policy was tight because of some receivables problems we'd had a couple of years before.

This particular year, however, we changed our strategy to ramp up sales rapidly and increase market share. Our commission structure and budgets were all built around this VFO, but we didn't realize how misaligned our credit policy was until the sales staff complained that the tightness of the policies was a huge turnoff to many good customers.

Sometimes, policy misalignments are hard to spot. For example, some strategies call for specialized levels of professional expertise or competence which require higher compensation, and yet restrictive

---

* I'll bet there are some great stories out there! If you've got some good examples of either wonderful policies or poor policies in action, please send them to policy@SixDisciplines.com. I promise I'll read every one. Maybe we'll do another edition of this book and incorporate them!

*compensation* policies may be causing the best candidates to be filtered out. In this case, the consequence may take a couple of years to rectify because of the time required to spot the problem and hire someone else.

A well-implemented policy has the following characteristics:

❑ **It is necessary**—the existence of the policy helps people do their jobs more effectively. Ask yourself the question, "If this policy were eliminated, what would happen to company performance over the long-term?" If the answer is "not much," get rid of it.

❑ **The intent is clear**—the reason *behind* the policy is clear to those enforcing it.

❑ **The intent is honored**—people who enforce the policy have the freedom and aptitude for adjusting its implementation to better meet the *intent* in individual situations.

❑ **It is aligned**—the policy is designed in such a way that the results it produces support the goals of the company, as opposed to being at cross-purposes.

❑ **It is measurable**—just as with processes, the best policies are those which have results that can be measured. For example, the results of a credit policy can be measured both in terms of *lost sales* and *bad debt* over time.

## Hints and Tips

❑ Formal policies should only be created where they truly add value. Too many policies are burdensome. The approach suggested is to identify the critical few policies that will drive the success of the business, and give a lot of thought to those few. Get them right. This is in contrast to investing a little in developing a lot of policies that aren't well-thought-out.

❑ Keep policies short, simple and easy to interpret. Many policies can be documented right inside the procedure itself, if the policy is brief. A simple log allows for a very quick review of all policies (see example).

❑ Make policies flexible by providing the principle behind the policy, and give people freedom to vary it if they think that makes sense. Discuss variations later, and coach them if you want them to do it differently the next time.

❑ There are many policies that don't have to be in written form. If you want to approve any check over $1,000, that only needs to be known by a few people. Why put it in writing? The important thing is that the policy is clear and is known by those who need to know it. If you have trouble getting consistent implementation, then consider putting it in writing for the sake of clarity.

❑ Remember that almost all policies are implemented as part of a process. When you're evaluating a policy that isn't working effectively, you often end up looking at the process, too.

## Process for Aligning Policies

| | Process for Aligning Policies[*] | |
|---|---|---|
| **STEP** | **RESPONSIBILITY** | **DESCRIPTION** |
| 1 | Author | Determine the purpose of the policy. Why do you want to create this policy? What's the real intent behind it? |
| 2 | Author | Closely examine whether a formal policy on this topic is necessary. What will happen to the long-term performance of the business if this policy is not implemented? Every policy that is implemented introduces some overhead for monitoring it, measuring it, teaching people to follow it, managing exceptions, etc. |
| 3 | Author | Evaluate what company goals this policy is designed to support, and make sure its purpose aligns with those goals. |
| 4 | Author | Determine who's affected by this policy and gather their input. Most policies have unforeseen long-term consequences the author doesn't predict. Get the input of those who should know best. |
| 5 | Author | Decide how exceptions to the policy are to be handled. This will determine how much latitude people should have in interpreting the policy, so they can use their judgment to better meet the intended purpose. Ranges of "exception handling" include:<br>User discretion: no approval or reporting<br>Report exceptions: no approval required, but must report exceptions later<br>Prior approval required |
| 6 | Author | Decide how the effectiveness of the policy will be measured. Often, the measures for a policy and the process within which it's used are the same or closely related. |
| 7 | Author | Draft a simple statement of policy that includes:<br>Purpose of the policy: what it's really trying to achieve<br>Statement of the policy: short and to the point<br>Measures<br>Exception handling |
| 8 | Author | Have the draft policy reviewed by people affected by it. Ask for their feedback and any necessary approvals. |
| 9 | Author | Incorporate any changes and issue a final version. |
| 10 | Author | Train people who have to enforce the policy about its proper implementation and the purpose behind it. |

---

[*] Although this process is for defining a new policy, an existing policy can be reviewed by checking it against these process steps.

# Example of Policies Documented in Table Form

| | | | | | | |
|---|---|---|---|---|---|---|
| **Policies** | | | | | | |
| **POLICY NAME** | **POLICY** | **PURPOSE** | **MEASURE** | **EXCEPTION HANDLING** | **OWNER** | **DATE REVISED** |
| **Service Policies** | | | | | | |
| Return call standard | Return service calls within 30 minutes | Premier service strategy | % of calls outside target Customer satisfaction service | User discretion | | |
| Calls on hold standard | Average < 2 minutes | Premier service strategy | Average time on hold Customer satisfaction service | User discretion | | |
| **Development Policies** | | | | | | |
| Release standard | Software released only when no severity 1 or 2 defects found in QA cycle | Maximize long-term sales Cost of service Overall profitability | Cost of support Returns Customer satisfaction | Pre-approval | | |
| Code inspections | All code will be inspected before check-in | Increased quality Lower costs | Number of errors Cost of errors | Pre-approval | | |
| **Personnel Policies** | | | | | | |
| Headcount | No hires that will cause sales per employee to fall below $125k | Productivity Stop low priority activity Profitability | Sales per employee | Pre-approval | | |
| Hiring standards | Permanent hire may only be made after all standard test results are evaluated | Zero wrong hires Lower turnover Higher productivity | Employee satisfaction Turnover Sales per employee | Pre-approval | | |
| **Financial Policies** | | | | | | |
| Operating margins | Maintain operating margins above 10% annually | Disciplined approach to business Strong balance sheet | Operating margin | Report exceptions | | |

## STEP III-D
# Align Measures

Measurement is part of the culture of an excellent organization. Excellence implies having a standard—knowing what you want to be good at. Measurement tells whether you are. For example, at school, our children study and then have a quiz, to see if they've learned the material. Clearly, no quiz is a perfect measure of a child's knowledge, but it does provide meaningful feedback, which guides future actions (study more, get assistance, etc.). In the business world, measurement accelerates learning and stimulates innovation.

Measurement frees us to try new things, because with measurement as a "tool at hand," we have a way of managing the risk of failure in a controlled setting. We can try a new idea on a limited basis, measure the results, and know with comparative certainty whether it works or not. We can then confidently rollout those ideas that work.

Clear measures help people to move toward a goal, giving them tangible feedback on their innovation and effort. There are many different types of measures. Some measures are *leading* (e.g., number of complaints predicts repeat sales), some *lagging* (sales lag sales leads). Some are highly *summarized* (e.g., return on investment), and some are very *detailed* (e.g., number of phone calls Sally handled from 10 to 11 A.M.). Some are notably *strategic*, like customer satisfaction, and some are *tactical*, such as the average length of a service call.

In Discipline II—*Set Goals That Lead*, attention was given to defining a very short list of strategic measures. Here in Discipline III—Align Systems, we're evaluating whether adequate measures are in place to manage key business processes in the day-to-day operation of the business.

People will focus on what you choose to measure, so choose wisely. For example, the person managing cash would make very different decisions, given two very different measures: Cash on Hand or Sales Days of Cash (see charts). Cash on Hand is an *absolute* measure of the total amount of cash on hand; Sales Days of Cash is a *relative* measure that divides total cash by the average *daily* sales for any time period.

The *relative* approach shows that cash reserves are actually declining relative to the growing business, which will eventually become a problem. Choosing appropriate measures is a learned skill. You won't get it right the first time, every time. But gradually, as better measures are put in place, the innovative capability of your team, will be more and more aligned with the priorities of the company, and performance will improve significantly.

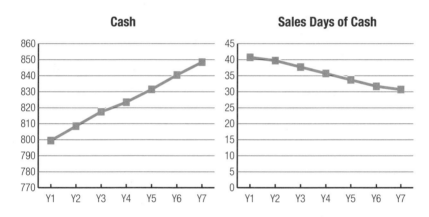

## Hints and Tips

❑ Use the fewest number of measures possible to manage a particular process. Simpler is better. Having too many measures reduces the value of them all.

❑ Make sure the measure is appraising the correct facet of the company's activity. Think about the most basic purpose of the process, and see if the measure is reflecting that purpose (as in the cash example above).

❑ Measures should be presented as trended data because the meaning is much greater. For example, in the chart below, a business leader looking at the 2004 rating of 84% customer satisfaction would realize the trend is severely down, but also realize satisfaction is approaching the lowest levels the company has ever had. In the past, these same low levels of customer satisfaction have correlated with some of the most difficult years, both in terms of sales and profitability. Obviously, evaluating measures in context of history adds a great deal of understanding.

**Customer Satisfaction**

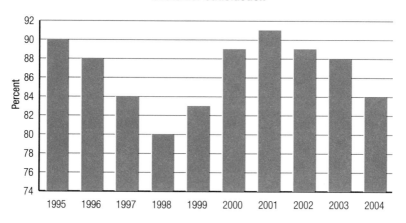

❑ Because trended data is so valuable, you should consider carefully before changing the definition of the measure. Otherwise, historical trends are interrupted. Of course, if you must change a measure, the sooner the better, so a new trend can be started.

❑ Be cautious about measures that use absolute values. Often, a relative measure (ratio) provides a more meaningful perspective over time. The cash example in the graphs on page 137 illustrates this point. Total cash (an *absolute* measure), in most cases, isn't as relevant as sales days of cash (a *relative* measure).

## Process for Aligning Measures

| | Process for Aligning Measures | |
|---|---|---|
| **STEP** | **RESPONSIBILITY** | **DESCRIPTION** |
| 1 | Author | Think through carefully what the purpose of the related process or policy is. Choose a measure that will lead people to take action that aligns with this purpose. Sometimes, it requires more than one measure; if at all possible, pick only one. |
| 2 | Author | Establish a name for the measure that's clear. For example, "Market Share" isn't as clear as "New Site $ Unit Market Share." "Market Share" can be based on dollars or on number of units sold. Be specific. |
| 3 | Author | Evaluate whether the measure is best expressed as a "relative" or an "absolute" measure. (See graphs on page 135 for example.) |
| 4 | Author | Write down how the measure is to be calculated. For example, unit market share might be calculated like this: number of units shipped/number of units shipped by competitors |
| 5 | Author | Evaluate the sources available for the data. Are they accurate enough to serve your purposes? Will they be consistent over time? Depending on the measure, determining how to get the data can take significant research. If the source of the data is too difficult or expensive to attain, then consider changing the measure. For example, it's often easier to get dollar sales data than unit sales. Ask yourself whether unit market share is worth the expense, when compared to dollar market share. |
| 6 | Author | Evaluate whether the sources of data are dependable enough to build long-term trends based on these numbers. Multi-year trended data increases the value of the data, because it allows leadership to see the long-term effects of decisions. For some types of decisions, the consequences don't become clear until years later. However, this data can provide some of the most valuable feedback. |
| 7 | Author | Decide what the frequency of reporting is. Some measures are best done monthly, some quarterly, some annually. There may even be some that are best done daily. |
| 8 | Author | If the data collection is not automated, someone will have to be made responsible for producing the data and calculating the measure. This is another reason to be sure the measures you ask for are important; they cost money to produce. |

## Examples

Following are a *few* examples of different types of measures that could be used. Many measures apply to many different types of businesses. There are also many measures that are unique to a particular type of business, such as a services business (percentage of hours billable), or a company that does research and development (e.g., software companies). Your list of measures should be as short as possible to do the job, and tailored to the needs of your specific business.

| Measures Checklist (Example) | |
| --- | --- |
| **Financial Measures** | |
| ❑ Cash | ❑ Operating Return on Sales (operating margin) |
| ❑ Sales Days of Cash | ❑ Return on Assets |
| ❑ Current Assets to Liabilities Ratio | ❑ Return on Equity |
| ❑ Sales Days of Receivables | ❑ Sales Growth Rate |
| ❑ Sales Days of Inventory | ❑ Gross Profit Growth Rate |
| ❑ Direct Cost Days of Payables | ❑ Interest Income as % of Revenues |
| ❑ Total Liabilities to Total Assets Ratio | ❑ Interest Expense as % of Revenues |
| ❑ Operating Profit-to-Interest Expense | |
| **Production Measures** | |
| ❑ Sales Days of Order Backlog | ❑ $ Leads Pipeline Value-to-Sales Ratio |
| ❑ Days to Ship | ❑ Days to Close Leads |
| ❑ Direct Labor as % of Revenue | ❑ Leads Close Rate |
| ❑ Indirect Labor as % of Revenue | ❑ Support Calls per Customer |
| ❑ Overtime Labor as % of Revenue | ❑ Time per Support Call |
| ❑ Receiving Cost as % of Revenue | ❑ Time to Close Support Issue |
| ❑ Shipping Cost as % of Revenue | ❑ Complaints-to-Customer Ratio |
| ❑ Marketing Expense as % of Revenue | ❑ Project Estimate vs. Actual Variance |
| ❑ Selling Expense as % of Revenue | ❑ Revenue Per Project |
| ❑ R&D Expense as % of Revenue | ❑ Gross Profit Per Project |
| ❑ IT Expense as % of Revenue | ❑ Average Sales Per Order |
| ❑ Training Expense as % of Revenue | ❑ Acquisition Cost Per New Customer |
| ❑ Administrative Expense as % of Revenue | |

### Customer Measures

- ❏ Market Share
- ❏ New Customers Added
- ❏ Customers Lost
- ❏ Total Customers
- ❏ Customer Retention Rate
- ❏ Average Sales Per Customer
- ❏ Average Profitability Per Customer
- ❏ Overall Customer Satisfaction Rating
- ❏ Lifetime Value of a Customer

### People Measures

- ❏ Sales Per Full-Time Equivalent (FTE)
- ❏ Payroll & Benefits Per FTE
- ❏ Revenue Per Sales & Marketing Employee
- ❏ Billed Hours as % of Billable Hours
- ❏ Employee Additions
- ❏ Employee Losses
- ❏ Total Employees
- ❏ Employee Turnover Rate
- ❏ # Customers Per Sales & Marketing Employee
- ❏ Employee Benefits as % of Revenue
- ❏ Total Benefits & Compensation as % of Revenue
- ❏ Cost of Training Per Payroll Hour
- ❏ Employee Satisfaction
- ❏ Performance Appraisal Scores

III.
ALIGN
SYSTEMS
III-A Identify Misalignments
III-B Align Processes
III-C Align Policies
III-D Align Measures
*III-E Align Technology*
III-F Align People

# STEP III-E
# Align Technology

During a time of rapid growth at Solomon, we were challenged to maintain the standards of service levels our customers expected. In an attempt to solve this problem, we decided to invest heavily in a service management software product. After using the new system for a while, we realized we weren't getting the results we expected.

After many months and much effort, we gradually began to understand the problem wasn't the technology. The problem was that our services operation was growing so fast we had to approach call management differently. We had to get better at bringing new people up to speed more quickly, we had to match types of calls with the proper expertise, and we had to have ways of cataloging and retrieving information that would work with a larger call group.

Once we realized what the problems were, *then* our top priority became aligning our computer system, software systems, phone systems, training systems and people with the new way we wanted to manage support. It was a major effort to rework all these systems to get them working together. But once they were aligned, we got great results!

This story illustrates several principles about aligning technology. First, throwing technology at a problem before you understand what you really need is a waste of time and resources. Second, once you know what you want, getting technology aligned with it can be a major effort that requires sustained management focus for a significant period of time. Third, once alignment is achieved, the payoff can be enormous.

Align Systems comes after Disciplines I and II to ensure that the organization understands its strategy before choosing where to make alignment investments. The purpose of the Align Technology step is to identify the technology investments that would provide the best return on investment to the company. When we use the term *technology,* we mean things like credit card systems, computers, software, phone systems, web sites, copiers, bar code readers, even production equipment. It is employed by the company to automate all or parts of individual business processes.

> *Throwing technology at a problem before you understand what you really need is a waste of time and resources.*

The last 30 years has brought an explosion in technology that touches our lives at home and in the office. However, lost in the headlines is the fact that technology is still a means to an end. At Solomon, we implemented more than 60,000 business systems. We learned that the organizations that received the greatest value from their business systems were those that focused on applying technology to their business priorities—whether in marketing, production or customer services.

Theodore Levitt was prophetic when, in his 1974 book *Marketing for Business Growth,* he explains the challenge we all face:

> The enormous prodigality of the computer has so accelerated the process of data accumulation that we often actually know less than we did before. Great masses of data are disgorged. . . . Yet the more abundant the information, the less meaning it will yield. We know that the surest way to destroy a man's capacity for discrimination is to overwhelm his senses with relevant stimuli. The greater the variety of food consumed at a meal, the less you appreciate each dish. The louder the noise, the less impressive the message . . . Abundance is not a liberator. It is a suffocator.[3]

By following the Six Disciplines Methodology, an organization gradually learns *how to make technology investments that serve the long-term purposes of the organization.* This is one of the *key* differences between organizations that last and those that don't.

## Hints and Tips

❑ Plan! Small incremental implementation steps are the right approach with technology, but it's important to look ahead several years so that your technologies will all fit together well. Get the advice of professionals to figure out how to sequence investments that fit your goals.

❑ Trade feature depth for technologies that work together so processes and information flow smoothly and flexibly, and good measures can be produced. The ability to work together well is more important than having the absolute deepest feature set in some particular area.

❑ Select technologies that help you measure the effectiveness of key processes. Examples of the types of things you might like to measure include: time it takes to close a lead, employee turnover trends, and average duration of projects.

❑ Leverage the Internet. Information technologies should leverage the Internet so your people can work anywhere and get easy access. This will ultimately enable you to streamline communication with your customers and suppliers. The biggest payoff for using the Internet for most small businesses isn't selling over the Internet; it's using the Internet to be better at strategy execution.

❑ Don't underestimate the investment required to get value out of the technology. More is usually invested in the ongoing cost of maintaining/using technology than the initial cost of acquiring it.

❑ Build lasting relationships with experts in this area, so that over time they come to know and understand what your priorities are. They can provide advice without having to come up to speed on your business. Like all professional advice, the more the advisor understands about the background and context of the business, the better the advice will be.

## Process for Aligning Technology

| | Process for Aligning Technology | |
|---|---|---|
| **STEP** | **RESPONSIBILITY** | **DESCRIPTION** |
| 1 | Facilitator | Have the leadership team review the System Alignment Survey to forge a preliminary draft of the processes, policies and measures that you want your long-term technology priorities to support. |
| 2 | Facilitator | Have the leadership team examine the Technical Review, conducted as a part of Discipline VI (Chapter 9), to identify any existing shortcomings in the basic technology infrastructure that need to be considered in the priorities. |
| 3 | Facilitator | Have the leadership team prepare and prioritize a list of technology investments using the Quick ROI Analysis (Chapter 8). |
| 4 | Facilitator | Have the leadership team prioritize those requirements into items to focus on in the next year and those covering the 3-5 year timeframe. Work with a consultant, if necessary, to figure out which technology investments should be done in what order, based on technical reasons. |
| 5 | President | Assign responsibility for current year projects, so they can be folded into the quarterly planning process (Discipline IV) for implementation. This person will develop budgets, requirements, etc. as the project progresses. |
| 6 | Project Manager | If you need to consider acquiring new technologies, have someone conduct a review of products and services that can address your long-term requirements. There are many detailed things to consider, but major considerations are: <br>• How well-integrated are all the components of the system? Do they share one database so information can be easily accessed? <br>• Does the system make it easy to define and measure processes? <br>• Is there local service available? Commitment to a major technology equates to developing a new strategic relationship with the provider. You want a long-term, trusted relationship. <br>• Are there services available to help adapt the system to future needs, e.g., new or revised reports, measures, processes, etc.? <br>• Is the system designed for Internet access anywhere? <br>• Is the security model practical? Does it provide adequate security without cumbersome administrative costs? <br>• Will the system handle your growth needs for the next 5-7 years, in terms of volume, process needs, measures, reports, etc.? |
| 7 | President | Make sure your organization selects the very best technology partner you can find. Focus on building a long-term relationship to help you apply the technology to your strategy. |

## Examples of Technology Investments

Following is a list of common technologies relevant to small businesses. Note that this list is not the same as the list of key processes described earlier, although there *is* some overlap. The reason is that some technologies end up automating more than one process, and frequently, one process requires more than one technology to implement. There isn't a one-to-one relationship.

| Technology Checklist | |
| --- | --- |
| **Basic Infrastructure** | |
| ❑ Internal network, including workstations available to all workers | ❑ Offsite data backup to protect data in the event of hardware failure, fire, site disaster |
| ❑ Internet connections | ❑ Security management—even more critical in the Internet era |
| **Basic Productivity** | |
| ❑ Word processing | ❑ Company web site—public access |
| ❑ Spreadsheet | |
| ❑ E-mail | ❑ Internal web site—employees only |
| ❑ Calendaring | |
| ❑ Web browser | ❑ Phone system |
| **Business Process Automation** | |
| ❑ General Ledger & Financial Reporting | ❑ Customer Relationship/Leads Management |
| ❑ Accounts Payable | ❑ Customer Service Management |
| ❑ Accounts Receivable & Credit Management | ❑ Market Research/Surveying |
| ❑ Billing | ❑ Strategy—Development & Execution |
| ❑ Cash Management | ❑ Budgeting |
| ❑ Inventory | ❑ Recognition |
| ❑ Shipping/Receiving/Warehouse Management | ❑ Suggestion Management |
| ❑ Purchasing | ❑ Learning Systems |
| ❑ Order Processing | ❑ Payroll |
| ❑ Project Accounting | ❑ Recruiting/Selection |
| ❑ Time and Billing | ❑ Performance Management |
| | ❑ Document Management |

### III.
### ALIGN SYSTEMS

III-A Identify Misalignments
III-B Align Processes
III-C Align Policies
III-D Align Measures
III-E Align Technology
*III-F Align People*

# STEP III-F
# Align People

The greatest wins in business I've ever experienced have been rooted in getting the right people in the right spots with a clear understanding of their priorities. The reason Solomon Software was so successful, after we reorganized, was that we had a very clear picture of what our goals were, and we drew what we thought would be the ideal organization chart for meeting our goals. This chart had no names on it.

Then, we went through our roster and picked who we thought would best fit each position in the chart. The results were outstanding! Our sales, profitability and overall ability to execute were actually substantially better with a much smaller organization, because *we narrowed our focus and had such clear organizational alignment around that focus.* *

Clearly, having to get alignment the way we did was only the course of last resort. A much better approach is to continually groom an organization and its people so investments and adjustments are made in small increments, instead of having to go through the process of a complete financial and organizational restructuring. The "Align People" step, working in conjunction with the rest of the Six Disciplines Methodology, is designed to help organizations get the right people in the right spots, and help them learn and grow faster.

Sometimes, this too feels like you're "trying to whistle a symphony." Not only does every person have different skills, abilities and personality, but each one is learning, growing and changing every day. This makes aligning people the most challenging of all the steps in "Aligning Systems," but also, by far, the most rewarding.

---

* A great deal of the credit goes to Brian Clark, who assumed the role of general manager at this time and brought about the alignment that produced such great results

So what exactly does *Aligning People* mean? It means bringing the right people into the organization in the first place. It means creating an environment that helps accelerate their growth; it means channeling the amazing ability of every person in the organization to innovate in ways that contribute to the organization's priorities; and it means structuring the organization so that the mission of individuals and teams are clear and complementary.

It means helping people find and fulfill the responsibilities that are the best fit for their passion and makeup. All of this isn't somehow "magically" achieved. Following the suggestions in this step, in combination with all of the other steps in the Six Disciplines Methodology, will move your team in the right direction!

## Hints and Tips

❑ Invest as much in making a hiring decision as you would if you were buying a $1 million piece of equipment. Over a 15- to 20-year period, the cost of an average employee, including salary, benefits and training, will be well in excess of that amount.

❑ Establish a rigorous hiring process. It should include the following elements: a clear definition of position, use of assessments to evaluate whether a person has the basic suitability to enjoy such a position and the skills to be successful at it, and very thorough interviews by people above, below and at the same level as this person. Use every means available to be able to say with integrity to the candidate, "We believe you are the right person to join our team."

❑ Invest heavily in understanding the strengths and performance of every team member, with the motive of helping him or her leverage those strengths.

❑ Be clear about the goals of the company and an employee's specific responsibilities. You can't expect people to be aligned if they don't know what to align to.

❏ Don't look for the ideal long-term organizational structure. No such thing exists. Every structure has its strengths and weaknesses. Be willing to change structure periodically to fit the current priorities, and to keep the weaknesses of the current structure from getting too ingrained.

❏ Build the kind of culture where organizational changes are a normal part of doing business, and not viewed as surprising or a sign that something's wrong. Instead, help people see this as a normal part of getting and staying aligned.

❏ Once the top priorities for process improvements and technology investments are identified, make sure people are well trained to implement and use the new processes effectively. A common error is to invest heavily to acquire a new technology, and then underinvest in learning how to use it.

## Process for Aligning People

| | Process for Aligning People | |
|---|---|---|
| **STEP** | **RESPONSIBILITY** | **DESCRIPTION** |
| 1 | Leadership Team | Prior to meeting, Review Team Member Survey Results summarized by department (Discipline VI—Chapter 9). Review a summary of individual performance ratings and 360° feedback (Discipline VI—Chapter 9), looking for people who are ready for new responsibility or are being underutilized. |
| 2 | Facilitator | After process, policy, measurement and technology priorities (step III-A) are established, lead a brainstorming exercise on the question, "What investments in team-member training would give us the greatest return?" |
| 3 | Facilitator | Lead the team on a brainstorming exercise on the question, "What changes in organizational structure might improve the effectiveness of the organization in pursuing its goals?" This includes forming cross-functional teams, reorganizing departments or forming new functions. |
| 4 | Facilitator | Lead the team on a brainstorming exercise on the questions, "What individuals are being underutilized, have demonstrated they're ready for new responsibilities, or may not be in a job that's the best fit for what they're doing?" |
| 5 | Facilitator | Lead the team on a brainstorming exercise on the question, "What new hires should be considered over the next couple of years?" |
| 6 | President | Gather and review the input from above. Spend time alone considering which of these ideas are the best and how they all fit together. (Structure changes, personnel moves, personnel additions, training emphasis, etc.) This work is really organizational design work and is often best done alone, with occasional advice from individuals on specific issues. Because personnel issues are often private matters, group discussion may not be the best way to make many of these decisions. |
| 7 | President | Document the organizational strategy changes that are planned and set the time frame for each. (Again, this could include structure changes, personnel moves, hiring plan, training priorities, etc.) |
| 8 | President | Make sure the organization defines and follows a rigorous hiring process for every new hire. |
| 9 | President | Invest in a high-quality set of personnel assessment tools, and help every individual learn how to use them to better understand their own characteristics and traits. |
| 10 | Team Leaders | Make sure individuals incorporate into their quarterly plans (Discipline IV—Chapter 7) training priorities that align with the company priorities. |
| 11 | Team Leaders | Follow the processes outlined in Discipline IV and Discipline VI for providing feedback to every team member through quarterly and annual appraisals. |

III.
ALIGN
SYSTEMS

III-A  Identify Misalignments
III-B  Align Processes
III-C  Align Policies
III-D  Align Measures
III-E  Align Technology
III-F  Align People

RECAP OF DISCIPLINE III

# Align Systems

Of all the Disciplines, this is the one that can seem like a "jungle" to the typical small business leader. It seems like a lot of discussion of technical and systems "mumbo-jumbo." And yet, it's this unfamiliarity and discomfort that's the very *proof* of the need to master it. Systems exist all over *every* business and many of them aren't designed—they just happen.

There's no way these systems are going to line up with the priorities of the company unless you diligently work to make them line up. And the more "out of line" they become, the more difficult it becomes to execute your strategy. If that weren't enough of a challenge, add the human element of people who are all different and learning and growing at different rates and in different directions.

In this chapter, we've described some practical steps for getting the orchestra playing your "symphony." These steps include:

- ❑ III-B Identify Misalignments
- ❑ III-C Align Processes
- ❑ III-D Align Policies
- ❑ III-E Align Measures
- ❑ III-F Align Technology
- ❑ III-G Align People

At last we are ready to move on to where everything comes together! Read on to find out how the individual on a daily basis connects his or her work with the priorities of the company.

## CHAPTER SEVEN

## DISCIPLINE IV
# *Work The Plan*

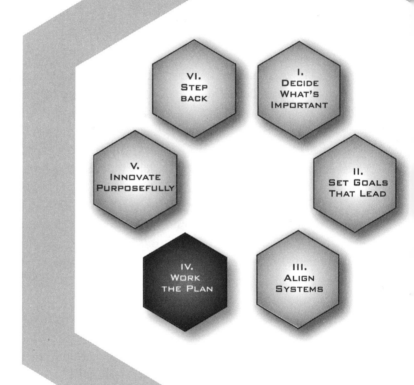

*It's about
learning how to do,
on a day-to-day basis,
the things required to build
sustainable leadership in your
chosen area.*

IV.
WORK
THE PLAN

IV-A Define IPs Quarterly
IV-B Review IPs Weekly
IV-C Rate IPs Quarterly
IV-D Prioritize Daily
IV-E Monitor Measures

# Overview

This is where all the other disciplines come together and the work gets done. In this discipline, every individual worker connects what he or she is doing on a daily basis with the long-term goals of the company. This is where the difficult work of figuring out who's responsible for what, on a daily basis, is ironed out. This is where people learn how to develop plans and take responsibility for executing them, learn how to coordinate with others and self-manage.

This is where people learn to anticipate and set realistic expectations for themselves and others. This is where constructive accountability is developed, which provides the focus needed to keep the "urgent" tasks from overriding the "most important" tasks. The result is an organization that has the most vital core competence of all—the ability to execute its strategy, to *be* excellent.

To achieve this, every team member prepares a one-page IP *(Individual Plan)* quarterly. On a daily basis, team members are taught to self-manage by monitoring their progress against their IP and other measures relevant to their job. Each week, the IP is used as a template for preparing a status report, which takes no more than five minutes to read and fifteen minutes to prepare. Each team member's IP Status report is reviewed with the team leader.

At the end of the quarter, the achievement of quarterly goals is rated by the team member and team leader, to learn what could be done better. Then, a new IP is prepared for the next quarter and the process continues. Eventually, the team leader grows into a coaching role, as the team member learns to plan better and take responsibility for innovating to stay on plan.

Practicing this discipline improves communication, helps people learn how to continually align their work with company priorities, and empowers them to innovate to do so. Whereas Disciplines I, II, and III are part of the annual planning process, Discipline IV is lived out every day in the company by every person.

Since alignment is a never-ending battle, there must be a systematic way of counteracting the forces of organizational entropy discussed earlier. Discipline IV provides the tools to do just that on a day-to-day basis. Stephen Covey likens living in integrity with your purpose to trying to walk in a straight line through deep water with large waves. You get tossed back and forth. There are major forces at work slowing you down, knocking you backward and every which way.

It's tough enough for an individual to stay on course in such an environment. Keeping a *whole team* of people on course is even more difficult!

*The result is an organization that has the most vital core competence of all—the ability to execute its strategy, to be excellent.*

Remember that the research showed that "fewer than 10% of effectively formulated strategies were successfully implemented."[1] Learning how to work the plan, day in and day out, overcoming the obstacles and getting back on course when the inevitable surprises come, is where the Six Disciplines Methodology is lived out, moment by moment.

This is the essence of what *Six Disciplines for Excellence* is all about. It's not some short-term fad that quickly fades; rather, *it's about learning how to do on a day-to-day basis the things required to build sustainable leadership in your chosen area.* It's all about learning how to work *on* the business—to be great at executing plans, whatever they may be. And, indeed, the results are transforming!

For people who haven't seen the benefits of such an approach, there may be considerable skepticism and resistance to a disciplined process. At the Six Disciplines headquarters, we follow this same process ourselves. When "Randy" joined our organization as manager of software development, we introduced him to this process and he was openly skeptical.

He felt it was going to be almost impossible to develop goals each of his team members could meet. His belief was that the software development process was too "unpredictable." But we asked him to focus his plans on what he knew, not on what he didn't know.

My weekly meetings with Randy were very valuable because they frequently revealed misunderstandings between the two of us. I thought a certain goal meant one thing; he understood it differently. Eventually, our communication improved. The first couple of quarters, we hit about 80 percent of our goals, but each quarter, he and I both got better at setting goals, and his team got better at eliminating reasons their goals were missed.

*Since alignment is a never-ending battle, there must be a systematic way of counteracting the forces of organizational entropy.*

After about four quarters, the people on his team started hitting 95 to 100 percent of their goals. This has now become a habit for Randy and his team, and our weekly meetings take just a few minutes. In fact, I recently heard him say, "I don't know how I ever managed without this process." He has become the biggest advocate in the company.

This process works! The productivity of our team is much higher than that of any organization I've worked in before. However, to make it work takes both a *firm commitment* from the top of the organization and *leadership by example,* to overcome the natural resistance to defining and sticking to a plan.

Following this discipline provides the following benefits:

❑ Productivity and quality are higher, and wasted time and effort are lower. Paperwork is very low and meeting time is reduced, because communication is greatly improved.

❑ Team members grow in their sense of responsibility for meeting clearly defined goals. They turn into problem solvers, using their innovative abilities to overcome challenges and meet goals.

❑ Learning for team members *and* team leaders is accelerated. Both get better at their jobs faster. This discipline is one of the greatest "people development" tools you can implement.

❑ Team members are getting four quarterly abbreviated performance appraisals, so when annual appraisals come along, there are seldom surprises. The latter are much easier to prepare, because of the existence of the four quarterly appraisals.

❑ Plans are executed more predictably. Individuals and the organization, as a whole, stay more focused on long-term goals and are less susceptible to the interruptions and distractions of everyday business.

❑ Problems and barriers are spotted much earlier, and there's more time to deal with them.

In summary, this discipline is where the carefully formed company vision and goals meet every worker, every day. They help each worker align their energy, skill and creativity with the mission of the organization. As stated earlier, the results are transforming!

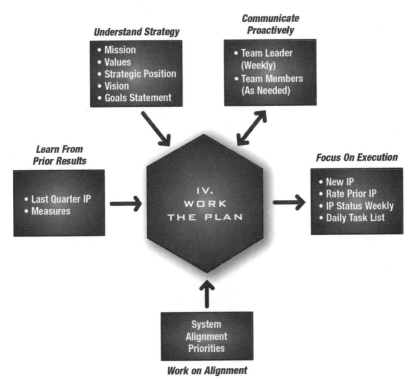

IV.
WORK
THE PLAN

IV-A *Define IPs Quarterly*
IV-B Review IPs Weekly
IV-C Rate IPs Quarterly
IV-D Prioritize Daily
IV-E Monitor Measures

## STEP IV-A
# Define IPs Quarterly

## Introduction

The real challenge in business is not how to get people to work harder. Instead, it's figuring out how to get a larger percentage of the potential ability of each person aligned with the priorities of the company. "Work smarter, not harder," as the saying goes. This step helps each team member spend one to two hours per quarter to develop an individual plan (IP) that reflects company goals.

The creation and monitoring of quarterly IPs force team members and their team leaders to communicate with each other about their priorities. Experience teaches that the discipline of defining IPs for every team member surfaces a lot of misunderstandings, identifies areas of misalignment, and reveals resource issues much sooner.

This is a true "win-win" situation. It *helps people understand how they improve company performance, and improves team member satisfaction.* In essence, *this step is at the heart of the process for achieving lasting excellence.*

## Hints and Tips

❑ Expect resistance at first. Concerns about practicality, difficulty in setting realistic goals, time required, etc. are normal. Explain that this is a learning experience, and allow two or three quarters as a trial run to get used to the process.

❑ The team leader's role is to make sure individual goals align with company priorities. Ownership of the plan rests with the individual; responsibility for *alignment* rests with the team leader.

❑ Get the team members to take as much responsibility as possible in defining and setting the goals for the quarter. This helps them grow professionally and learn to plan.

❑ The number of goals should be kept small. We recommend five summary goals as a maximum. Sometimes, it's useful to break a summary goal into smaller tasks for better clarity of what's in the goal.

❑ One of the five goals should be related to individual/personal development, such as completing a training course, reading a book, etc.—any of a myriad of activities that expand the individual's professional capability. Such investments should connect with current or planned responsibilities.

❑ Goals will typically be a mixture of ongoing activities, like *number of sales orders processed*, and one-time projects, like *complete competitive pricing analysis.*

❑ Goals should describe deliverables produced, *not* the activity that produces the deliverable. For example, *redesign the sales process* describes an activity, whereas *first draft of sales process reviewed by Tom* describes a deliverable.

❑ Sometimes, the responsibility for one goal is shared by multiple people. In these cases, a team goal is defined and this goal appears on each of their IPs. It's better if individual responsibilities can be defined, but this isn't always practical.

❑ For jobs that are highly routine, just meeting the day-to-day expectations is often considered "success." However, consider asking team members to identify something they can improve during the current quarter: reduce supply costs, increase discounts taken on payables, improve the filing system, etc. There's *always* something to improve.

❑ Once goals are set, the team leader's role is to help individuals meet their goals. Setting and tracking goals should not be adversarial, or an opportunity to look for failure; rather, it's a shared "win-win" mindset, because team leaders can't meet their goals if the team doesn't.

❑ If you want to attach cash incentives to quarterly goals, we suggest you wait until the process is working relatively smoothly, *and* that you keep the percentage of compensation involved small. Too much emphasis on monetary matters reduces openness and leads to less challenging goal-setting. Non-cash compensation, such as gift certificates for team members, works well.

❑ Resist changing goals once they're set. There are cases where a team leader may need to change priorities for some reason, but changing goals frequently sends the message that it's okay if you don't plan well ahead of time. It actually weakens the organization's development.

## Process for Defining Quarterly IPs

| STEP | RESPONSIBILITY | DESCRIPTION |
|---|---|---|
| 1 | Team Leader | Make sure the team member understands the goals statement for the company for the current year, the team's goals and how it affects their priorities, *before* planning. |
| 2 | Team Member | Make sure you understand what your team leader's goals for the upcoming quarter are, so you can be sure that anything you have to do to meet those is included in your plan. |
| 3 | Team | If you have a team of people who are working on the same projects, it's useful for the group, as a whole, to: (1) discuss goals for the quarter, (2) work out who's best to work on which task, or which tasks should be shared, and (3) identify any dependencies among the team. |
| 4 | Team Member | Identify potential problems and barriers to the goals, and figure out how to plan for addressing them. A significant part of successful plan development and execution is identifying risks, whether internal or external, and managing those risks proactively and aggressively. |
| 5 | Team Member | Write down four or five goals and make sure they're in the form of deliverables. If necessary, summary goals can be broken into more detailed deliverables. Make sure one of the goals is related to personal development. |

| 6 | Team Member | Write down "sustaining responsibilities" in the area provided. These are the everyday types of responsibilities that have to be completed every quarter, regardless of projects. The intent of this IP process is to bring more focus to the *non-sustaining* responsibilities and make sure they get done, assuming the sustaining activities are more routine and easier to handle. |
| 7 | Team Member | For each goal, write down a proposed weight (Wt) to be given to it. The collective weight for all items should total 100 percent. Weighting is related to importance, not necessarily to effort. Weighting can be used in computing incentive awards. |
| 8 | Team Member | Indicate the rough number of hours expected to be invested in completing the task under consideration this quarter. This field can be a great help in getting clarification on the scope of projects. I've frequently thought I was clear with a team member as to what needed to be done; when I saw the estimate of the work, however, it was multiples of what I expected. This enabled us to drill down and realize we had very big differences in scope. |
| 9 | Team Member | For each goal, enter the target completion date. Usually, this is set at the end of the quarter, unless there's some reason it has to be completed earlier. Using end-of-quarter dates reduces management overhead, by placing the responsibility on team members to manage their tasks. The alternative is to have different dates for each line item, but that reduces the flexibility of the team members to allocate their time. Sometimes this is necessary, but it should be an exception. |
| 10 | Team Member | For each line, you may optionally enter a comment to document assumptions, or possible issues or barriers associated with this goal. |
| 11 | Team Leader | Review the plan and check for alignment with company priorities and team goals, weightings, target dates and scope assumptions. Make sure the goal is realistic and possible barriers have been thought through. |
| 12 | Team Leader | Approve the plan. |

## Example of an IP (Individual Plan)

### Solomon Software
### Individual Plan

Name: John Smith                                          Quarter Ending xx/xx/xx

| GOALS (INCLUDE DELIVERABLES) | HRS | WT. | TARGET DATE | ACTUAL | AT RISK | NOTE |
|---|---|---|---|---|---|---|
| 1. Project plan for next generation product—Approved Includes budget, schedule, manpower plan in Microsoft Project format | 120 | 25% | 6/30/xx | | | |
| 2. Updated budget & staffing plan for next fiscal year | 30 | 15% | 6/30/xx | | | |
| 3. Reduce average time to correct errors from 11 days to 10 days | 30 | 20% | 6/30/xx | | | |
| 4. Complete hires in hiring plan for this quarter: 1 software engineer (entry level) 1 software tester | 100 | 25% | 6/30/xx | | | |
| 5. Take training and pass certification test for Microsoft SQL Server | 100 | 15% | 6/30/xx | | | |
| Sustaining Responsibilities | | | | | | |
| IPs completed for all team members before start of next quarter | 8 | | | | | |
| Manage relationships with outside contractor | 22 | | | | | |
| Vacation | 40 | | | | | |
| Other | 70 | | | | | |
| Total | 520 | | | | | |

---

The "at-risk" column (see example) is not used when setting a goal. This column is used later, when completing a status report.

IV.
WORK
THE PLAN

IV-A Define IPs Quarterly
*IV-B Review IPs Weekly*
IV-C Rate IPs Quarterly
IV-D Prioritize Daily
IV-E Monitor Measures

## STEP IV-B
# Review IPs Weekly

## Introduction

This step in the Methodology is designed to encourage every team member *and* team leader to review progress toward quarterly goals on a regular basis, preferably weekly. This report (as mentioned earlier) is designed to be read in five minutes, and filled out in less than fifteen.

This process makes it evident whether the team member is focusing on the agreed-upon goals. It also becomes clear whether progress is being made toward those goals at the pace expected. Misunderstandings are identified, and problems, resource issues, priority changes, etc. all surface early and in a proactive manner, *while there's still time to do something about them.*

From personal experience, I know this process leads to much better communication and understanding between team members, and provides many great opportunities for constructive coaching as well.

The process uses a quarterly IP plan as a template. It allows the team member to record progress for each person in the plan, and whether there are any barriers that threaten the quarterly goals. It should be short and to the point. Sending the report, however, isn't enough.

It's strongly suggested that there be a face-to-face meeting (or phone call for remote workers) to review status every week: certainly no less frequently than every other week. The frequency depends on how well the projects are going, how many people report to the team leader, and whether the projects are at a stage of great unpredictability or not.

It's surprising the issues that turn up in live conversations which aren't picked up by reading a report. The existence of the report, however, makes the meetings much shorter and more focused. Frequently, they can be 30 minutes or less. Team leaders should think about these meetings as "staff development" opportunities.

This process teaches people to think ahead and anticipate problems. It makes them consider their work, and it causes them to declare when something is at risk, which requires judgment. The goal is to get to the point at which people are *anticipating* problems, and are already proposing solutions.

The fact that you're willing to spend time every week checking on their progress sends a huge message about the importance of what they're doing, and how seriously you take their goals. In the end, this doesn't cost you time; it *saves* you time, because there are fewer fires to put out.

## Hints and Tips

❑ Remember the goal is "5–15"—read under five minutes and keep preparation time under fifteen minutes.

❑ Strive to identify problems as early as possible. Teach team members that anticipating problems is part of their job, and those who are unable to consistently do this are not fully developed.

❑ Establish a routine for meeting together—the same time each week is best. Turn status reporting into a habit. Meet, even if you think there's nothing to discuss. Some of the biggest discoveries come during meetings when you think things are going well.

❑ Ask probing questions to see how well grounded they are. "What got accomplished this past week?" "Was it everything you expected ?" "Are you running into anything unexpected?" "How can I help make your job easier?" "What are you going to do next week?"

❑ When team members say a project is in trouble because someone else is late giving them a deliverable they need, remind them that it's *their* job to know the progress of deliverables they're dependent upon. They should raise such concerns in their status reports in advance of the issue. Proactive communication among the team members is the mark of a mature, self-managing team.

❑ When projects get off-schedule, make the focus of conversation how to get back on track. Try to avoid changing the deadline. Challenges like this are opportunities for innovation. Encourage them to talk with their peers to see if there's an easier way to get the job done, find someone who can assist, or put in overtime. Help them through the problem, but don't take "ownership" of the problem yourself.

❑ The IP doesn't replace more detailed project planning. Some goals are big enough that a more detailed project plan needs to be prepared. There the work is broken down further to know whether the quarterly goal can be reached. Some people use tools like Microsoft Project or spreadsheets to list more detailed steps and estimated effort to complete.

❑ Be patient. As stated earlier, it can take three to four quarters for a team to get good at this. *What's really happening is that you're teaching people to take responsibility for developing their plans and executing them.* Even when people are good at this process, the unexpected still occurs. This process helps detect and correct these inevitable challenges more proactively.

## Process for Preparing the IP Status

### Process for Preparing the IP Status

| STEP | RESPONSIBILITY | DESCRIPTION |
|---|---|---|
| 1 | Team Member | Open the copy of the last week's Status Report in your word processor, so you don't have to re-enter information that hasn't changed; then update the report date. |
| 2 | Team Member | Change any items that need to be updated. |
| 3 | Team Member | Mark any completed items by entering the *actual date*. |
| 4 | Team Member | If there are items that are *at risk* of not being completed on schedule, put an "X" in that column. |
| 5 | Team Member | Record any brief comments or concerns about progress on a particular item. Any item marked "at risk" should have an explanation of the problem. Keep explanations very brief. You can elaborate in your meeting with the team leader. |
| 6 | Team Member | Forward the report to your team leader the day before your regularly scheduled meeting. |
| 7 | Team Member | At the weekly meeting, walk through each item and discuss the progress and any issues or concerns. Focus should be on anticipating problems and finding solutions as early as possible. |

## Examples of IP Status Report (weekly)

### Solomon Software
IP Status Report

Name: John Smith                                                      Quarter Ending xx/xx/xx

| Goals (include deliverables) | Hrs | Wt. | Target Date | Actual | At Risk | Note |
|---|---|---|---|---|---|---|
| 1. Project plan for next generation product— approved Includes budget, schedule, manpower plan in Microsoft Project format | 120 | 25% | 6/30/xx | | X | Assessment of next generation tools is being held up due to pending version from Microsoft. Release is significant enough that it is worth an estimated delay of 6 weeks to get better information. |
| 2. Updated budget & staffing plan for next fiscal year | 30 | 15% | 6/30/xx | 5-15-xx | · | Completed |
| 3. Reduce average time to correct errors from 11 days to 10 days | 30 | 20% | 6/30/xx | | | Progress is good, expect to exceed the target by end of quarter. |
| 4. Complete hires in hiring plan for this quarter: 1 software engineer (entry level) 1 software tester | 100 | 25% | 6/30/xx | | | Strong pipeline of qualified people. Expect to have phone screened and be down to top 3 candidates for each position next week. |
| 5. Take training and pass certification test for Microsoft SQL Server. | 100 | 15% | 6/30/xx | | | Test scheduled for 6-15-03 to allow time for a retake if necessary. |
| Sustaining Responsibilities | | | | | | |
| IPs completed for all team members before start of next quarter | 8 | | | | | |
| Manage relationships with outside contractors | 22 | | | | | |
| Vacation | 40 | | | | | 5/20—6/3 |
| Other | 70 | | | | | |
| Total | 520 | | | | | |

IV.
WORK
THE PLAN

IV-A Define IPs Quarterly
IV-B Review IPs Weekly
*IV-c Rate IPs Quarterly*
IV-D Prioritize Daily
IV-E Monitor Measures

## Introduction

*The evaluation of Individual Plans at the end of each quarter is a critical step for any organization serious about building and sustaining excellence.* The process of formally comparing what was planned with what was delivered helps team members grow in *many* ways.

It helps people learn how to plan, to anticipate problems, to manage the unexpected, to identify dependencies, to communicate more clearly with team members, and, most of all, to take responsibility. When goals aren't met, this evaluation should help identify *why,* so the next plan can be better than the last one.

This process also helps identify areas where the team leader and team member are in agreement and where they're not. A wise team leader uses this process to coach, train and develop team members. The team leader sets appropriate expectations and shows that those expectations are important, formally evaluating them at the end of the quarter.

Finally, following this process provides much-needed feedback to team members four times a year, which is more effective than waiting until the annual performance appraisal. This way, there are no surprises, and there's time to respond to issues before that appraisal.

## Hints and Tips

❑ Complete the rating promptly at the end of the quarter. Any learning can be applied to the development of the next quarter's plan. Usually, you have a pretty good idea of the level of goal achievement before the quarter is ended and can draft next quarter's plan considering current quarter results.

❑ The team leader's job is to help the team member learn, grow, and maximize performance. Input provided should be constructive in spirit.

❑ If you're going to tie incentive payments to achievement of the IPs, it's recommended that you do it gradually. As mentioned earlier, have a couple of quarters of trials to allow people to get comfortable. Also, it's recommended that the dollar amounts involved be modest in terms of percentage of compensation. Putting too much economic pressure on this system can create an undesirable, fear-oriented environment. What's ideal is a climate that's open and based on high trust.

❑ Make good notes and comments on the form, so that at the end of the year you have information that can be incorporated into the annual performance appraisal.

## Steps for Rating Achievement of Quarterly IPs

| Process for Rating Achievement of Quarterly IPs | | |
|---|---|---|
| **STEP** | **RESPONSIBILITY** | **DESCRIPTION** |
| 1 | Team Member | Complete the self-rating column on the form and add comments about the performance on each goal, supporting why it was rated the way it was. These should be brief, a phrase or a sentence. This form is forwarded to the team leader. |
| 2 | Team Leader | Complete the leader-rating column on the form, and add comments about performance. |
| 3 | Team Leader | Return the form to the team member, and schedule a meeting (this can be the regular weekly meeting) to review the IP ratings and discuss any differences in views. |
| 4 | Team Member/ Leader | Meet to discuss the review, what went well, what could be improved and how. After discussion, both finalize their ratings (making changes if necessary) and both parties sign the form. A copy is provided to the team member, and the original goes to HR. |
| 5 | HR | If there's an incentive involved, HR computes the bonus according to the policy of the company and has a check prepared. |
| 6 | HR | The form is filed in the personnel file of the team member. |

## Example of IP Rating (Quarterly)

### Individual Plan Achievement Rating
#### Solomon Software

Name: John Smith                                                                 Quarter Ending xx/xx/xx

| GOALS (INCLUDE DELIVERABLES) | HRS | WT. | TARGET DATE | ACTUAL | TEAM MEMBER | TEAM LEADER | WT RATING | NOTE |
|---|---|---|---|---|---|---|---|---|
| Project plan for next generation product—approved Includes budget, schedule, manpower plan in Microsoft Project format | 120 | 25% | 6/30/xx | | 3 | 2 | .5 | JS: Delay due to waiting on Microsoft beta release not considered in developing the plan. GH: Agree with decision to delay, but strive to anticipate in future plans. |
| Updated budget & staffing plan for next fiscal year | 30 | 15% | 6/30/xx | | 4 | 5 | .75 | GH: Good job. Found ways to save more funds than expected. |
| Reduce average time to correct errors from 11 days to 10 days | 30 | 20% | 6/30/xx | | 5 | 5 | 1.00 | GH: Achieved 9.5 days This was better than expected. Very creative approach to getting team up to speed on new methodology. |
| Complete hires in hiring plan for this quarter: 1 software engineer (entry level) 1 software tester | 100 | 20% | 6/30/xx | | 4 | 4 | .8 | GH: Good job. These were critical hires for us staying on plan and you didn't compromise on quality. |
| Take training and pass certification test for Microsoft SQL Server | 100 | 10% | 6/30/xx | | 4 | 4 | .4 | JS: Passed on first try GH: Congratulations! You have great ability to span technical and managerial leadership. |
| Sustaining Responsibilities | | | | | | | | |
| IPs completed for all team members before start of next quarter | 8 | 5% | | | 4 | 3 | .15 | GH: Put more focus on personal development goals. Some people in your group aren't taking this seriously. |
| Manage relationships with outside contractors | 22 | 5% | | | 4 | 4 | .2 | GH: Nice job getting contractors on track after last quarter problems. |
| Vacation | 40 | | | | | | | |
| Other | 70 | | | | | | | |
| Total | 520 | 100% | | | | | 3.8 | |

Comments: Overall solid quarter. Good progress on everything. For our next significant project plan, before we set dates, let's identify the likely major external dependencies so our plans allow for those unexpected delays—or we qualify our schedule with the assumptions we're making to better set expectations. Let's just keep learning—you are progressing!

IV.
WORK
THE PLAN

IV-a Define IPs Quarterly
IV-b Review IPs Weekly
IV-c Rate IPs Quarterly
*IV-d Prioritize Daily*
IV-e Monitor Measures

# STEP IV-D
# Prioritize Daily

## Introduction

On a daily basis, each team member is encouraged to develop the discipline of maintaining a Task List (or "To Do" List). The point is to jot down commitments you make or tasks you need to do, whenever they occur to you, *so you don't forget them.* Then, each day, reprioritize your list for what you want to focus on that particular day, given your quarterly IP plan and other priorities that may come up.

Some prefer doing this the first thing every morning, while their mind has a fresh perspective; some prefer addressing it at the end of the day in preparation for the next day. Do whatever works for you. The point is to consciously choose your priorities and not let circumstances overwhelm you.

*All the planning, prioritization and goal setting in the Six Disciplines Methodology eventually comes down to choosing what action to take—what you're doing today, at this instant (see figure next page). Is this work aligned with what's important to the company, or not?*

Long-term excellence is about daily integrity in the little decisions. You can think of the significance of what you do today as an upside-down pyramid.

Choices made today determine whether you'll meet your quarterly plans. The quality and achievement of the quarterly plans determine whether the annual goals are met. Achievement of the annual goals determines whether the long-term goals are met, and

achievement of those determines whether the vision is met. The significance of what each individual in the organization does compounds up through the layers and determines what the organization becomes over the long-term.

## Hints and Tips

❑ Get in the habit of writing down commitments *every time* in the *same place*. A notebook, laptop or PDA—it doesn't matter. Find something that works and stick with it.

❑ Prioritize daily, allocating enough time to achieve quarterly goals and sustaining responsibilities. There will always be more on the list than you can do, so you have to choose which are the most important. Adopt a simple ranking system like *A* for "critical today," *B* for "important," and *C* for "can wait."

❑ When you consistently have more 'A' items than you can handle, you need to alert your team leader and ask for guidance on priorities. It's also possible you overcommitted on your quarterly plan, and you need to learn from that when preparing your next plan (although it's also possible something unpredictable has come up).

## Example of Task List

### Task List

John Smith                                                    Date xx/xx/xx

| DONE | RANK | DESCRIPTION | DUE |
|------|------|-------------|-----|
| X | A | Get agreement on team for next generation project | |
|  | A | Schedule kick-off meeting & set agenda | |
|  | A | Call Jamie Swanson regarding complaint 419-426-9999 | |
| X | A | Order flowers for anniversary | |
|  | B | Update position description for engineer position | |
|  | B | Update position description for tester position | |
|  | B | Prepare IP plan draft for next quarter—review by Susan | 6/20 |
|  | B | Select SQL Server training class & schedule | 4/15 |
|  | C | Respond to compensation survey request | |
|  | C | Review contract files and move closed files to storage | |

IV.
WORK
THE PLAN

IV-A Define IPs Quarterly
IV-B Review IPs Weekly
IV-C Rate IPs Quarterly
IV-D Prioritize Daily
*IV-E Monitor Measures*

# STEP IV-E
# Monitor Measures

## Introduction

One of the most important objectives of the Six Disciplines Methodology is helping organizations build a *measurement-oriented culture,* one that realizes learning is rooted in measuring or observing results. It's the results that tell us whether the innovations we try are working.

For example, testing the *close rate* (percentage of customers who buy) from two different direct mail lists would give evidence to which is a better list. *Organizations that want to accelerate learning should strive to have every person in the organization have a few key measures that help them do their job more effectively.*

These measures supplement the IPs and serve as "instrumentation," like those a pilot uses to fly a plane: fuel levels, direction, altitude, speed, hydraulic pressure, engine pressure, etc. For example, a sales rep may have on his or her IP a sales target for the quarter, but also have measures (not on the IP) that indicate how many leads are in the pipeline by level of qualification. Also, this rep may have measures about average deal size trends, customer satisfaction ratings, order backlog, average time to ship, etc.

## Hints and Tips

❑ Measures help promote innovation. People should be encouraged to try new things, but prove through measurement that they work, before general adoption.

❑ Measurement promotes empowerment. People have a clearer understanding of what's expected and are encouraged to self-manage in pursuit of those expectations.

❑ Measurement promotes learning. People learn from cause-and-effect observations. The greater the frequency of observations, the faster the learning.

❑ The real purpose of measurement is not to correct a particular defect in a product or service. It's to correct the process that caused the defect in the first place.

❑ Throughout a company there may be hundreds of measures, but for an individual, there should only be a few. Remember Theodore Levitt's observation: "The more abundant the information, the less meaning it will yield. We know that the surest way to destroy a man's capacity for discrimination is to overwhelm his senses with relevant stimuli."

❑ Be patient. It takes a long time to get the right measures in place for every job, but the payoff is huge, with an energized and aligned workforce. Start slowly—one measure for one person, and work gradually to expand it.

❑ Measures should be trended. The learning value of a measure is much greater when you can see changes over long periods of time *and* understand how today's performance compares to the past. When an organization commits to tracking measures, it's building an asset that will increase in value as time passes.

❑ To be effective, measures need to be easily accessible. The organization needs to develop a technology strategy that facilitates the tracking of measures. For example, don't buy contact management/sales software, *unless* it will provide the measures for tracking leads through your qualification stages, and shows the percentage that are moving from one stage to the next.

❑ Get rid of measures that don't add value. Remember that every measure you track takes time and effort to produce and analyze.

## Process for Monitoring Measures

### Process for Monitoring Measures

| STEP | RESPONSIBILITY | DESCRIPTION |
|------|----------------|-------------|
| 1 | Team Member | Establish a routine for reviewing measures. For most jobs, weekly, monthly or quarterly measures are the norm. There are a few situations, like phone support, where there may be a need for daily (or even more frequent) measures. |
| 2 | Team Leader | At the appropriate time, the measure should be checked. The measure is ideally presented in trended graph form (see example). Questions should be asked, such as, "Is the value higher or lower than expected?" and "Why?" |
| 3 | Team Leader | Sometimes in diagnosing root causes, it's useful to be able to drill into the data to see how the value was calculated. For example, if you're monitoring total sales leads and they're lower than expected, you might want to look at leads by sales region, to see if the problem is isolated in one or more geographic areas. |
| 4 | Team Member | Unacceptable trends should be reviewed with your team leader and corrective actions agreed upon. Be proactive in notifying your team leader. |
| 5 | Team Member & Team Leader | Be on the alert for better ways to define the measures. Sometimes, it becomes evident that the current measure isn't really the best one. When that occurs, old measures should be replaced with new and better ones. Remember to keep the total number per team member small (five to seven maximum). |

## Example

Average order size may be a measure a sales manager monitors. In this example, the company had offered discount coupons to its most loyal customers and given each person until May 31st to redeem them. Because of the discounted prices, the average price per order went down. However, the volume of orders went up, which isn't shown on this measure. The expiration date was extended six weeks, due to popular demand, and amount per order returned to normal by mid-July.

**Average Order Size**

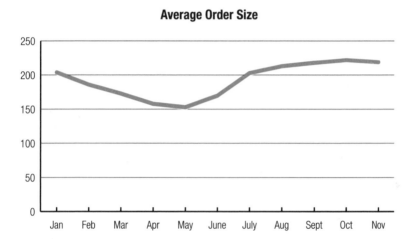

IV.
WORK
THE PLAN

IV-A Define IPs Quarterly
IV-B Review IPs Weekly
IV-C Rate IPs Quarterly
IV-D Prioritize Daily
IV-E Monitor Measures

## RECAP OF DISCIPLINE IV
# Work The Plan

We all talk and think much about the future; yet to achieve our most desirable future, we must master the moment at hand. Every team member, each day, is spending the most precious asset any organization has—time and energy. Whether or not that time and energy are being well-spent is a very important question.

This *Discipline* is designed to teach individuals and organizations how to invest in each moment in such a way that they build the most preferred future for the company, *and* make life and work more fulfilling for the individual. The key steps to doing this are:

- ❑ IV-B Define IPs Quarterly
- ❑ IV-C Review IP Status Report Weekly
- ❑ IV-D Rate IPs Quarterly
- ❑ IV-E Prioritize Daily
- ❑ IV-F Monitor Measures Regularly

In the next chapter we address how to harness the creativity of every individual in the organization so that it is applied to the purposes of the company.

## CHAPTER EIGHT

## DISCIPLINE V

# *Innovate Purposefully*

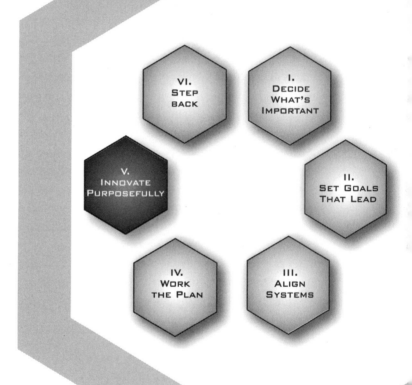

*One small idea implemented is
more valuable than an incredibly
"big" idea that never gets acted upon.*

## V.
### INNOVATE
### PURPOSEFULLY

V-A Brainstorm
V-B 100-Point Exercise
V-C Quick-ROI Analysis
V-D 5-Step Problem Solving
V-E Champion Your Ideas
V-F Recognize Contributions

# Overview

Growing up in an agricultural community, I learned that a farmer can do many things to improve a crop—proper preparation of soil, fertilization, weed control, irrigation—but one thing a farmer can't provide is the "life" that exists only inside the seed.

Similarly, a business leader must properly "prepare the soil" in order for innovation to thrive. In the same way that life is in the seed, creative ability is within the individual. It's a part of the human design. All six of the Six Disciplines are designed to help take advantage of this innate ability to think, to dream and to solve problems, by focusing these priceless resources toward the goals of the company.

*Discipline V—Innovate Purposefully* is unlike the other five disciplines, because it *primarily* provides principles and tools that are used in the day-to-day execution of the steps in the *other* disciplines. In other words, "innovating purposefully" is not an isolated event in an annual or quarterly cycle; it's a mindset that permeates the culture of an excellent organization.

Principles like *Engaging Everyone* and *Embracing Constraints,* and tools like *brainstorming* and the *100-Point Exercise,* are meant to be lived out as you practice the other disciplines. Discipline V is like the yeast in bread: it's a small but critical ingredient spread throughout the loaf.

To achieve the kind of excellence that lasts requires a continuing stream of new services, new products and new ways of delivering them. Globalization and virtual relationships are changing the competitive landscape. Under this pressure, many people in leadership positions have, at one time or another, felt like "jumping on their horse and riding off in all directions at once."[1] I know I have.

And I've certainly struggled with questions like, "How do I get people to learn faster?" "How do I find more creative people?" "How do I nurture the creativity we already have?" "How do I channel creativity in the right direction?" Or there's the opposite problem: "How do I respond to all the creative ideas people come up with, which I don't have time to think about?"

Most of us place great value on creativity, but sometimes we forget that, in a business setting, it's a means to an end. If creativity isn't properly channeled to contribute to the company's mission and vision, then it can actually be detrimental.

As Theodore Levitt pointedly says, "Whatever the goals of a business may be, it must make money. To do that, it must get things done. But having ideas is seldom equivalent to getting things done. . . . Since business is a uniquely 'get things done' institution, creativity without action-oriented follow-through is a uniquely barren form of individual behavior."[2]

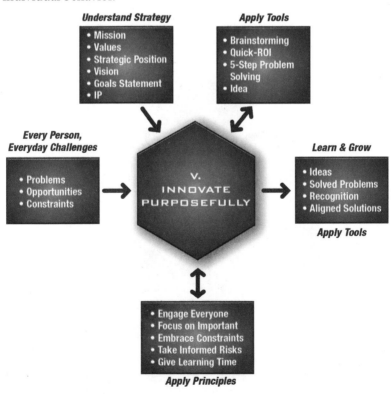

In this chapter, and throughout all the Six Disciplines, we describe how to build an organization that has a culture where everyone is engaged in using his or her potential to contribute to the organization's goals. Described are five keys to innovating purposefully and six tools that, when used in conjunction with the other disciplines, help build an innovative culture that unlocks the potential of all workers.

## Innovation Principles

### Engage Everyone

For small businesses, creativity is not a specialized talent that belongs primarily in a research department. Innovation is not about the pursuit of the next "big idea"—the *single transforming thought* that will change the company's prospects. A far larger payoff for most businesses lies in figuring out ways to get *all* staff members engaged in improving the business *in their own respective work areas*. Unless your firm's mission is pure research, you don't need, and probably don't want, *specialists* in creativity.

**INNOVATION PRINCIPLES**

Although not everyone has the same creative and learning abilities, the good news is that we each have more than enough. Peter Senge points out that deep down, we're all learners. "No one has to teach an infant to learn. In fact, no one has to teach infants anything. They are intrinsically inquisitive, masterful learners who learn to walk, speak, and pretty much run their households all on their own."[3]

This creative nature is alluded to in the Bible, which records that God created people in His image and gave the human race the mission (and ability) to rule (bring order) over all the earth. The idea that people are designed for a purpose, designed to problem solve, has forever changed the way I view other people and myself.

*Every* individual has God-given value, capability, and purpose, and there's no greater adventure than finding and fulfilling that purpose and helping others do the same. So, if you, as a business leader, want to nurture and harness the full potential that exists inside your organization, the number one principle to be learned and applied is "*engage everyone in innovation.*"

## Focus on the Important

It's not enough, however, to just get people creating "new ideas." Such ideas must be *aligned with what's important to the company.* They must be usable. One small idea *implemented* is more valuable than an incredibly original "big" idea that never gets acted upon. Even worse is an idea that gets implemented, which *doesn't* contribute to the company's priorities. It's worse because it takes up the resources—time, attention, funds—of the company. At least the damage of an unaligned and unimplemented idea is minimal, depending on how much time was consumed to generate and evaluate it.

*Unless your firm's mission is pure research, you don't need, and probably don't want, specialists in creativity.*

Let me tell a true story about unbridled creativity that illustrates this point. At Solomon, one individual, "Mark" (not his real name), stood out as being one of the most creative people we ever hired. His breadth of knowledge was impressive, and he wielded a great deal of influence in his working area.

He was, however, so creative that he wouldn't (or perhaps couldn't) stay focused on any one issue for very long. He had many great ideas, but he had an extraordinarily negative impact on the organization. He'd continue to generate ideas, but never finished anything. His creativity turned whole teams of people into a non-productive churning mode. It took us way too long to figure out the impact this was having on our organization, and we never were able to figure out how to harness this person's potential.

Perhaps this type of individual would fit better in a pure-research function that's isolated from the rest of the organization. For most small businesses, it's better to have people who are normal idea *generators* and outstanding idea *implementers*.

With its emphasis on defining goals, aligning systems and working plans, one of the major design objectives of the Six Disciplines Methodology is to help businesses apply principle number two: *focus innovation on things that are important to the company*.

## Embrace Constraints

From childhood on, we grow up fighting limitations that constrain us. Yet there are many examples in history where severe constraints (problems) provided a setting that incubated great creative thinking. Sometimes, "necessity *is* the mother of invention."

The Apollo 13 mission in 1970 is a great example. When a spacecraft containing three astronauts had a malfunction that damaged their air supply halfway to the moon, the men's survival was unlikely. Yet NASA engineers on the ground accepted the limitations and used materials on board in a truly innovative way to save the three men's lives. In this situation, fighting the constraints would have wasted precious time.

A business example has ingrained this same principle in me forever. At Solomon in the early '90s, we were financially very weak and had to build a next generation product to survive. We didn't have the resources to do it. So we formed a small team and asked them to come up with a way to develop a new product line with ten people in two years, which is a much shorter time than we prefer.

A few years earlier, we would have thought such constraints were laughable. But this time, no one was laughing! For our small company, it was the Apollo mission: though no one's life was at stake, the company's was! This team, under the leadership of my partner, Vernon Strong, was forced to think about completely new ways of accomplishing these objectives—ways that we would have *never* considered without these constraints.

To pull this off, the team conceived a completely new way of building software. The resulting product was delivered on time and our business grew six-fold over the next 10 years.

If you want to foster breakthrough innovation, you must help people learn to practice principle number three: *embrace constraints.* Often it's the constraints that lead to "out-of-the-box thinking!"

### Take Informed Risks

Fear is crippling to individuals and to organizations. It's like a black hole that absorbs creativity and the drive to learn. When it comes to innovation, there are several things we face: fear of failure, fear of commitment, fear of the unknown, and even the fear of letting go. *A fundamental role of leadership is to foster a culture that is not afraid to fail, but is empowered to take informed risks.*

The most effective way to establish a work environment where team members are open to take educated chances is *not* by what you say, but by what you *do*. Leaders themselves should be open about their own failures and what they learned from them. Most of us don't have any shortage of material to share, if we'd just be honest.

Leaders also need to be involved, showing interest in the activities of their people. This shows both a helpful attitude and a desire to work with them, not against them. We're demonstrating that we want them to succeed, as opposed to sitting back and saying, "I told you so."

In truth, failure that comes out of informed risk-taking is just a step in the learning process. There should not only be no stigma attached. Such failures should be viewed as something of value that may pay dividends immediately, or down the road in future decisions. Our role as leaders and how we react to failure will be the primary determinant of whether people develop the willingness to apply principle number four: *take informed risks.*

### Give Learning Time

*Innovating Purposefully*—applying creativity to the purposes of the business—takes a lot of wisdom. And certainly, wisdom takes time to develop. A simplified view of how learning takes place posits the following cycle: we get an idea, we try that idea, and we observe the results produced. Often the results observed generate another idea, and the cycle continues.

The elapsed time for this "learning loop" may be mere *seconds* in some situations. For example, a toddler sees something shiny on the stove, reaches up to touch it, and gets burned. Learning of a kind has taken place; however, it may not be the "correct" learning. It may take several repititions through the loop for the child to figure out that *not all shiny objects are hot*; but any item on the stove, shiny or not, may

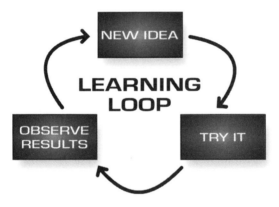

be hot. The rate of learning is related to the amount of elapsed time it takes to go through one cycle, and how many cycles it takes to get it "right."

In business, we have examples of many different types of learning loops with correspondingly different learning rates. From concept to understanding, the results of a *direct mail* advertising campaign may take four months, whereas an *awareness-building* campaign may take two years. An architectural project may take three to five years from conception to full use of a building, and the consequences of certain design decisions used in constructing the building may still not be fully understood. In this case, the learning "loop" could be years long.

At a business strategy level, sometimes it takes the senior leader many, many years to truly understand the consequences of certain decisions. If we're truly committed to developing an innovative culture, we have to recognize that different "learning loops" unfold over different periods of time. The recognition of this truth makes it easier to follow principle number five: *give learning time.*

## Recap of Principles

Although not an exhaustive list, organizations that learn how to: 1) Engage Everyone, 2) Focus on the Important, 3) Embrace Constraints, 4) Take Informed Risks and 5) Give Learning Time are creating the "fertile conditions" in which innovation can blossom. Experience working with many small businesses has revealed a handful of very practical tools for bringing some order to the creativity process. As mentioned earlier, if creativity isn't channeled properly, it can do more harm than good. Most of us have experienced meetings to discuss a problem, yet we left the room more confused and frustrated than when we came in.

Following are some practical steps for tapping the "creativity power" of people in constructive ways. I'm not the originator of many of the ideas covered in these steps. For many of them, I don't even know when I was first exposed to them. What I do know is that *they work!*

## STEP V-A
# Brainstorm

## Introduction

A tool for generating ideas, brainstorming has been around for decades. Even though it's not new, it's still underutilized and its underpinning principles are as valid today as they've ever been. The basic principle is that people are more willing to put forth ideas in an environment where their ideas aren't critiqued at the time. The brainstorming exercise described below is used throughout the Six Disciplines Methodology to generate and capture ideas quickly. After the ideas are on the table, they can be evaluated in a separate process, using either the 100-Point Exercise or the Quick-ROI Analysis.

## Hints and Tips

❑ Make sure there's a clear statement of what the brainstorming topic is. Be specific. For example, brainstorming on the topic, "How can we increase sales?" will produce a very different result than the topic, "How can we generate an additional $200,000 in sales in the next 90 days?"

❑ Do *not* permit evaluation or comments on the validity of ideas. Just capture the idea, regardless of how wild it may seem.

❑ Set a time limit and capture as many ideas as possible in the given time. You'll be surprised at how many ideas can be generated in just a few minutes. (You don't have to be bound to the time limit, if the ideas are still freely flowing.)

❏ Use a facilitator to record the ideas, and make sure the rules are followed.

❏ Keep the group small (under seven is recommended).

## Process for Brainstorming

| | Process for Brainstorming | |
|---|---|---|
| **STEP** | **RESPONSIBILITY** | **DESCRIPTION** |
| 1 | Facilitator | Make sure the group has agreement on what the brainstorming topic is, and that it's clearly defined. The way the question is phrased can lead to very different results. |
| 2 | Facilitator | Set a time limit. This helps people focus on idea *generation*, not evaluation. Five to ten minutes is usually enough time, but the limit can be relaxed if the ideas are still coming. |
| 3 | Facilitator | Remind people, as necessary, not to evaluate their ideas or those of others. |
| 4 | Facilitator | Record ideas on a wall board or easel pad that's visible to the group. Just write down enough words to remember the idea. |
| 5 | Facilitator | Review the list to make sure the descriptions are readable and contain enough information. Then proceed to the evaluation step. |

## Example of Brainstorming Exercise

| Brainstorming Exercise | |
|---|---|
| Solomon Software xx/xx/xx | |
| Brainstorming Topic: | What are the most important things we want this company to stand for over a 10- to 20-year period? |
| **Customer** | |
| Quality products and services | |
| Cost savings | |
| Better information | |
| Productivity | |
| Better quality of life | |
| More economic freedom | |
| Convenience | |
| Excellence overall | |
| **Employees** | |
| Job security | |
| Financial well-being via satisfying compensation | |
| Challenge | |
| Meaningful work | |
| Make a difference | |
| Be creative | |
| Respect for each worker | |
| Self-respect | |
| Growth/learning | |
| Quality of life | |
| **Shareholders** | |
| Fair return on investment | |
| Predictable cash flow | |
| Longevity | |
| Stability in the community | |
| Satisfied customers (especially locally) | |

V.
INNOVATE
PURPOSEFULLY

V-A  Brainstorm
*V-B  100-Point Exercise*
V-C  Quick-ROI Analysis
V-D  5-Step Problem Solving
V-E  Champion Your Ideas
V-F  Recognize Contributions

# STEP V-B

# 100-Point Exercise

## Introduction

The essence of decision-making and strategy formulation is making difficult trade-off decisions—saying "yes" to a few things and "no" to most things. The purpose of the 100-Point Exercise is to help a group of people use their individual judgment to prioritize choices, and then aggregate those individual judgments into a group perspective.

This technique can bring order to a chaotic process and save time. To illustrate, frequently at Solomon Software we convened an advisory group of the partners who sold our products. Their experience was valuable, so we'd often preview new ideas with them. Wild meetings with lots of debate often ensued.

Much of this dialogue was very valuable, but eventually, choices had to be made. One time, I walked into one of these sessions that had been grinding on for hours with no convergence of priorities. We stopped the meeting and used the 100-Point Exercise; within 30 minutes, we had agreement on our priorities.

This process works because it's a simulation of the judgments we must all make in decision-making—the choice between what we'd *like* to do and what we *can* do with limited resources.

## Hints and Tips

❏ This exercise is particularly useful when you have a lot of ideas to evaluate and want to get down to a shorter list quickly, without a big investment of time.

❑ A key assumption of this process is that the "experts" in a particular business are *the people who work in that business.* They have the most contact with their customers, and they know the capabilities of their organization better than "outsiders" do.

❑ Allow time for people to explain why they allocated points the way they did. Sometimes, the reasoning changes someone else's mind, thereby setting up a beneficial, synergistic effect.

## Process for Prioritizing with 100-Point Exercise

| | | **Process for Prioritizing with 100-Point Exercise** |
|---|---|---|
| **STEP** | **RESPONSIBILITY** | **DESCRIPTION** |
| 1 | Facilitator | Make sure the topic being addressed in the prioritization exercise is clearly stated. For example: "What's the best way for our company to grow the business 50% over the next five years?" |
| 2 | Facilitator | Make sure each participant has a copy of the ideas (brainstorming) to be evaluated. This could be on wall charts, computer screens or handouts. Each idea should be numbered so it can be easily referenced. |
| 3 | Facilitator | Allot each person 100 "points," which they can then allocate among the list of ideas, awarding the most points to the most important ideas. Each group member, theoretically, could put all 100 points on one idea, one point on 100 ideas, or any combination in between. This exercise simulates the real world of strategy formulation: you have limited resources (100 points), and you have to decide how to deploy those resources. You give everyone five to 10 minutes to write down their allocations on their own notepads, based on the number of items. (It's useful to limit the minimum number of points that can be allocated to increments of five or ten, to encourage people to focus on the most important issues.) |
| 4 | Facilitator | When everyone is finished, record the number of points beside each idea by person. There's no discussion of the ratings at this point. After the last person's points have been written down, the Facilitator totals the points to see which ideas received the most points (see example). You can then number the top five to seven ideas in order. |
| 5 | Facilitator | At this point, the group should discuss the resulting priorities and see who disagrees and why. Usually, there's pretty good consensus after this first round of prioritization; however, if there isn't, you can allow each person to explain the rationale of their votes. |
| 6 | Facilitator | Optionally, after discussion, you can return to Step 3 and repeat the process until there's better consensus. This can be done in the same meeting. Sometimes its better to give people time to think about what they've heard and repeat the process on another day. |

## Example of 100-Point Exercise

This example illustrates how a 100-Point Exercise could be used for agreeing on the key elements in a mission statement. The ideas for mission focus came from a Brainstorming Exercise. The 100-Point Exercise shows the five shaded areas that were the most important to the group overall. Of course, the topic could be any set of ideas a group is trying to prioritize.

| 100-Point Exercise | | | | | |
|---|---|---|---|---|---|
| Solomon Software | | | | | xx/xx/xx |
| Brainstorming Topic: | What are the most important things we want this company to stand for over a 10- to 20-year period? | | | | |
| | | POINTS AWARDED | | | |
| | JAN | SUE | STEVE | BRIAN | TOTAL |
| Customer | | | | | |
| Quality products and services | | | | | |
| Cost savings | | | | | |
| Better information | | | 10 | | 10 |
| Productivity | | 20 | | 40 | 60 |
| Better quality of life | 30 | 10 | 40 | | 80 |
| More economic freedom | 10 | | | | 10 |
| Convenience | | | | | |
| Excellence overall | | | | | |
| Employees | | | | | |
| Job security | | | | 20 | 20 |
| Financial well-being via satisfying compenstion | 20 | 30 | | | 50 |
| Challenge | | | | | |
| Meaningful work | | | 25 | | 25 |
| Make a difference | | | 25 | | 25 |
| Be creative | | | | | |
| Respect for each worker | | | | 10 | 10 |
| Self-respect | | | | | |
| Growth/learning | 30 | 20 | | | 50 |
| Quality of life | | | | | |
| Shareholders | | | | | |

| 100-Point Exercise (cont'd) | | | | | |
|---|---|---|---|---|---|
| Solomon Software | | | | | xx/xx/xx |
| Brainstorming Topic: | What are the most important things we want this company to stand for over a 10- to 20-year period? | | | | |

| | POINTS AWARDED | | | | |
|---|---|---|---|---|---|
| | JAN | SUE | STEVE | BRIAN | TOTAL |
| Fair return on investment | | 10 | | 30 | 40 |
| Predictable cash flow | | | | | |
| Longevity | 10 | 10 | | | 20 |
| Stability in the community | | | | | |
| Satisfied customers | | | | | |
| **TOTAL** | **100** | **100** | **100** | **100** | **400** |

V.
INNOVATE
PURPOSEFULLY

V-A  Brainstorming
V-B  100-Point Exercise
*V-C  Quick-ROI Analysis*
V-D  5-Step Problem Solving
V-E  Champion Your Ideas
V-F  Recognize Contributions

## STEP V-C
# Quick-ROI Analysis

## Introduction

Often, the best business ideas are ones that produce the most revenue or earnings increases, in the shortest amount of time, with the smallest investments. The *Quick-ROI Analysis* is based on this assumption. This exercise is useful when you'd like to develop priorities *explicitly* considering three factors: impact of the idea in terms of *revenue (or earnings)*, *time to market*, and *cost* of implementation.

With the 100-Point Exercise, these factors *may* be considered *implicitly* in the points an individual awards to an idea, but such assumptions aren't visible in the process. The Quick-ROI approach makes assumptions more visible and helps people communicate more effectively. A significant part of the value is the improved understanding that results among the team members.

## Hints and Tips

❑ For this exercise, estimates of revenue, cost and time to market are just rough approximations based on the experience of the people involved. They're not based on bottom-up plans.

❑ You should have people in this evaluation process who represent all functions of the business, so that all business perspectives are reflected in the analysis.

❑ Start with a list of items that's fairly short—10 to 15 items. If the list is too long, use the 100-Point Exercise to narrow the list.

## Process for Quick-ROI Analysis

| | Process for Quick-ROI Analysis | |
|---|---|---|
| **STEP** | **RESPONSIBILITY** | **DESCRIPTION** |
| 1 | Facilitator | Select a group of three to seven people who have the most relevant background to consider the questions at hand. Make sure that what's being evaluated is clearly defined; e.g., "What are the best short-term revenue generation products?" |
| 2 | Facilitator | Ask each person to rate each item according to the following criteria. Note that the group needs to agree on the thresholds being used. The numbers found in the parentheses are *suggested* amounts to consider, but different businesses have different thresholds, depending upon size and profit margins of their industry. Participants also need to observe that, regarding the numeric ratings, "1" is considered *less* desirable and "3" is *most* desirable. For example, a 3 in sales means high sales, and a 3 in cost means low cost. The point is to find projects that are all ranked 3s or a mixture of 3s and 2s.<br><br>Sales (cost savings):<br>1: low impact (<$100,000 sales or <$20,000 cost savings)<br>2: medium impact (100-$500k sales or $20-100k cost savings)<br>3: high impact (> $500k sales or >$100k cost savings)<br><br>Cost to implement:<br>1: high cost (>$100k)<br>2: medium cost ($25-100k)<br>3: low cost (<$25k)<br><br>Elapsed time:<br>1: long time (> 4 quarters)<br>2: medium time (1-4 quarters)<br>3: short time (<1 quarter)<br><br>Have the individual add up his/her ratings for each project. For example, +2 medium sales impact; +2 low cost to implement; +3 short elapsed time = rating of 7. |
| 3 | Facilitator | On a wall pad, write down the total rating from each participant and total these ratings by person. |
| 4 | Facilitator | Give each person the chance to explain his or her assumptions. In this exercise, certain people may have more expertise than others. For example, the sales manager may rate the sales potential as "high" and the cost to implement as "low," whereas the production manager may do the opposite. This exercise helps to get all the assumptions on the table, drawing out the group's different perspectives. |
| 5 | Facilitator | Repeat steps 2-4 if the discussion has led to new thinking by the team on how they rated their individual priorities. |

## Example of Quick-ROI Analysis

### Quick-ROI Individual Worksheet

Short-Term Revenue Generation Projects                    xx/xx/xx

| ITEM | HIGH SALES | SHORT TIME | LOW COST | TOTAL |
|------|------------|------------|----------|-------|
| Introduce low-end product as a downsized version of Solomon IV | 2 | 2 | 1 | 5 |
| Increase recruitment of new channel members | 2 | 1 | 1 | 4 |
| Increase sales force to gain mind share of current partners | 2 | 1 | 1 | 4 |
| Install base promotion for add-on modules | 2 | 3 | 3 | 8 |
| Module bundle pricing to show more value vs. lower price | 2 | 3 | 2 | 7 |
| Raise software prices | 1 | 3 | 3 | 7 |
| Raise service plan prices | 2 | 3 | 3 | 8 |
| Introduce partner-funded seminars | 3 | 2 | 3 | 8 |
| Form team to focus on major accounts | 1 | 1 | 1 | 3 |
| OEM licensing of products | 1 | 1 | 1 | 3 |

### Quick-ROI Summary

Short-Term Revenue Generation Projects                    xx/xx/xx

| ITEM | TOM | SUSAN | AMY | TOTAL |
|------|-----|-------|-----|-------|
| Introduce low-end product as a downsized version of Solomon IV | 5 | 4 | 6 | 15 |
| Increase recruitment of new channel members | 4 | 5 | 6 | 15 |
| Increase sales force to gain mind share of current partners | 4 | 5 | 5 | 14 |
| Install base promotion for add-on modules | 8 | 7 | 5 | 20 |
| Module bundle pricing to show more value vs. lower price | 7 | 8 | 6 | 21 |
| Raise software prices | 7 | 8 | 6 | 19 |
| Raise service plan prices | 8 | 7 | 6 | 21 |
| Introduce partner-funded seminars | 8 | 6 | 7 | 21 |
| Form team to focus on major accounts | 3 | 4 | 5 | 12 |
| OEM licensing of products | 3 | 4 | 5 | 12 |

## STEP V-D
# 5-Step Problem Solving

## Introduction

Whereas earlier exercises are designed to help groups sort through a collection of ideas and come to agreement on priorities, *5-Step Problem Solving* is an approach for thinking through a solution to a particular problem or opportunity *in more detail*. The output of this process is typically a 2-3 page document that describes what the problem is, its root causes, possible solutions and implementation considerations.

*This tool can be used by an individual or a team working together.* The advantage of this approach is that it provides a checklist of issues to address and questions to ask so that creativity is channeled in the right direction. This is an easy template to place in a word processor document and make available to your whole organization.

## Hints and Tips

❑ This tool can be used as a way to kick off projects that have been chosen as a priority, based on the 100-Point Exercise or *Quick-ROI Analysis.*

❑ This document should be short: 2-3 pages is typical. It provides a great training tool to help people be thorough when analyzing a problem or opportunity.

❑ Don't hesitate to modify this template to better fit your organization's needs. This approach should serve as a practical checklist for making better decisions more quickly.

❑ 5-Step Problem Solving can employ brainstorming to gather ideas and the 100-Point and *Quick-ROI Analysis* to identify root causes, possible solutions, etc. The 5-Step Problem Solving Template provides a great format to document the outcome of such group exercises when teams of people are involved in defining and solving the problem.

## Process for 5-Step Problem Solving

| | Process for 5-Step Problem Solving | |
|---|---|---|
| **STEP** | **RESPONSIBILITY** | **DESCRIPTION** |
| 1 | Person with Idea | Start with a blank copy of the 5-Step Problem Solving word-processing template and fill it in, following the remaining steps (see example). |
| 2 | Person with Idea | *Define the problem.* Record a clear statement of the problem, who is impacted and how, history leading up to the problem, the gap between current and desired results, how you'd know if the problem were resolved and who should be involved in solving the problem. |
| 3 | Person with Idea | *Identify root causes.* List the obvious contributing causes *and* the causes behind the causes. One technique is to ask "Why?" seven times, to get at the root issue. For example: *(1) Why do we have severe cash flow shortage?* Because of slow receivables collections. (2) *Why are collections slow?* Because customers are dissatisfied. (3) *Why are customers dissatisfied?* Errors in their software. (4) *Why are there errors in the software?* Because products are shipped with unknown errors. (5) *Why are they shipped with unknown errors?* Because there aren't clear specifications for what to test. (6) *Why are specifications not clear?* Because the people designing the systems don't understand what users do with the software. (7) *Why don't designers know what users do with the software?* Because we're not hiring people who have experience with the target market. After seven levels of "drill down," chances are pretty good that you're close to the real root cause. |
| 4 | Person with Idea | *Develop the requirements for the solution.* Determine the key deliverables required for the solution; the amount of improvement of "product quality," Identify constraints the solution must fit: time, dollars, manpower, etc. |
| 5 | Person with Idea | *Develop the solution.* List alternatives considered and describe the recommended solution. |
| 6 | Person with Idea | *Implementation Plan.* Identify who is responsible, clarify what's included and not included in the solution, key steps, resources (people, funds, etc.) and schedule, and how results will be measured. |
| 7 | Person with Idea | *Evaluate results after implementation.* Gather feedback from team members and affected stakeholders and identify how well goals were met, including what worked and what didn't work on the project. |

## Example

### 5-Step Problem Solving Template

#### 1. Define the problem.
- ❏ Problem statement.
- ❏ Impact—who will be impacted, when and how much, if not resolved?
- ❏ History—specify any relevant history leading up to this problem.
- ❏ How will you know if the problem is resolved? How will it be measured?
- ❏ Who should be involved in solving the problem?

#### 2. Identify root causes. (ask "Why?" seven times)

#### 3. Develop the solution.
- ❏ Key deliverables (outputs) required for the solution.
- ❏ Constraints the solution must fit: time, dollars, manpower, etc.
- ❏ Final decision-maker for proceeding to implementation.
- ❏ Alternatives considered.
- ❏ Recommended solution.

#### 4. Implementation Plan.
- ❏ Who is responsible?
- ❏ Scope clarification—What will and will not be addressed?
- ❏ Resources required: people, funds, etc.
- ❏ Key steps and schedule.
- ❏ How will results be measured?

#### 5. Post-Implementation Findings.
- ❏ Summary of stakeholder feedback (customers, employees, etc.).
- ❏ How well were the goals met? (planned vs. actual)
- ❏ List what worked on this project.
- ❏ List what didn't work or could have been done better.

V.
INNOVATE
PURPOSEFULLY

V-A Brainstorm
V-B 100-Point Exercise
V-C Quick-ROI Analysis
V-D 5-Step Problem Solving
*V-E Champion Your Ideas*
V-F Recognize Contributions

## STEP V-E
# Champion Your Ideas

## Introduction

Once again, one small idea well implemented is worth more than a "big" idea that never gets acted upon. The problem in most organizations isn't coming up with ideas. The problem is coming up with ideas that are well-considered—first, in terms of how they fit into the company priorities, and second, in terms of how the idea would be implemented. The purpose of this step is to encourage people to generate ideas, and to take responsibility for championing the idea through evaluation *and* implementation.

Different organizations have different approaches to idea generation. Some have no process at all, and ideas are handled informally through conversation. In other organizations, there's a "suggestion box" concept, in which people can submit ideas and it becomes *someone else's* problem to figure out what to do with them. Organizations that take the informal approach often tend not to focus much on idea generation. People tend to do their own work, and ideas that come up that aren't related to the immediate work at hand are lost.

The suggestion box approach has a different problem, in that more ideas are generated (at least when the box is first implemented), but the responsibility for doing something about the idea is frequently transferred to leadership. Because of the typical workload of leaders, good ideas often get passed over for lack of attention. If suggestions aren't acted on, then gradually submissions stop.

The "champion your ideas" approach to idea generation offers a middle ground between these two approaches. It presents a formal mechanism for capturing ideas, but puts responsibility for evaluating the idea, and working to advocate the implementation of the idea, on the person generating it.

This approach helps people develop professionally as well. For example, they may have to do some work outside their normal area of responsibility, thereby meeting, working with and leading new people. They learn the business better by evaluating the idea from different angles and perspectives. In general, they grow through taking responsibility for implementing ideas.

For this process to work, there has to be a genuine support in the company for trying new things and taking reasonable risks. Building such a culture may feel "messy," but the payoff is the unleashing of a great deal of innovation and professional development. Gradually, you can build a workforce that has the mindset and skill to consistently improve products and services, lower costs and drive revenue, *and* enjoys themselves doing it!

## Hints and Tips

❑ Don't solicit suggestions if they're not going to be evaluated seriously. Doing nothing is better than setting up a formal system that isn't really supported or fully implemented.

❑ Help people understand that many small, easy-to-implement ideas are often better than trying to "hit home runs." At the company-wide level, only a very few strategic level priorities can be focused on, but small improvements can often be acted upon quickly.

❑ Formal suggestion processes don't replace simply listening and respecting people's ideas.

❑ In most cases, leaders should avoid letting the person generating the idea "delegate up" responsibility for the idea. Instead, encourage the person to talk to someone (arrange an introduction, if necessary) in the organization to better understand its feasibility. The key is to be encouraging and supportive, without taking ownership of the idea.

❏ Those submitting the ideas should ask themselves if they believe enough in the ideas to fight for them. In a well-managed organization, people are already busy with high-value activity. Someone must be willing to make the case that this idea is worth the distraction of evaluating and implementing. If you're not willing to do this, then don't waste people's time. If *you* don't believe in it, why should they?

## Process for Assuming Responsibility for Ideas

| STEP | RESPONSIBILITY | DESCRIPTION |
|------|----------------|-------------|
| 1 | Idea Owner | Complete a simple one-page idea form (see example). This is typically a template available to everyone on their word processors. |
| 2 | Idea Owner | Discuss the idea with your team leader and get advice as to who in the organization would have the best input on the value of this idea, and who would have to approve implementing the idea. |
| 3 | Idea Owner | Talk informally with some of those people about your idea, soliciting input and interest in the idea. For bigger ideas, ask them to do a Quick-ROI rating with you while you're meeting. (This would provide a quick read of their view of the opportunity.) |
| 4 | Idea Owner | As you get more information, continue to check whether you're willing to make the investment to carry this forward. If not, drop it. |
| 5 | Idea Owner | Be aware that sometimes in this process, someone else will see the benefit of the idea and be willing or want to take ownership of it, because he or she is in a better position to make it happen. You should view this as success. Your goal should be to see that a good idea gets implemented for the benefit of the company, and it shouldn't matter whether you or someone else does it. |
| 6 | Idea Owner | For bigger ideas that affect the strategy of the company, you may be asked (or choose) to complete a 5-Step Problem Solving Analysis and present it to the leadership team as they're evaluating other priorities for the company. |
| 7 | Idea Owner | Be willing to let go of ideas that are not at the top of the priority list. Many people have many ideas and sometimes the time and resources aren't available to act on them. There's a fine line between knowing when to keep fighting for an idea and when to let it go. |

## Example of Idea Form

---

### IDEA

Owner: Joe Smith               Date: xx/xx/xx
Short Description Seminar Marketing Program

**Describe the Idea in a Few Sentences:**
Create a seminar marketing program where we manage the lists,
mailings and national promotion of seminars in exchange for a
fee from partners. There will be a controlled number of seminars
per market region per month. This will motivate partners to
participate because, if they don't, their competitors will be more
visible than they are.

**Benefits (in terms of revenue, cost savings, customer
satisfaction, etc.)**
- Local, qualified leads leading to more sales
- Greater mindshare of our partners
- High leverage for our marketing. Cost of administering
  program is fixed, but the number of people reached is very
  high
- Ads serve as image builders—national publications with
  40 seminars listed contribute to image and awareness of
  significant player

**Rough estimate of cost to implement
(time in man-weeks/months, out of pocket $):**
- 2 man-months of preparation
- 40 hours per month to administer seminars
- $30,000 to create direct marketing materials and partner
  marketing kits

**Rough estimate of total elapsed time to implement
(assuming fully resourced):**
- 4 elapsed months from decision to initial seminar

**Feedback received from reviewers.**

**Rated as a 7 on the Quick ROI Exercise by Susan
(marketing director).**

---

V.
INNOVATE
PURPOSEFULLY

V-A Brainstorm
V-B 100-Point Exercise
V-C Quick-ROI Analysis
V-D 5-Step Problem Solving
V-E Champion Your Ideas
*V-F Recognize Contributions*

## STEP V-F
# Recognize Contributions

## Introduction

A truth written thousands of years ago says that ". . . a good word makes the heart glad."[4] The purpose of this step is to help people give a *good word* to each other—to recognize the contributions individuals and teams make to the mission of the organization. Honest praise and acknowledgement are among the most satisfying gifts we can give to each other. It's not only good for the individual involved, but it reinforces, to everyone in the company, behavior and character traits that align with company values and mission.

There are many different types of recognition systems that are used. Following is a small sampling:

- ❏ Awards issued anytime, anywhere, by anyone who spots someone doing something that exemplifies company values (see Way-to-Go Award below)

- ❏ Quarterly recognition programs as part of company meetings

- ❏ Major annual awards at a company banquet where spouses are in attendance

- ❏ Employee of the month awards—preferred parking space, picture on the wall, etc.

- ❏ Displaying key metrics (sales calls, leads, service levels, etc.) for individual or team performance

- ❏ Anniversary of hire recognition, tenure awards

- ❏ Incentive/bonus programs

You could use one or all of these, or other approaches that better fit your organization. The approach you use is *not* critical, but having some defined approach *is*. If you want to sustain excellence, it's important to build a culture that recognizes and affirms examples of excellence.

We're going to illustrate one recognition program called *the Way-to-Go Award*. The purpose of this award is to engage everyone in the company in the process of acknowledging examples of excellence that reinforce company values. This could include putting in overtime to get a project back on schedule; investing significant time helping another team member; championing a new idea that made a big difference and getting it implemented; willingness to take on a high risk project even if it failed; a money-saving idea, etc.

As a specific example, the Way-to-Go Award is the exact opposite of the "big bang" employee of the year award. This is a small award that can be issued in two minutes and is a formal way of just saying "nice job." It also engages everyone in building a culture of recognition and appreciation.

## Hints and Tips

- ❑ Keep the award process simple, so that a nomination can be completed in less than five minutes.

- ❑ Make it everyone's job to nominate award winners. This builds a culture of trying to catch people doing something "right." For this to catch on, *you* must set an example by doing this yourself.

- ❑ Remember to recognize the people who nominate others for awards, perhaps quarterly or annually.

- ❑ Don't start this process until you can focus on making it a habit in your company. It's better to have no process than to set the expectation of a process and not follow it.

- ❑ Make sure people are recognized publicly for the award—for example, read them at company meetings, email copies, post them on bulletin boards, etc.

## Process for Using the Way-to-Go Award

### Process for Using the Way-to-Go Award

| STEP | RESPONSIBILITY | DESCRIPTION |
|------|----------------|-------------|
| 1 | Nominator | Use a word processing template for the Way-to-Go Award, and document very briefly the action or result you want to recognize. |
| 2 | Nominator | E-mail the award to the recipient, and copy the award to the recipient's team leader and the team leader's team leader. In a small company, there's no reason that notification shouldn't go all the way "up" to the president. |
| 3 | Team Leader(s) | The team leader should stop by in person the same day if possible. Also, there should be a standing item in team meeting agendas to mention Way-to-Go Awards that were issued since the last meeting. |
| 4 | President | At the next company meeting (quarterly), all awards should be read aloud in front of the group and the recipient formally recognized and thanked. You could provide a small gift to the top award recipient for the quarter—for example, two tickets to the movies or a lunch gift certificate. |
| 5 | HR | A copy of the award should be placed in the person's personnel file. |
| 6 | President | At the end of the year, the company can recognize the person who received the most Way-to-Go Awards for the year and the person who submitted the most Way-to-Go Awards. It's suggested that some "special bonus" be given, such as a gift certificate for dinner for two at a nice restaurant. It is a good idea to structure the gift so that if the person is married, the spouse feels a part of the award as well. |

## Example of Way-to-Go Recognition Form

### Way-to-Go Award

**Person Nominated:** Susan Thompson
**Nominated by:** Davy Jones          **Date:** 10/15/xx

**Reason for Award:**

On Wednesday afternoon, August 9th, I was scheduled to have a follow-up call from a client who was very upset. About thirty minutes before the call, I received a call from school that said my daughter Anna was sick and needed to be taken to a doctor soon. Susan overheard me describing my predicament to my Team Leader and offered to handle the call for me. I provided her with a brief background and referred her to the file on this client. She prepared for the meeting and handled the client professionally, and worked out what the next steps would be for addressing the client's concerns.

Thanks, Susan, for bailing me out without me even asking! I needed help and you volunteered to do something that is not easy—talking with an upset client.

V.
INNOVATE
PURPOSEFULLY

V-A   Brainstorm
V-B   100-Point Exercise
V-C   Quick-ROI Analysis
V-D   5-Step Problem Solving
V-E   Champion Your Ideas
V-F   Recognize Contributions

RECAP OF DISCIPLINE V

# Innovate Purposefully

Building an organization that excels over the long term requires a team of people who know how to apply their innate ability to innovate toward the goals of the company. Included in this chapter were several key innovation excercises upon which the Methodology is based, and several tools that, if practiced faithfully, will harness the amazing potential that exists in all of us to improve the success *of* and satisfaction *with* your business!

- ❑ V-B   Brainstorm
- ❑ V-C   100-Point Exercise
- ❑ V-D   Quick-ROI Analysis
- ❑ V-E   5-Step Problem Solving
- ❑ V-F   Champion Your Ideas
- ❑ V-G   Recognize Contributions

We're now ready to move into the last discipline. It shows organizations and their personnel some practical, annual steps for stepping back from all the urgent issues of work life and gaining some perspective on exactly where they are. This prepares you for revisiting where you want to go next.

# CHAPTER NINE

## DISCIPLINE VI

# *Step Back*

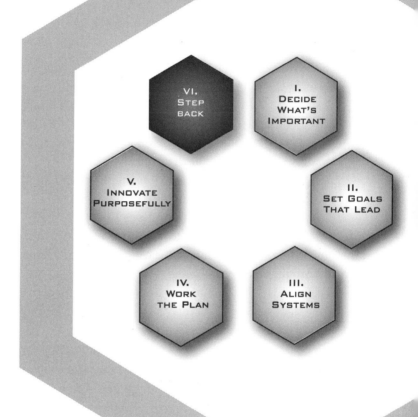

"... *examine everything carefully;*
*hold fast to that which is good.*"
—1 THESSALONIANS 5:21

VI.
STEP BACK

VI-A  Review Externals
VI-B  Review Internals
VI-C  Recap SWOT
VI-D  Review Individuals

# Overview

One spring, our family was walking in the surf at Amelia Island, Florida. Looking down, trying to spot shells, we noticed we couldn't walk in a straight line. As the surf washed in and then receded into the ocean, we'd drift toward the ocean as we walked. Our eyes were using the receding waterline to establish the direction in which we should walk. It was amazing how powerful the draw toward the water was. The only way we could walk straight was to stop looking down and lift our eyes to look 100 yards down the beach at something stationary.

Businesses operate in a continually shifting "surf" of daily activities that occupy our time and attention, and this "surf" has an impact on us we sometimes don't detect. If we want to move our businesses toward our long-term priorities, we must learn how to *step back* from all the activity occasionally, so that we gain a broader view. Most of us agree that we need to do this, yet we frequently don't take the time, or do it in a thorough and systematic way.

*Discipline VI—Step Back* is an *annual,* step-by-step process designed to help organizational leadership and individuals withdraw from the press of everyday business, thereby gaining a clear picture of factors inside and outside the business that should be examined before updating strategy. Most of Discipline VI takes place in a 4-6 hour retreat with the leadership team.

The end result of this once-a-year "mega-review" is an updated list of Strengths, Weaknesses, Opportunities and Threats (*SWOT*). During this discipline, external trends (competitors, industry, etc.), goal achievement, key measures, and stakeholder feedback (customers, team members, etc.) are explored. Expert reviews of critical areas (financial, technological, legal, risk, etc.) can also be conducted yearly or as needed.

All this feedback is consolidated into a SWOT statement which can be easily referenced by everyone in the company. Last of all, individual team members are encouraged to *step back* by completing a 360° survey as part of the annual performance appraisal.

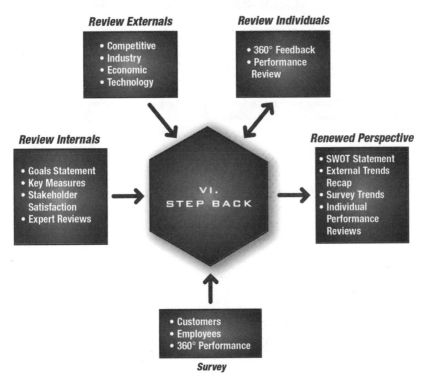

Although Discipline VI is focused on the annual process of stepping back, you should be aware that integrated into the rest of the disciplines are other cycles that help gain perspective. For example, *quarterly* goal setting is a brief but critical process of looking up from your detailed work and recalibrating your priorities according to longer-term goals.

The *weekly* IP Status Report also helps team members step back from the detail and check how they're progressing toward quarterly goals. There's even a *daily* reassessment that takes place by maintaining a Task List for the day's activities. Organizations that learn to systematically focus their resources on their goals, not allowing the urgent to overwhelm the important, will be dramatically more successful over the long term.

## STEP VI-A
# Review Externals

## Introduction

A key part of gaining perspective for any business is periodically identifying and prioritizing the external factors that have the potential to influence company performance and strategy the most over the next few years. External factors are forces that are not controlled by the company. Which factors are most important varies by industry, company and even stage of life of a given business. Printing businesses might be highly vulnerable to technological advances, whereas consulting businesses might be more dependent on local economic trends, depending on how widely dispersed their client base is.

## Hints and Tips

❑ The people who know the most about your business are already working for you. Your sales staff and customer support staff are a veritable fountain of information about competitive issues and trends.

❑ If there are areas that need more research, have someone on your own staff spend some time gathering information relevant to your business.

❑ As a last resort, you can engage outsiders or buy industry analysis reports from market research firms.

❏ All key departments in the company should be present in these exercises, so that all functional perspectives are considered.

❏ Keep in mind that the purpose is only to *identify top issues*, not to develop strategies for responding. That will come later in Disciplines I and II.

## Process for Reviewing Externals

| | Process for Reviewing Externals | |
|---|---|---|
| **STEP** | **RESPONSIBILITY** | **DESCRIPTION** |
| 1 | President | Decide which two or three topics need to be examined—such as Competitive, Industry, Technology, Economic, Regulatory or any other external trends relevant to the business. |
| 2 | President | Send an e-mail and ask the leadership team to gather information on these selected topics from their staff, websites, etc. Often they already know this information because of their day-to-day interaction with customers, team members or competitors. |
| 3 | Facilitator | At a meeting of the leadership team, lead a brainstorming exercise on the first topic—e.g., competitive trends. |
| 4 | Facilitator | Repeat step 3 for each of the topics until they're all completed. |
| 5 | Facilitator | Lead the group through a 100-Point Exercise for each of the topics. The objective is to come to agreement on the top three items for each category that should be considered in Discipline I (when deciding what's important and what's not). |
| 6 | Facilitator | Get agreement on who's going to recap the results of these trends and distribute them to the leadership team. |

## Examples of External Trends Summary

### Solomon Software Company—External Trends

### December 19 [XX]

**Competitive Trends**

1. Consolidation of the industry is accelerating quickly. Five competitors in the past 12 months have been acquired.
2. The average list price of offerings by our competitors and us has risen by about 10% in the past year. This continues the trend of the past several years.
3. The breadth of product lines continues to expand. Most competitors have either announced or introduced major new suites of applications that attempt to position them as offering an enterprise-wide solution.

**Industry Trends**

1. The post-Y2K growth rate has been about half the growth rate of the two years preceding Y2K. It's estimated the growth rate for U.S.-based companies is currently 5%.
2. There's an increasing focus in the media on Application Service Provider (ASP)-based offerings for our class of product. There are no sales being lost to the ASP model, but there's certainly a lot more talk.
3. There's an increased rate of roll-ups taking place in the channel, including our own channel. Primary motivations appear to be: a) to provide an avenue to liquidity, b) scale to deal with larger, more complex applications, and c) centralizing administrative functions, like billing, recruiting, services, etc.

VI.
STEP BACK

VI-A  Review Externals
*VI-B  Review Internals*
VI-C  Recap SWOT
VI-D  Review Individuals

# STEP VI-B
# Review Internals

Have you ever noticed that when you get a good physical exam, you end up with most or all of your clothes off at one time or another? A good physician either looks at or touches almost every part of your body. In like manner, if we want to have healthy businesses, we need to thoroughly poke and probe the internals of our business once a year, even at the risk of a little embarrassment or discomfort.

The review of External Trends in the previous step examined factors outside the control of the business (economic, competitive trends, etc.). This step is focused on the things that we do have control over—our own internal operations. A thorough *internal review* should examine:

❑  Achievement of current-year goals

❑  Key performance measure trends

❑  Stakeholder satisfaction: customers, employees, vendors, etc.

❑  Financial condition and controls (outside expert)

❑  Information Technology (outside expert)

❑  Risk/insurance (outside expert)

❑  Legal issues (outside expert)

❑  Six Disciplines Methodology (outside expert)

Any organization that doesn't have a systematic way of gathering and periodically analyzing vital information, like stakeholder satisfaction and other key measures, is "flying blind."

## Hints and Tips

❑ Assess performance openly, without assigning blame. Ask "how can we, as a team, plan AND execute better next year?"

❑ Keep surveys to outside stakeholders short (under 10 questions). The purpose is to identify problems, not diagnose them.

❑ Surveys should be changed *infrequently*, so the results can be trended from-year-to-year. Changing a question breaks the trend.

❑ For valid results, design surveys so you get a minimum of 30 responses for each category you want to break down: sales region, product type, etc.

❑ Leverage the Internet. Surveys are much less expensive to send and respond to if done electronically.

❑ Don't be frustrated by the lack of measures you have in place. As described in Discipline III, add a few measures each year.

❑ Be willing to live with approximations or rough estimates until you get better data. For example, a sampling of product quality is better than no data at all.

❑ Top-performing businesses (Chapter 1) learn how to develop and effectively use the advice of outside experts. Most small businesses need outside advisors in the areas of accounting, finance, technology, legal, risk/insurance and a business improvement methodology.

❑ Select outside advisors/reviewers who have the ability to understand your long-term goals, and who can help you take *short-term* steps that fit into a *long-term* plan. This is particularly true when it comes to information technology.

## Process for Reviewing Internal Performance

### Process for Reviewing Internal Performance

| STEP | RESPONSIBILITY | DESCRIPTION |
|---|---|---|
| 1 | President | Three months before the review meetings are scheduled, decide what items are going to be included in this year's Internal Performance Appraisal. Recommended items include:<br>Achievement of current year goals<br>Key performance measure trends<br>Stakeholder satisfaction: customers, employees, vendors, etc.<br>Financial condition and controls (outside expert)<br>Information Technology (outside expert)<br>Risk/insurance (outside expert)<br>Legal issues (outside expert)<br>Six Disciplines Methodology (outside expert) |
| 2 | President | Assign responsibilities for preparing the content for each of the areas chosen. |
| 3 | Person Responsible | Develop a schedule for what needs to be done for your particular area of responsibility. For example, for goal achievement, actual results may need to be pulled together and put on a report; for key performance measures, information may need to be gathered and analyzed. Satisfaction surveys will have to be reviewed for changes, distribution lists prepared, survey sent and compiled. |
| 4 | Person Responsible | A week before the appraisal meeting is scheduled, distribute a short report (1-3 pages) of the information needed to the leadership team so they have time to read it before the meeting. |
| 5 | Leadership Team | Review all materials before the leadership meeting and, if you have questions about the material, ask the person who prepared it for explanations. Come to the appraisal meeting prepared to discuss positives and areas of concern for each report. |
| 6 | Facilitator | Have the group list on an easel pad what went well with the current year's company goals execution and what could be improved next year in terms of planning and execution. This should be a thorough walk-through of each VFO, measure, target and initiative. |
| 7 | Facilitator | Repeat step 6 for each of the areas to be reviewed in step 1. |
| 8 | Facilitator | Make sure all the easel pad information is visible on the walls in preparation for the SWOT Recap step coming up. |

## Examples of Key Measures

| Key Measures | | | | | |
|---|---|---|---|---|---|
| | 1998 | 1999 | 2000 | 2001 | 2002 |
| **Financial View** | | | | | |
| Cash | 810 | 820 | 822 | 841 | 850 |
| Sales Days of Cash | 43 | 41 | 38 | 36 | 33 |
| Current Assets-to-Liabilities Ratio | 2.0 | 1.9 | 1.8 | 1.7 | 1.6 |
| Sales Days of Receivables | 35 | 36 | 35 | 37 | 37 |
| Sales Days of Inventory | 159 | 163 | 157 | 154 | 150 |
| Direct Cost Days of Payables | 40 | 38 | 38 | 38 | 40 |
| Total Liabilities-to-Total Assets Ratio | 1.3 | 1.4 | 1.4 | 1.5 | 1.5 |
| Operating Profit-to-Interest Expense | 10 | 15 | 20 | Na | na |
| Operating Return on Sales (operating margin) | 7% | 8% | 8% | 8.5% | 8% |
| Return on Assets | 13% | 14% | 14% | 15% | 15% |
| Return on Equity | 14% | 14% | 13% | 14% | 16% |
| Sales Growth Rate | 5% | 5% | 6% | 6% | 6% |
| Gross Profit Growth Rate | 5% | 6% | 7% | 6% | 5% |
| Interest Income as % of Revenues | 2% | 2% | 2% | 1.5% | 1.4% |
| Interest Expense as % of Revenues | 1% | 1% | 1% | 0 | 0 |
| **Customer View** | | | | | |
| Market Share | 8% | 9% | 9% | 10% | 10% |
| New Customers Added | 49 | 51 | 55 | 60 | 58 |
| Customers Lost | 7 | 9 | 11 | 10 | 7 |
| Total Customers | 615 | 657 | 701 | 751 | 802 |
| Customer Retention Rate | 99 | 99 | 98.5 | 99 | 99 |
| Average Sales Per Customer ($1000) | 10 | 10 | 10 | 10 | 10 |
| Average Profitability Per Customer | 780 | 781 | 779 | 775 | 770 |
| Overall Customer Satisfaction Rating | 88% | 89% | 90% | 91% | 92% |
| Lifetime Value of a Customer ($1000) | 78 | 78 | 52 | 52 | 77 |
| **Production View** | | | | | |
| Sales Days of Order Backlog | 40 | 40 | 41 | 41 | 43 |
| Days to Ship | 4 | 4 | 3.5 | 3.5 | 3 |
| Direct Labor as % of Revenue | 25% | 25% | 25% | 25% | 25% |
| Indirect Labor as % of Revenue | 10% | 9% | 8% | 8% | 8% |
| Overtime Labor as % of Revenue | 2% | 2% | 2% | 2% | 3% |
| Receiving Cost as % of Revenue | 1% | 1% | 2% | 3% | 2% |
| Shipping Cost as % of Revenue | 1% | 1% | 1% | 1% | 1% |
| Marketing Expense as % of Revenue | 3% | 3.5% | 3.5% | 3% | 3% |
| Selling Expense as % of Revenue | 18% | 18% | 17% | 17% | 17% |

## Key Measures (cont'd)

| | 1998 | 1999 | 2000 | 2001 | 2002 |
|---|---|---|---|---|---|
| R&D Expense as % of Revenue | 8% | 8% | 9% | 9% | 9% |
| IT Expense as % of Revenue | 5% | 5% | 4% | 5% | 5% |
| Training Expense as % of Revenue | 2% | 2% | 2% | 2% | 2% |
| Administrative Expense as % of Revenue | 15% | 15% | 15% | 14% | 14% |
| $ Leads Pipeline Value-to-Sales Ratio | 3.0 | 2.9 | 3.0 | 3.0 | 3.3 |
| Days to Close Leads | 57 | 58 | 58 | 59 | 60 |
| Leads Close Rate | 5% | 4% | 5% | 6% | 6% |
| Support Calls per Customer | 4 | 5 | 4 | 4 | 3.8 |
| Time per Support Call–minutes | 7 | 7.4 | 7.5 | 7.4 | 7.0 |
| Time to Close Support Issue–days | 4 | 3.9 | 3.8 | 3.6 | 3.5 |
| Complaints-to-Customer Ratio | .005 | .005 | .006 | .004 | .01 |
| Project Estimate vs. Actual Variance | -5% | -5% | -4% | -2% | -1% |
| Revenue Per Project | 25k | 27k | 29k | 30k | 32k |
| Gross Profit Per Project | 15kk | 16k | 14k | 14k | 15k |
| Average Sales Per Order | 17k | 18k | 18k | 19k | 19k |
| Acquisition Cost Per New Customer | 5k | 4.9k | 4.8k | 4.5k | 4.4k |
| People View | | | | | |
| Sales Per Full Time Equivalent (FTE) | 125 | 127 | 127 | 128 | 128 |
| Payroll & Benefits Per FTE | 47k | 49k | 50k | 51k | 51k |
| Revenue per Sales & Marketing Employee | 600k | 612k | 613k | 618k | 616k |
| Billed Hours as % of Billable Hours | 68% | 71% | 71% | 70% | 73% |
| Employee Additions | 5 | 6 | 5 | 6 | 7 |
| Employee Losses | 3 | 4 | 3 | 3 | 3 |
| Total Employees | 40 | 42 | 44 | 47 | 51 |
| Employee Turnover Rate | 7.5% | 10% | 7% | 6.8% | 6.3% |
| # Customers Per Sales & Marketing Employee | 25 | 27 | 28 | 28 | 30 |
| Employee Benefits as % of Revenue | 5% | 4% | 4% | 5% | 5.5% |
| Total Benefits & Compensation as % of Revenue | 35% | 35% | 35% | 35.5% | 36% |
| Cost of Training Per Payroll Hour | $1.25 | 1.20 | 1.25 | 1.25 | 1.50 |

## Example of a Stakeholder Survey (Customer)

### Customer Survey

To: ABC Distribution
2300 Commerce Parkway
Findlay, OH 45840

| PART A—PLEASE RATE YOUR SATISFACTION WITH THE FOLLOWING: | POOR | FAIR | GOOD | VERY GOOD | EXCELLENT | DON'T KNOW |
|---|---|---|---|---|---|---|
| 1. Quality of products/services | O | O | O | O | O | O |
| 2. Value received considering the price | O | O | O | O | O | O |
| 3. Friendliness, attitude | O | O | O | O | O | O |
| 4. Overall satisfaction | O | O | O | O | O | O |

| PART B—PLEASE ANSWER THE FOLLOWING QUESTIONS: | YES | NO | NOT SURE |
|---|---|---|---|
| 5. Do you plan to continue purchasing from us? | O | O | O |
| 6. Would you recommend us to others? | O | O | O |

**PART C—PLEASE ANSWER THE FOLLOWING:**

7. How long have you been using our products? ___Less Than 1 year ___1-3 Years ___More than 3 years ___Not Applicable

8. Your company revenues ___ Less than $5 M ___$5-10 M ___$11-25 M ___More than $25 M

9. What type of business: ___Manufacturing ___Distribution ___Service ___ Other_____

10. Your Role (select best fit): ___Owner/President ___Accounting-related ___IT-related ___Other_____

11. What is the most important thing we could do to improve your satisfaction with us?

_____

_____

_____

_____

12. Your Name _____Date_____

## Example of a Stakeholder Survey (Team Member)

| PLEASE RATE THE FOLLOWING: | POOR | FAIR | GOOD | VERY GOOD | EXCELLENT | DON'T KNOW |
|---|---|---|---|---|---|---|
| **Team Member Survey** | | | | | | |
| **Leadership** | | | | | | |
| My knowledge of my organization's mission (what it is trying to accomplish) | 0 | 0 | 0 | 0 | 0 | 0 |
| My senior leaders' use of our organization's values to guide us | 0 | 0 | 0 | 0 | 0 | 0 |
| My senior leaders' creation of a work environment that helps me do my job | 0 | 0 | 0 | 0 | 0 | 0 |
| My organization's leaders' effectiveness at sharing information about the organization | 0 | 0 | 0 | 0 | 0 | 0 |
| My senior leaders' encouragement of learning that will help me advance in my career | 0 | 0 | 0 | 0 | 0 | 0 |
| My organization's leaders informing me about what they think is most important | 0 | 0 | 0 | 0 | 0 | 0 |
| My organization's leaders' consistency in asking what I think | 0 | 0 | 0 | 0 | 0 | 0 |
| **Strategic Planning** | | | | | | |
| As it plans for the future, my organization's leaders ask for my ideas. | 0 | 0 | 0 | 0 | 0 | 0 |
| I know the parts of my organization's plans that will affect me and my work. | 0 | 0 | 0 | 0 | 0 | 0 |
| I know how to tell if we're making progress on my work group's part of the plan. | 0 | 0 | 0 | 0 | 0 | 0 |
| **Customer and Market Focus** (customers are those who use your work products) | | | | | | |
| I know who my most important customers are. | 0 | 0 | 0 | 0 | 0 | 0 |
| I keep in touch with my customers. | 0 | 0 | 0 | 0 | 0 | 0 |
| My customers tell me what they need and want. | 0 | 0 | 0 | 0 | 0 | 0 |
| I ask if my customers are satisfied or dissatisfied with my work. | 0 | 0 | 0 | 0 | 0 | 0 |
| I'm allowed to make decisions to solve problems for my customers. | 0 | 0 | 0 | 0 | 0 | 0 |
| **Information and Analysis** | | | | | | |
| I know how to measure the quality of my work. | 0 | 0 | 0 | 0 | 0 | 0 |
| I know how to analyze the quality of my work to see if changes are needed. | 0 | 0 | 0 | 0 | 0 | 0 |
| I know how the measures I see in my work fit into the organization's overall measures of improvement. | 0 | 0 | 0 | 0 | 0 | 0 |
| I get all the important information I need in order to do my work. | 0 | 0 | 0 | 0 | 0 | 0 |
| I get the information I need to know how my organization is doing. | 0 | 0 | 0 | 0 | 0 | 0 |

## Team Member Survey (cont'd)

Solomon Software
Page 2

| PLEASE RATE THE FOLLOWING: | POOR | FAIR | GOOD | VERY GOOD | EXCELLENT | DON'T KNOW |
|---|---|---|---|---|---|---|
| **Human Resource Focus** | | | | | | |
| I can make changes that will improve my work. | O | O | O | O | O | O |
| The people I work with cooperate and work as a team. | O | O | O | O | O | O |
| My boss encourages me to develop my job skills so I can advance in my career. | O | O | O | O | O | O |
| I am recognized for my work. | O | O | O | O | O | O |
| I have a safe workplace. | O | O | O | O | O | O |
| My boss and my organization care about me. | O | O | O | O | O | O |
| **Process Management** | | | | | | |
| I can get everything I need to do my job. | O | O | O | O | O | O |
| I collect information about the quality of my work. | O | O | O | O | O | O |
| We have good processes for doing our work. | O | O | O | O | O | O |
| I have control over my work process. | O | O | O | O | O | O |
| **Business Results** | | | | | | |
| My customers are satisfied with my work. | O | O | O | O | O | O |
| My work products meet all requirements. | O | O | O | O | O | O |
| I know how well my organization is doing financially. | O | O | O | O | O | O |
| My organization uses my time and talents well. | O | O | O | O | O | O |
| My organization removes obstacles that get in the way of progress. | O | O | O | O | O | O |
| My organization obeys both governmental and industry laws and regulations. | O | O | O | O | O | O |
| My organization has high standards and ethics. | O | O | O | O | O | O |
| My organization helps me help my community. | O | O | O | O | O | O |
| I am satisfied with my job. | O | O | O | O | O | O |
| **Information Technology Support** | | | | | | |
| Availability of the computer-related tools I need to do my job | O | O | O | O | O | O |
| Reliability of the tools I have | O | O | O | O | O | O |
| Effectiveness of the tools I have in making me productive and efficient | O | O | O | O | O | O |
| Access to information I need when traveling or working at home | O | O | O | O | O | O |
| Adequacy of the amount and quality of training needed to use my tools | O | O | O | O | O | O |

## Team Member Survey (cont'd)

Solomon Software
Page 3

| PLEASE RATE THE FOLLOWING: | POOR | FAIR | GOOD | VERY GOOD | EXCELLENT | DON'T KNOW |
|---|---|---|---|---|---|---|
| Integrity with Company values | | | | | | |
| How well does the company as a whole follow its stated value of "Teamwork?" | 0 | 0 | 0 | 0 | 0 | 0 |
| How well does the company as a whole follow its stated value of "Quality in the eyes of the customer?" | 0 | 0 | 0 | 0 | 0 | 0 |
| How well does the company as a whole follow its stated value of "Integrity and Honesty?" | 0 | 0 | 0 | 0 | 0 | 0 |
| I rate my own practice of our company's stated value of "Teamwork". . . | 0 | 0 | 0 | 0 | 0 | 0 |
| I rate my own practice of our company's stated value of "Quality in the eyes of the customer". . . | 0 | 0 | 0 | 0 | 0 | 0 |
| I rate my own practice of our company's stated value of "Integrity and Honesty". . . | 0 | 0 | 0 | 0 | 0 | 0 |
| What are the company's greatest strengths? | | | | | | |
| In what areas can the company improve the most? | | | | | | |

Most of the questions on this survey were derived from the Baldrige National Quality Program Assessment. This survey should be adapted to the specifics of your particular business.

## Example of Financial Review Checklist (outside expert)

### Financial Review Checklist

### Financial reporting

- ❑ Timely, accurate interim financial statements
- ❑ Audited or reviewed annual financial statements
- ❑ Personal financial statements of owners
- ❑ Internal control system (to provide accurate accounting and prevent loss)
- ❑ Compliance with accounting standards

### Tax compliance

- ❑ Appropriate tax structure (C corp., S corp., partnership, sole proprietor)
- ❑ Income tax return preparation (federal, state and local)
- ❑ Timely income tax estimates
- ❑ Quarterly and annual payroll tax reports
- ❑ Timely payroll tax deposits
- ❑ Annual forms 1099 preparation
- ❑ Tax planning

### Financial management

- ❑ Lease vs. buy analysis
- ❑ Cash flow projection and/or budget preparation
- ❑ Banking relationships
- ❑ Business succession planning

---

Provided by Jim Thomas of Thomas Ridge CPAs, Findlay, Ohio

## Example of Technology Review Checklist (outside expert)

| Technology Review Checklist |
|---|

**Verify that Backup Policies are being followed**

- ❏ Check daily backup of data files (monitored by in-house staff).
- ❏ Weekly cleaning of backup system (executed by in-house staff)
- ❏ Backup media is being rotated to secure off-site location for protection against fire, flood, etc. (performed by in-house staff)
- ❏ Monthly verification that anti-virus, backup, security software are operating properly (usually done by consultant)
- ❏ Full archive backup performed monthly and taken offsite (in-house staff)

**Processes are in place and being followed for "real-time" monitoring**

- ❏ Anti-virus scanning
- ❏ Anti-spam scanning
- ❏ Log file monitoring
- ❏ Server process monitoring
- ❏ Intruder detection (Internet) monitoring
- ❏ Content filtering (Internet)
- ❏ Performance metrics gathering

**Year-End Activities**

- ❏ Perform year-end archive backup (executed by in-house staff)
- ❏ Update inventory of company's hardware: servers, workstations, network infrastructure, electrical power
- ❏ Update inventory of company's software: server and workstation operating systems; commodity software, such as word processing and spreadsheets; server-based software, such as e-mail servers, SQL servers or web servers; business system software, such as ERP or CRM systems
- ❏ Update inventory of utility software in use at your company: tape backup, anti-virus, anti-spam, monitoring software
- ❏ Update schematic of company's Wide Area Networking (or WAN) environment (including utilization statistics): T1 or frame relay
- ❏ VPN point-to-point
- ❏ Update schematic of company's Internet environment (including utilization statistics): T1 or frame relay, broadband, dial-up
- ❏ Update schematic of company's remote connectivity: dial-up, VPN (secure remote connections), web-based e-mail, terminal services
- ❏ Update inventory of security systems in use at company: firewalls, IDS (Intruder Detection Systems), audit logs, content filters

## Technology Review Checklist (cont'd)

**Conduct Technology review meeting to review current status of the company's IT infrastructure, and to determine the company's hardware and software needs for next fiscal year.**

- ❑ Determine if any hardware systems need to be replaced or upgraded.
- ❑ Determine if any software systems need to be replaced or upgraded.
- ❑ Determine if any additional software licenses need to be purchased.
- ❑ Determine if additional WAN/Internet/LAN bandwidth needs to be brought online.
- ❑ Review the company's IT security requirements and whether additional security hardware or software are required.
- ❑ Review the company's IT processes. Do they need to be modified?
- ❑ Review the company's IT performance against last year's plan. Did IT meet the plan's expectations?
- ❑ Create the IT performance plan for the upcoming year.

Provided by Bryan Hunt, EIS Group, Inc, Toledo, Ohio

## Example of Risk/Insurance Checklist (outside expert)

### Risk/Insurance Checklist

**❑ Insurance to Value**

| | |
|---|---|
| ❑ Building | ❑ Personal property |

**❑ Leasing Requirements**

| | |
|---|---|
| ❑ Heating and A/C | ❑ Building glass |
| ❑ Tenant legal liability | ❑ Signage |

**❑ Liability**

| | |
|---|---|
| ❑ Commercial umbrella | ❑ Professional liability |
| ❑ Directors and officers | ❑ Employment discrimination |
| ❑ Employee benefit | |

**❑ Building Insurance**

| | |
|---|---|
| ❑ Building ordinance | ❑ Building glass |
| ❑ Boilers | ❑ Outdoor property |
| ❑ Heating and A/C | |

**❑ Business Income & Extra Expense**

**❑ Flood & Earthquakes**

**❑ Valuable Papers**

**❑ EDP Hazards**

| | |
|---|---|
| ❑ Mechanical breakdown | ❑ Computer virus |
| ❑ Electrical injury | |

**❑ Life Insurance**

| | |
|---|---|
| ❑ Business continuation fund | ❑ Split dollar agreements |
| ❑ Key person | ❑ Disability income |
| ❑ Supplemental executive compensation | |

**❑ Payroll Deduction Insurance**

Provided by Copeland-Lewis, Findlay, Ohio

## Example of Legal Review Checklist (outside expert)

### Legal Review Checklist

**State and Federal Compliance**

- ❑ Election of directors and approval of financial statements required for corporations
- ❑ Transactions with related parties, such as shareholders, are always approved by corporate action in order to minimize possibility of IRS re-characterizing the transaction
- ❑ Qualified to "do business" in states where property or personnel reside
- ❑ Shareholder and director minutes up-to-date

**Tax Issues**

- ❑ Legal structure is appropriate; as business grows, it may be advantageous to change the structure or tax elections (for example: C corporation vs. S corporation, or corporation instead of single-member LLC)
- ❑ Estate plans are up-to-date relating to business entity, particularly succession planning for the business
- ❑ Tax planning and employee benefits are reviewed—use of pre-tax, instead of after-tax dollars; compliance with federal and state requirements in the case of certain benefits, such as retirement plans and medical reimbursement plans

**Employment Issues**

- ❑ Employee handbook is up-to-date—changing landscape of job discrimination and harassment, employee safety requirements, drug testing, etc.
- ❑ Hiring, discipline and firing procedures are up-to-date
- ❑ Employment agreements, non-competition are up-to-date and in use
- ❑ Contracts related to stock-options grants, phantom stock plans, bonuses, are up-to-date and in use
- ❑ Safety issues to minimize liability for intentional torts are being properly managed

**Contracts**

- ❑ Documentation and procedures are in place and in use to protect intellectual property (copyright, trade secrets); failure to actively protect those rights can result in loss of protection
- ❑ Systems for tracking key renewal dates or other significant contractual obligations are in place and in use
- ❑ Standard contracts are up-to-date for changes in the law

Provided by Douglas Huffman of Firmin, Sprague, and Huffman Co. L.P.A.

## Example of Six Disciplines Methodology Review Checklist

| Six Disciplines Methodology Review Checklist ||
|---|---|
| **Mission** ||
| ❏ Company is on a mission (has a clear sense of purpose)<br>❏ Mission statement reflects the mission | ❏ People in the company understand the mission<br>❏ People in the company believe in the mission |
| **Values** ||
| ❏ The values are documented<br>❏ The values are known by people in the company<br>❏ The values are lived in the company | ❏ People are reviewed based on the values<br>❏ People are recruited based on the values |
| **Strategic Position** ||
| ❏ Leadership has developed a clear strategic position<br>❏ The strategic position is stable | ❏ People in the company understand what the strategic position is<br>❏ Work in the company is aligned around the strategic position |
| **Vision Statement** ||
| ❏ The vision is documented<br>❏ The vision is guiding the decisions of leadership | ❏ The vision is understood by people in the company<br>❏ The vision is stable for long periods of time |
| **VFOs** ||
| ❏ Clearly defined<br>❏ Fewer than 10<br>❏ Aligned with each other (not conflicting) | ❏ Aligned with strategic position<br>❏ Stable (not changing every year) |
| **Measures** ||
| ❏ Clearly defined<br>❏ Aligned with intent of VFO | ❏ Measure is tracked (data is available) |
| **Targets** ||
| ❏ Targets for every measure | ❏ Attainable |

| Six Disciplines Methodology Review Checklist (cont'd) | |
|---|---|
| **Goal Engagement of Team Members** | |
| ❑ Team members understand the goals<br>❑ Can "tell" the strategy from the goals statement | ❑ Can articulate how their work relates |
| **Alignment Self-Assessment** | |
| ❑ Survey conducted annually | ❑ Progress being made on top priority items |
| **Processes** | |
| ❑ Percent realigned/redefined<br>❑ Well designed | ❑ Measures are in place |
| **Policies** | |
| ❑ Necessary ones are documented | ❑ Well designed |
| **Measures** | |
| ❑ Adequate measures in place | ❑ Measures are well designed |
| **Technology** | |
| ❑ Long-term strategy in place<br>❑ Annual audits conducted | ❑ Key processes are automated |
| **People** | |
| ❑ Robust hiring process<br>❑ People in roles that fit their strengths | ❑ IPs used by everyone, on time<br>❑ Annual appraisals are conducted on time |
| **IPs** | |
| ❑ Goals are met<br>❑ Appropriate number of goals<br>❑ Appropriate blend of change Initiatives vs. sustaining activities | ❑ Personal development goals utilized<br>❑ Few changes in goals |
| **Status Reporting** | |
| ❑ Completed regularly (weekly preferred)<br>❑ Face-to-face meeting to review | ❑ Evidence of self-management<br>❑ Problems identified proactively— few surprises |

## Six Disciplines Methodology Review Checklist (cont'd)

### Initiatives

| | |
|---|---|
| ❑ Clear responsibility<br>❑ Due date identified | ❑ Align with targets |

### Monitoring Measures

| | |
|---|---|
| ❑ Everyone has appropriate measures<br>❑ Easily accessible | ❑ Used to improve work |

### Innovation

| | |
|---|---|
| ❑ Everyone is engaged in problem solving<br>❑ Innovation is focused on company priorities<br>❑ People accept reasonable constraints | ❑ Willing to take informed risks<br>❑ Patient—willing to keep trying and give themselves time |

### Appropriate Use of Tools—Brainstorming, 100-point, etc.

| | |
|---|---|
| ❑ Structured approach used when needed—people are assuming responsibility to champion ideas through implementation | ❑ Recognition is a basic part of the culture—broad involvement top to bottom |

### External Trends

| | |
|---|---|
| ❑ Key trends are identified and prioritized as part of planning process | |

### Stakeholder Surveys

| | |
|---|---|
| ❑ Surveys administered annually | ❑ Trended results maintained |

### Measures

| | |
|---|---|
| ❑ Key measures available to diagnose issues/problems | ❑ Easily accessible |

### 360° Performance Feedback

| | |
|---|---|
| ❑ 100% participation<br>❑ Trended results maintained | ❑ Feedback is constructive |

### Performance Appraisals

| | |
|---|---|
| ❑ Conducted on-time<br>❑ Incorporates quarterly IPs, 360s and team leader feedback, personality profiles | ❑ Constructive |

| Six Disciplines Methodology Review Checklist (cont'd) | |
|---|---|
| **External Audits** | |
| ❏ Financial <br> ❏ Legal <br> ❏ Technology | ❏ Risk/insurance <br> ❏ Six Disciplines Methodology |
| **Strengths, Weaknesses, Opportunities, Threats** | |
| ❏ Written statement prepared | ❏ Considers external trends, company goal achievement, stakeholder surveys, measures, external audit |

VI.
STEP BACK

VI-A Review Externals
VI-B Review Internals
*VI-C Recap SWOT*
VI-D Review Individuals

# STEP VI-C
# Recap SWOT
(Strengths, Weaknesses, Opportunities, Threats)

## Introduction

Remember the comments earlier that good strategy is rooted in defining what to do and what *not* to do. Because all organizations have limited time and resources, one of the primary roles of the leadership team is to help narrow the focus upon which those limited resources are applied. However, up until now, the steps in Discipline VI have been expansive. We have looked thoroughly at lots of different areas—factors outside the company, such as competitive and industry trends, and factors inside the company, including stakeholder satisfaction and other critical indicators of performance.

The purpose of the SWOT step is to get the leadership team to use their experience and judgment to begin narrowing the focus of planning toward the most important strengths, weaknesses, opportunities and threats. The year's stategy should be based upon these. This SWOT statement is one of the primary inputs into Discipline I, where this same leadership team will begin to update the goals of the company for the next year as the Six Disciplines cycle begins again.

## Hints and Tips

❑ Trust your judgment. There's no team in the world that knows more about your business than you do.

❑ Be concise. The recap should fit on a page or two, and should focus on the most important three to five items in each category.

❏ Be candid. The success of the company depends on the ability of the leadership team to trust each other and be open. Hidden agendas or "sacred cows" should be brought into the light.

## Process for Preparing a SWOT Recap

| STEP | RESPONSIBILITY | DESCRIPTION |
|------|----------------|-------------|
| | | **Process for Preparing a SWOT Recap** |
| 1 | Facilitator | Make sure the information produced from the Internal Appraisal step is available—the easel pad notes should still be on the wall or a typed summary in hand. (Ideally this step occurs immediately after the Internal Review step in the same meeting, so everything is fresh in the minds of the leadership team.) |
| 2 | Facilitator | Lead the group through a Brainstorming Exercise on the following topics: What are our greatest strengths? What are our greatest weaknesses? What are our greatest opportunities? What are our greatest threats? |
| 3 | Facilitator | Use the 100-Point Exercise to develop a prioritized list of the topic issues for each of the questions in Step #1 above. Allow enough time for people to explain their answers. |
| 4 | Facilitator | Review last year's SWOT statement and see how it compares. |
| 5 | Facilitator | If there's any significant change in views, the 100-Point Exercise can be repeated to see if the team would prioritize their responses differently. |
| 6 | President | Assign someone responsibility to summarize the results into a statement of Strengths, Weaknesses, Opportunities and Threats. |

## Example of SWOT Recap

**Solomon Software SWOT Recap**

xx/xx/xx

**Strengths**
1. Market leadership in technical innovation and feature breadth, as validated by customer surveys
2. Partner loyalty
3. Whole product flexibility leadership, including field services
4. 40,000+ customers actively using the product
5. Committed and capable team of people

**Weaknesses**
1. Product development processes that deliver predictable schedules
2. Leads generation and qualification processes for selecting best customers
3. Leadership development processes for team members
4. Low accountability culture doesn't challenge people to be their best

**Opportunities**
1. Dramatically increase sales volume by lowering cost of implementation and ownership
2. Double mindshare of partners by having fully integrated suite—covering distribution, project and financial suites—all built with the same tools. This provides the best ROI to partners, and crowds out attention to competitors
3. First to market with a next generation Internet-optimized product, designed to cut by 70% the time to solution, and remove all barriers to remote accessibility

**Threats**
1. Size and visibility of larger publicly traded companies. Their marketing budgets are significantly larger than ours
2. Industry consolidation could suddenly change the competitive landscape

## VI.
## STEP BACK

VI-A Review Externals
VI-B Review Internals
VI-C Recap SWOT
*VI-D Review Individuals*

# STEP VI-D
# Review Individuals

## Introduction

For years before I began practicing the Six Disciplines approach, as a manager I worried about the annual appraisal process. I seldom had the confidence that I was fulfilling my responsibility for giving accurate feedback to those who reported to me. Part of this was due to my lack of maintaining good records to support the appraisal process, and part of it was due to the reality that I had only my own perspective on a person's performance, which I knew wasn't the whole picture.

The problem is compounded by the situation any of us as an *employee* is in. Not one of us *fully* understands how our work and our attitude affect others. In some ways, it's like the color blindness I was born with. I don't see colors the same way as other people do (so my wife reminds me). But I have no idea what I'm missing, because my mind can't imagine colors I haven't seen. Others have likened this to a fish that doesn't know what water is, because it's never been outside of water. We're all swimming in a bowl filled with our own experiences, but we really aren't able to see ourselves as others do without help.

Unfortunately, the response of many business people to these realities is to delay appraisals as long as possible, not do them at all, or to do them reluctantly and poorly. Fortunately, there *is* a better way. The purpose of this step is to lay out an approach that allows team leaders and team members to approach appraisals openly, with confidence, integrity and with no significant surprises.

Following the Six Disciplines approach, you'll go into an appraisal with:

❑ the prior year's appraisal

❑ four completed and rated IPs that show clearly what has been accomplished, along with coaching tips

❑ a profile that helps explain the person's natural preferences and aptitudes

❑ a current 360° survey that shows feedback from the five to ten co-workers who rely on this person the most

❑ a list of personal development goals and attainment over the past year

Using this process, the Individual Performance Appraisal doesn't take much time to prepare. More importantly, it *helps each individual gain the broader, more far-reaching perspective that can only be achieved by stepping back from the day-to-day activities that occupy our thoughts.*

The fact that all people in the company, and the company itself, are doing this at approximately the same time provides an atmosphere of openness and opportunity to improve the alignment of people and their priorities with the priorities of the company.

## Hints and Tips

❑ We recommend that the performance appraisal occur as part of the annual planning cycle.

❑ Compensation decisions should be based on multiple factors, including appraisal ratings, economic trends, company performance, seniority, etc.

❑ Conducting quality performance appraisals is the responsibility of the team leader. All of this input is just that—input. This is not review by committee.

❑ Participants in a 360° survey should be no fewer than six, and no more than 10, including your boss and yourself. They should represent a good sampling of people: those who report to you, your peers, and those who use your work product.

❑ Pick people who will be candid with you about strengths and weaknesses. A bunch of inflated ratings won't help you grow.

❑ The individual being surveyed should recommend the list of people to include in the survey, but the team leader should review and approve.

❑ Participation in the survey should be anonymous, except for your boss. This helps remove barriers to candor.

❑ Don't assume or try to figure out who said what on your surveys. Time and time again, people have jumped to wrong conclusions, so don't go there.

❑ Survey contents should be standardized for all participants. Job-specific goals are addressed by quarterly IP results.

## Process for Reviewing Individuals

### Process for Reviewing Individuals

| STEP | RESPONSIBILITY | DESCRIPTION |
|------|----------------|-------------|
| 1 | HR | Update the schedule (from prior years) for the Individual Appraisal process and communicate it to the team, so everyone knows what the schedule is and can plan his or her own involvement. |
| 2 | HR | Finalizes the questions that are going to be included on the 360° survey. It would be good if these questions could be fairly static from year to year, so trended analysis of the results can be performed. |
| 3 | HR | Initiate an e-mail reminding team members of their role in the 360° process and their responsibilities in the process. |
| 4 | Team Member | Prepare a proposed list of reviewers, including your team leader, team members and peers. The point is to get people involved who best understand your work. |
| 5 | Team Leader | Review the proposed reviewer list and forward it to HR for processing. |
| 6 | HR | E-mail is sent to distribution list providing instructions for completing the 360° form (see example). |
| 7 | Reviewer | Complete the survey promptly, explaining with comments any unusually high or low marks, and return it to HR. |
| 8 | HR | When the deadline is passed, prepare a confidential report to the employee and team leader, including the ratings and comments of reviewers (see example report). |
| 9 | HR | Review Performance Appraisal forms, making any necessary changes and setting the schedule. |
| 10 | HR | Send instruction to all team leaders, or set up a meeting with team leaders to review the purpose, importance and process being followed for appraisals. |
| 11 | Team Leader | Gather and review all pertinent input: last year's appaisal, IPs, 360° results, personality profile, etc., and draft a Performance Appraisal form, including an overall rating. |
| 12 | Team Leader | Set up a meeting with the team member and review the draft of the Performance Appraisal, soliciting input, concerns and questions. This should be a very open and constructive process. |
| 13 | Team Leader | After the meeting, the Performance Appraisal is finalized by the team leader and sent to the team member to add any comments of his or her own about the appraisal itself; He or She then returns it to the team leader. |
| 14 | Team Leader | Add any final comments and forward it to HR for processing and filing. |

## Examples of Individual 360° Feedback

### Team Member Survey

Name _____  **Sample 360° Survey**  Date _____

| PLEASE RATE THE FOLLOWING: | POOR | FAIR | GOOD | VERY GOOD | EXCELLENT | DON'T KNOW |
|---|---|---|---|---|---|---|
| **Integrity with Company Values** | | | | | | |
| Practices consistently our value of "Teamwork" | O | O | O | O | O | O |
| Practices consistently our value of "Quality in the eyes of the customer" | O | O | O | O | O | O |
| Practices consistently our values of "Integrity" (keeping your word) and "Honesty" (candor, truthfulness, openness) | O | O | O | O | O | O |
| Understands & supports company mission & vision | O | O | O | O | O | O |
| Appears fulfilled in his/her work | O | O | O | O | O | O |
| **Knowledge & Skills** | | | | | | |
| Has necessary knowledge & skills to fulfill responsibilities | O | O | O | O | O | O |
| Invests time in growing knowledge & skills through training, reading, research, etc. | O | O | O | O | O | O |
| Asks questions when needing additional information | O | O | O | O | O | O |
| Work is completed on time (project management skills) | O | O | O | O | O | O |
| Work is completed in a high-quality manner | O | O | O | O | O | O |
| Talents are well utilized | O | O | O | O | O | O |
| Anticipates issues and works proactively to resolve (self-manages) | O | O | O | O | O | O |
| Written communication skills | O | O | O | O | O | O |
| Verbal communication skills | O | O | O | O | O | O |
| **Customer and Market Focus (customers are those who use your work products)** | | | | | | |
| Seeks feedback and stays in touch with customers | O | O | O | O | O | O |
| Customers are satisfied with his/her work | O | O | O | O | O | O |
| **Information and Analysis** | | | | | | |
| Knows how to measure the quality of his/her work | O | O | O | O | O | O |
| Innovates to improve performance, according to measures | O | O | O | O | O | O |
| **Team Leader (completed only if person is a team leader)** | | | | | | |
| Creates work environment that helps team do its job effectively | O | O | O | O | O | O |
| Involves team members in planning/estimating their own work | O | O | O | O | O | O |
| Helps team members understand how their work aligns with company strategy | O | O | O | O | O | O |
| Provides constructive accountability for team members | O | O | O | O | O | O |
| What are this person's greatest strengths? | | | | | | |
| What are suggested areas for improvement? | | | | | | |

## Team Member Survey Results Summary

Name _____ **Sample 360° Feedback Report** Date _____

| PLEASE RATE THE FOLLOWING: | DIRECT REPORTS | PEERS | TEAM LEADER | AVERAGE | SELF | GAP |
|---|---|---|---|---|---|---|
| Integrity to Company Values | | | | | | |
| Practices consistently our value of "Teamwork" | | 3.5 | 3 | 3.4 | 4 | -18% |
| Practices consistently our value of "Quality in the eyes of the customer" | | 4 | 4 | 4 | 4 | |
| Practices consistently our value of "Integrity" (keeping your word) and "Honesty" (candor, truthfulness, openness) | | 3 | 3 | 3 | 4 | -33% |
| Understands & supports company mission & vision | | 4 | 4 | 4 | 3 | +25% |
| Appears fulfilled in his/her work | | 3 | 4 | 3.2 | 3 | +6% |
| Knowledge & Skills | | | | | | |
| Has necessary knowledge & skills to fulfill responsibilities | | 5 | 5 | 5 | 4 | +20% |
| Invests time in growing knowledge & skills through training, reading, research, etc. | | 4 | 4 | 4 | 4 | |
| Asks questions when needing additional information | | 4 | 3 | 3.8 | 4 | -5% |
| Work is completed on time (project management skills) | | 4 | 3 | 3.8 | 4 | -5% |
| Work is completed in a high-quality manner | | 4 | 5 | 4.2 | 4 | 5% |
| Talents are well utilized | | 5 | 5 | 5 | 3 | +40% |
| Anticipates issues and works proactively to resolve (self-manages) | | 4 | 3 | 3.8 | 4 | -5% |
| Written communication skills | | 4 | 4 | 4 | 4 | |
| Verbal communication skills | | 4 | 4 | 4 | 4 | |
| Customer and Market Focus (customers are those who use your work products) | | | | | | |
| Seeks feedback and stays in touch with customers | | 4 | 4 | 4 | 4 | |
| Customers are satisfied with his/her work | | 4 | 5 | 4.2 | 4 | +5% |
| Information and Analysis | | | | | | |
| Knows how to measure the quality of his/her work | | 4 | 3 | 3.8 | 3 | +21% |
| Innovates to improve performance, according to measures | | 4 | 3 | 3.8 | 4 | -5% |
| Team Leader (completed only if person is a team leader) | | | | | | |
| Creates work environment that helps team do its job effectively | | | | | | |
| Involves team members in planning/estimating their own work | | | | | | |
| Helps team members understand how their work aligns with company strategy | | | | | | |
| Provides constructive accountability for team members | | | | | | |
| Total | | 3.8 | 3.8 | 3.8 | | |
| What are this person's greatest strengths? | | | | | | |
| | | | | | | |
| What are suggested areas for improvement? | | | | | | |

## Examples Performance Appraisal

### Performance Appraisal

Name: Susan Thomas  Job Title: Marketing Manager

Appraisal Period  From 1/1/xx Through 12/31/xx

**Key Accomplishments (list 3-5 most significant accomplishments)**
1. Reduced cost per closed lead by 10%
2. Increased productivity, as evidenced by 14% increase in sales with no staff increases
3. Completed all quarterly plans with 100% achievement

**Greatest Strengths**
1. Ability to build vision within the Sales & Marketing team about what can be accomplished & gets full commitment in doing so
2. Measurement-driven approaches to processes, which enable people to both self-manage and learn
3. Great verbal and written communications skills, which are used effectively with team members and customers
4. "Can do" attitude—it's a pleasure to work around someone who always finds a way to solve problems and move forward

**Areas for Improvement**
1. Occasionally, enthusiasm can cause overly optimistic assessments of the time and effort to achieve desired results.
2. We are behind competitively in applying technology to leads management. This is an area to increase leadership.

## Suggested professional development activities

1. Involve others in developing plans in order to catch things that might be missed, before expectations are set on schedule and effort.
2. Visit some other businesses that are leaders in applying technology to marketing, to build knowledge and conviction as to what could be done here.

**Overall Comments:** (Leader and Team Member)

GMH: Susan, you have been a great addition to our team over the last two years. You have quickly earned the respect of others in the company, and the improvement in our marketing shows why. . . You have gotten people engaged and excited about leads generation and shown how big a difference it makes in the success of the company. With additional growth on your part in the areas suggested, you can lead our performance to whole new levels over the next few years. Thanks for being a high performer with an infectiously great attitude!

ST: Am enjoying my time here and thank you for your increasing trust in me and my sometimes-crazy ideas. Your openness to trying new things builds my confidence in myself, and I find myself growing more than I have for years. The suggestions for improvement make sense to me and I look forward to focusing on both of these areas this year. Before coming here, I would have rated my performance as excellent; but with your input and support, I know I can move to a whole new level of performance and even greater fulfillment. Thanks for the opportunity to contribute here!

Performance Rating:

❏ Poor  ❏ Fair  ❏  Good  ■  Very Good  ❏  Excellent

Team Member Signature <u>Susan Thomas</u>  Date <u>1/4/xx</u>

Team Leader Signature <u>Gary Harpst</u>  Date <u>1/4/xx</u>

HR Signature _____  Date _____

**VI.**
**STEP BACK**

VI-A Review Externals
VI-B Review Internals
VI-c Recap SWOT
VI-D Review Individuals

RECAP OF DISCIPLINE VI

# Step Back

For a company in pursuit of excellence, it's not at all contradictory to say that a key component in the process of moving ahead is *stepping back*. Even seemingly insignificant changes in day-to-day activities can gradually shift a business from the course that was originally charted for it to reach its long-term objectives.

Each year, the leadership team needs to step back and take a close look at what's taking place, both internally and externally, and to make whatever mid-course corrections are needed to keep the business headed in the desired direction. The key steps in this process are:

- ❑ VI-B Review Externals—competitive, industry, technology, etc.
- ❑ VI-C Review Internals—goals, measures, stakeholders, etc.
- ❑ VI-D Recap SWOT—(Strengths, Weaknesses, Opportunities, Threats)
- ❑ VI-E Review Individuals

This *Discipline* ends the *Six Disciplines* cycle and, at the same time, paves the way for starting the cycle all over again . . . with Discipline I – Decide What's Important. The best news of all, really, is that with each passing cycle, your organization becomes better and better at achieving lasting excellence!

## CHAPTER TEN

# *Putting It All Together*

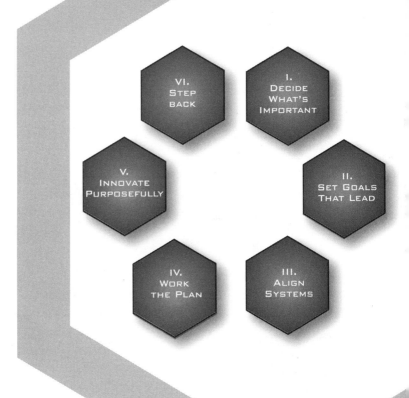

VI.
STEP
BACK

I.
DECIDE
WHAT'S
IMPORTANT

V.
INNOVATE
PURPOSEFULLY

II.
SET GOALS
THAT LEAD

IV.
WORK
THE PLAN

III.
ALIGN
SYSTEMS

*The seed you sow today will not
produce crop till tomorrow. For this
reason, your identity does not lie in your
current results. This is not who you are.
Your current results are who you were.*
—JAMES A. RAY

## Learning to work on your business

James A. Ray's quote on the previous page says it well: translated to the business sector, the identity of your business does not lie in current results, it lies in what you do in the future. The Six Disciplines Methodology is all about what you want your business to become. There are many who talk about excellence, there are some who achieve it for a moment, but there are a few who are *willing to learn how to deliver excellence that lasts.*

The Six Disciplines Methodology is many different things. It incorporates elements of strategic planning, quality management, business process automation, a healthy amount of measure driven improvement and some people management to round it all out. But more than anything else, Six Disciplines is an integrated *learning system.* It is a systematic way for the whole organization to learn how to set, and more

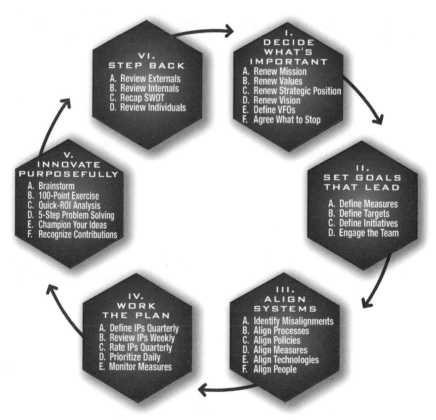

importantly, *execute* strategy. By following its repeatable annual, quarterly, weekly and daily cycles, people continue to learn and grow at their own pace. It's a way for every team member to continue to increase in understanding about how to work *on* the business, not just in it.

It's surprising that in almost all professions, there are accepted methods and processes for becoming proficient. Think of what it takes to become an *expert* engineer, cabinetmaker, architect, graphics designer, lawyer or accountant. It takes years of education, mentoring and on-the-job training. Yet for small businesses, until now, there has really been *no* practical way to learn how to build an excellent business and keep it that way.

The Business Excellence Sustainability Model introduced in chapter three helps convey the magnitude of the challenge. And with that realization comes the understanding of the value of having a step-by-step approach already tuned for small businesses.

| **Business Excellence Sustainability Model** | | | | | | |
|---|---|---|---|---|---|---|
| | **CAPABILITY LEVELS** | | | | | |
| **MAJOR DISCIPLINE AREAS** | **UNDEFINED** (0) | **DEFINED** (1) | **ALIGNED** (2) | **MEASURED** (3) | **IMPROVEMENT** (4) | **PROVEN** (5) |
| **I. Decide What's Important** (mission, values, vision…) | | | | | | ✓ |
| **II. Set Goals That Lead** (1 to 5 year goals, with measures, targets…) | | | | | | ✓ |
| **III. Align Systems** (processes, policies, people, technology…) | | | | | | ✓ |
| **IV. Work the Plan** (individual plans, measures, review, assessment…) | | | | | | ✓ |
| **V. Innovate Purposefully** (problem solving, idea ownership, recognition) | | | | | | ✓ |
| **VI. Step Back** (competitive, industry, stakeholders, measures) | | | | | | ✓ |

This methodology in the hands of the right organization that is properly trained and coached will methodically improve their capabilities, leading to further separation from the rest of the pack. The question becomes: "Is this for you?"

## Is this for you?

If you've read all the way to this point in the book, then *at least the concept* of this Methodology and its promise must hold some interest for you. Now, a key question for you to ask is: "How can I best apply the Methodology to my company?" One of the first things to do is to develop an honest assessment of how "ready" you think your organization is for this type of challenge.

Here's a checklist of things to think through to help you gauge readiness:

- ❑ There's a hunger or passion for excellence in the company, especially among the leadership. Usually this exists in the very beginning for an entrepreneur, before the pressure of survival, paying bills, etc. becomes a higher priority. However, often this passion reemerges when the business gets stable and there's some time to truly think about the future.

- ❑ Leadership gets the idea of the difference between working *in* the business and working *on* it; they're also the primary champion and driving force for the organization's learning how to make the switch to "working *on* it."

- ❑ The size of the business is sufficient that people are beginning to see the difficulties and challenges growth brings. Usually this awareness starts to emerge in businesses that are larger than 15 people in number, because new layers of management are typically added. There are other "pain points" as size increases: 30-40 people, 75-100, 200-250, etc. It's the pain involved that makes people appreciate having a more systematic way of working *on* the business.

❑ A "high trust culture" exists. People believe and respect the leadership and each other. The Six Disciplines Methodology is *not* designed for a radically broken culture, where workers are suspicious of leaders. One piece of evidence of a high trust culture is that the organization is able to attract and retain high-quality people.

❑ The business is stable. This means it has been profitable for several years and has a decent balance sheet to weather storms and make investments. Overall business levels are sustained or growing. This is critical, because adopting the Methodology is best done when the leadership isn't under the pressure of crisis.

❑ The company uses technology effectively. People at all levels are connected to the network and the Internet, and are used to using common productivity tools like word processing, spreadsheets, accounting, e-mail, etc.

❑ The company has learned how to use outside experts—accountants, lawyers, bankers, technology consultants, etc. Small businesses can't have all this expertise in-house, and it's a learned skill to use such know-how effectively.

For those of you who sense you want to move forward,* I want to challenge and encourage you, right now.

*First, the challenge.* Business survival itself is rare. Remember that 96% of all businesses fail within ten years. Frankly, only those who start and run businesses know just how difficult merely *surviving* is. Now, you're about to undertake something even *more* rare and *more* rewarding—moving beyond survival *to excellence* and moving beyond excellence *to lasting excellence.*

*Second, the encouragement.* If you follow the Six Disciplines Methodology faithfully, you'll transform your organization into a place where the leadership team becomes expert at setting the vision for the company and engaging people in the pursuit of that vision.

---

\* Listed in the Appendix are additional resources available from Six Disciplines Leadership Centers to help apply the Methodology.

Your team members will learn how to be more self-managed, using their innovative capability to increase company success.

Yours will be an organization that has the integrity to know what expectations to set with customers and other stakeholders, and has the competence to meet those expectations, *consistently.* You'll be part of an organization that's disciplined and able to adapt to the unexpected quickly. It will be a company where the best people want to work, because they know their abilities will be challenged, respected and utilized to contribute to something meaningful—the mission of your company. In addition, yours will be a business whose overall intrinsic value will continue to increase because profitability is stronger, more predictable and sustainable.

Putting it all together, your overall "return" on investment for applying the principles embodied in the Six Disciplines is very high. It's a blend of more satisfied customers, learning and growing employees, better profitability and the deep personal fulfillment that comes from building an  excellent business. For those of you who are ready to take the next step in this journey of learning how to lead and last, I salute you. In my book, you truly are heroes! May *Six Disciplines for Excellence* guide you in your quest. For additional resources in your quest, turn to the "Resources" section in the Appendix.

But first is the conclusion to "Hancock Enginering". . . .

# Hancock Engineering
## (continued . . .)

On Monday morning, just as Brian was walking into his office, Steve called on the phone. "I read the book over the weekend, Brian, and I'd like to take you up on your offer to get a first-hand look at the way you implement this Six Disciplines Methodology. When can we get together?"

Pleased to hear Steve had already finished the book and was eager for more, Brian said, "All right, Steve. How about Friday at 3:00 P.M.? The person I want you to talk to will be available then."

"Great," Steve replied. "I'll see you then."

On Friday, when Steve arrived, his smile conveyed the sense of gratitude he felt. "Brian, thanks for investing so much time with me. After reading *Six Disciplines*, I see what you meant about the book. In some ways I found it a little overwhelming, because it made me realize I haven't really thought very thoroughly about all that's involved in working *on* my business.

"On the other hand, seeing the whole picture, as it was organized in the book, gave me *hope*—hope that I could bring more order to my business and not leave its development to chance." Steve sat down and continued, though changing to a slightly doubtful tone of voice.

"I've got to admit, I *want* to believe this will work for me, but I'm *also* skeptical. I don't know how many seminars and programs I've been involved with, where I get all fired up and then the reality of everyday business takes over. Also, it seems like there could be a lot of paperwork and busywork in this thing. Preparing weekly reports seems like a stretch."

He paused, somewhat flustered. "Do you guys *really* do this? How long does it take? Y'know, it would help me a *lot* if you could walk me through what it was like implementing this, *and* what it's like using it on a day-to-day basis."

With a wry grin, Brian said, "You wouldn't be worth much as a business leader if you *didn't* have some healthy skepticism. Look, I'll tell you the good *and* the bad of our experience, Steve."

Taking a deep breath, Brian began telling Steve what he had asked to hear. "I want to say *right off* that there are *no* miracles here. Building a business is an enormous challenge and we *still* have lots of problems and issues to face every day. But we're much more effective at identifying them early and managing our way through them." Then he paused a moment, looked at his watch, and said, "Let's go down the hall and get something to drink. This discussion may take us a while."

*Seeing the whole picture, as it was organized in the book, gave me hope—hope that I could bring more order to my business and not leave its development to chance.*

When they got to the break room, they each grabbed a cup of coffee and sat down by a large wall of windows facing the woods behind the office. Steve asked, "So after reading the book, where did you start?"

"First, I went to the web site for the Six Disciplines Leadership Center," Brian replied. "It has a lot more information about how to go about implementing the Methodology. It provides word-processing templates for the forms in the book for "do it yourselfers," but what piqued my interest was the services of the local Six Disciplines Leadership Center located not far from here. I thought we could probably implement this ourselves, but I also realized that working with someone who has done this before would save us a lot of time and mistakes."

Steve nodded and Brian continued, "I called the Leadership Center and ended up speaking with Susan Christopher, who's a very energetic and enthusiastic facilitator for Six Disciplines."

Steve commented, "I saw the term *facilitator* mentioned a lot in the book. Exactly what does a facilitator do?"

Brian responded, "Her primary job is working with companies like yours and mine to help us use the Six Disciplines effectively year in and year out. She leads us through the annual planning meetings each year and coaches us on how to apply the Methodology to different situations that arise. She also introduces us to new ideas and best practices as they emerge. I think as we talk you'll get a better idea of what Susan does."

He continued, "OK, let's get back to what happened next. Susan explained to me that one of the most important steps in adopting the Methodology was to determine whether the organization was *really* ready to adopt it, whether there was sufficient buy-in at the leadership level, in particular.

"She then laid out typical implementation steps that involve increasing levels of commitment. At each step, the organization can assess whether to continue or not. I remember Susan saying, 'Our fee structure is based on a long-term relationship. A monthly fee covers our standard services, and we don't really make a profit on a client relationship for a couple of years. We only take on a couple of clients a month at a local office, so you can imagine that we're very careful about the clients we engage.' Anyway, the implementation steps were well defined. I'll give you a quick overview of the process we went through and then I'll let you talk to Diane, our marketing/sales manager."

Brian got up and refilled his coffee. "Susan suggested I have all my key leaders read the book to make sure there was openness to considering this new approach. All my department heads read it and, one day, we got together to discuss it. In general, I sensed a true openness in almost everyone, but with some healthy questions and concerns. Diane was one person who seemed to be openly resistant. She felt this would be a distraction and that we wouldn't get a return out of it. However, she at least agreed to go to the next step to get more information."

Sitting back down, Brian explained, "Next, Diane and I attended a two-day training session on the Six Disciplines Methodology conducted at the local Leadership Center. We knew this was a significant step because we were investing high-value people's time, plus paying a fee for the training. It was in this seminar that the Methodology became more real.

"We got to hear 'war stories' from the facilitator; we went through some sample exercises; and we saw how the software implementation could save a lot of time. People also got to air their questions openly. Diane, in particular, got some of her questions answered. All in all, those two days were a good step forward.

"The next step recommended by the Leadership Center involved a three day 'Private Seminar' for our whole leadership team. Whereas the two day 'public' seminar gave us a theoretical overview of how the Methodology works, the 'Private Seminar' used our actual business issues as exercises. In reality, it was really the first pass cycle for Disciplines VI, I, and II. This allowed our whole team to see how the Methodology would work in our company, get experience with our facilitator, Susan, and it showed the Leadership Center our commitment to this process. After this meeting our Leadership Center was enthused about moving forward, and so were we.

"We then reviewed a contract in detail, discussed the implementation steps and who was responsible for what. It was a very clear and open process. What also became apparent was that this was going to be a significant investment, in terms of dollars and time. But the fact that most of their costs were included in a monthly fee made me realize they really *were* in it for the long run.

"There was a significant initial fee to set up the relationship, but it was reasonable, given the size of the project. There was *no* doubt in my mind that they weren't going to make money unless they kept me as a long-term client. I liked their willingness to bet on providing me with a thoroughly satisfying program."

Leaning back, Brian continued, "Soon, we had a company-wide meeting, at Susan's suggestion, to brief our team and preview what we were proposing to do and why. In general, we had good support and those who were more skeptical agreed to give the *Six Disciplines* approach a fair chance. I was comfortable moving forward, and so was Susan.

"After that, a technology audit was performed by our IT consultants to make sure we were ready to implement Six Disciplines. To make things easier, the Six Disciplines Leadership Center has put everything a small business needs to implement the Methodology into this device they call the *SixBox™*. It's a device that contains all the software and learning systems for automating the Methodology and tracking many of the key measures most businesses should track, but don't."

"In addition, it provides a secure place for data about our company to reside—information on measures and plans, etc. I like having the SixBox™ here at the office, because all our data stays here and, in case the Internet is ever down, we can still run our business.

"From this point forward, the process was as the book describes. The only difference was that in the book it seems more complex than it is, because you're not being led by a facilitator who has done this before.

*I thought we could probably implement this ourselves, but I also realized that working with someone who has done this before would save us a lot of time and mistakes.*

"Now, a few weeks before the end of every fiscal year, we kick off our planning cycle. Susan comes in and leads us through a half-day meeting where our leadership team reviews competitive, industry and technology trends. We survey all customers, vendors and employees and review those results, and we check out how we did compared to last year's plans. We look at other critical performance measures. We wrap that all up with a one- or two-page list of strengths, weaknesses, opportunities and threats."

Steve asked, "How long does it take to pull together the information you need for this meeting?"

Brian replied, "Not long. The survey information, goals and most of the key measures are maintained in the SixBox™. The first year, of course, we didn't have any of this information, so we just worked with what we had. Every year, however, we get more and more measures in place, and it just gets easier and better."

Continuing on, Brian said, "Next, in a separate meeting facilitated by Susan, we review mission, values, vision, etc., and then update our VFOs. That first year, one of biggest surprises was dealing with "what to stop." The idea of actually stopping some activities really was foreign to us. It took us a while to learn the power of freeing up resources for higher-priority initiatives.

"This second meeting typically runs for about a half day as well. Sometimes, if we're having a significant change in strategy, it takes a little longer. I like having Susan facilitate these meetings, so I can focus on our strategy and not managing the meeting. She keeps us on track and saves us a lot of time.

"Once the VFOs are nailed down, we have another planning session, about a week later, to review measures, set targets and identify initiatives for reaching those targets. This meeting can take anywhere from four to six hours. We usually have a larger group in this meeting, because we want the people who are going to be involved in implementation to participate.

"This is a key meeting, because we're getting down to measurable goals for the next year. That first year or two, we weren't great at defining good measures, but we gradually learned the power of picking measures that provide more guidance to our team as to what they should do."

Steve said, "I guess the Align Systems Discipline must be next. How does that work?"

"Well," Brian reflected aloud, "before we launch into Discipline III, we have a company-wide meeting to explain our goals statement and get everyone on board with what we're trying to do. Then we move ahead. More than any other discipline, Discipline III has helped us get a better return for our investments in training and technology. It's helped everyone in the company begin to think about how to make our processes, measures and technology serve our goals.

"What I like is the employee survey, because it gets everyone involved in thinking about these issues. Gradually, people learn to think strategically about the business and its investments. By the way, you definitely have to go slow with this one. The first year or two, it can definitely be overwhelming to see all the things that aren't well aligned, but Susan was great at reminding us to stick to just one or two items and go slow."

*In the book it seems more complex than it is, because you're not being led by a facilitator who has done this before.*

Steve got up and refilled his coffee, while Brian briefly gathered his thoughts. "The last thing we tackled in our initial implementation cycle," he said, "was the most challenging. It was Discipline IV—Working the Plan. Nobody in the company had ever developed a quarterly plan, including *me*. Some were open to trying it and some were very reluctant.

"In some ways, all the other disciplines are designed to pave the way for this. The first thing we noticed was the reluctance of people to take responsibility for dates. It made them nervous to commit to a due date for something, when they felt they weren't in control of all the factors that affected them." Both men nodded, acknowledging they could identify with that.

Brian went on, "Susan coached us to go slow and give people time to try the system for a couple of quarters. So about two weeks before each quarter began, we made sure people had copies of company goals. I sat down with the people who reported to me, and asked them to provide me with a list of the top five things they thought they needed to get done in their departments over the next quarter. We'd review that list together, and sometimes I'd spot something they missed.

"Frequently, during the first few quarters, I realized that I, too, had missed important items in my plans. Also, we struggled with when to allow people to change their goals during the quarter. Susan counseled us to try to minimize the number of changes and learn to do a better job of thinking ahead.

"At first it was awkward, but each quarter we got better at setting goals. I noticed my communication with my team was improving. We were learning to be clear with each other. We worked hard to get people to take responsibility for their goals, including checking with others they were dependent upon, and making sure those plans aligned with their own.

"This eventually led to much more of a self-management approach. Instead of the manager trying to spot all those problems, responsibility was shifted to the individuals. After a few quarters, we could really see the people who were *getting it* and taking responsibility. This became a good indicator of people who were ready for more responsibility. We coached the others, and trained and helped them grow.

"We had a couple of people leave, but most of our staff have come to like this approach. They know what's expected of them. You'll frequently hear people say things like, 'I need this to meet a quarterly goal.' Or they push back on some change, because it affects a goal. It forces us all to pay more attention to what we're doing."

Steve interrupted and said, "It sounds good, but how long does this really take? The status reports sound like a lot of work."

Brian replied, "That's the most common question I get about this Methodology. I think the best person to answer this is Diane, the skeptic I told you about earlier. Let's go talk to her. She heads up our sales and marketing operation. She's got three account managers, who work in the field most of the time making presentations. Two others on her team develop our marketing materials, maintain our web site and produce success stories and other brochure-type information. Last, she has three people who are responsible for taking incoming calls to qualify clients, and making telemarketing prospecting calls. All direct mail leads are handled by them, as well."

Brian tapped on Diane's door. She turned from some papers she was working on and stood up to greet Steve. Diane appeared to be in her early forties, and her dress, friendly smile and firm handshake reinforced Brian's characterization of a veteran, get-things-done kind of person. After chatting informally for a couple of minutes, she asked Steve how she could help him. Brian excused himself, saying he'd return in a few minutes.

Steve said, "I told Brian I wanted to talk to someone who had to live with the Six Disciplines Methodology every day, because I'm thinking about adopting it for our business. Would you recommend it?"

Diane smiled and said, "It depends. If your team understands they're making a long-term commitment and are willing to stick it out, then I heartily recommend it. I was on the fringe when we first talked about it. Frankly, I've seen too many 'great ideas' that end up wasting people's time. Six Disciplines turned out to be different, though.

"I think it's because of the way the author of the Methodology defined the problem to begin with. The key insight was that the problem wasn't *knowing* what to do; the real problem was *doing* it over a long period of time—making it last. As a result, the emphasis of the Methodology was focused more on making implementation easier, and less on theory. Let me show you what I mean." She turned away from Steve toward her computer desk.

"Take a look at my workstation," she said, motioning him to come around to get a better view. "This is the Six Disciplines home page. The top section is my Task List. It has all the documents and actions I've received from others in the company. Let's check out this first one. This is from Derek, one of my account managers. Derek is on the road so much he's hardly *ever* in the office. He's recently drafted a set of goals for next quarter.

> *The idea of actually stopping some activities really was foreign to us. It took us a while to learn the power of freeing up resources for higher-priority initiatives.*

"When I open this task, he's asking me to review and approve these goals. I can make changes or notes on this, or with a click of the button, see his current quarter goals *or* prior quarters, for as far back as I want. With another click of the button, I can forward this back to Derek. Because this system is Internet-based, it doesn't matter where Derek is. It's this kind of ease that makes the difference between quarterly planning working or not." She looked up at Steve, who was nodding his head with understanding.

"The next item is Karen's weekly status report. It's the status of how she's doing on her quarterly goals. It takes me less than five minutes to scan this report. I pay particular attention to whether the 'at risk' box is checked, or whether she has any comments. People in my group have been trained to be concise and to the point. If they need something, they'd better ask for it. That's their job. It's my job to get them help if they need it.

"The next item on my task list is a draft invoice for one of our key customers. Accounting is asking me to check it before it goes out. One of accounting's performance measures is the number of billing errors. This simple process saves time and errors.

"As you can see, I have a number of other tasks on my list. Here's one that's a reminder. I took a call from a client a week ago and promised to call back tomorrow. This task will sit here until I delete it. With one click of the button, I can see the customer record and notes about our conversation."

Steve pointed to the bottom of the screen and asked, "What's this?"

Susan replied, "This is the Methodology Viewer. This puts at my fingertips, as well as those of every employee, the current statement of our mission, vision, values, etc. And most importantly, it shows our *current* goals, including the VFOs, measures, targets and initiatives for achieving those goals.

"We expect people to understand these when formulating their quarterly goals. It's my job to see that their goals are aligned with company priorities. It's the *employee's* job to see that the goals get completed, or tell me ASAP if they aren't."

At this point, Steve interrupted her to say, "This seems like a super-efficient system. But is everyone *really* okay with the amount of scrutiny that seems routine around here?"

Diane replied, "That was a concern of *mine*, Steve, when I was first hearing about our implementing Six Disciplines here at Hancock. But you know, the way they presented the Methodology, and with the training and guidance that was provided, all of us have really bought into the value of following the Six Disciplines *and* using the system to its fullest. Besides, the results speak for themselves." She smiled at Steve and then turned back to the monitor.

"On the left part of the home page is the Measure Analyzer. This shows the key measures I want to monitor for my department. For example, the first is a graph of the number of leads we have in the pipeline, by category. The second is a trended graph of the number of unresolved client issues. As you can see, right now our client issues are at a 90-day high. If you open this and look back at last year's results, you realize this is a seasonal trend we see every summer, due to increased sales volume.

"The third graph is the average number of outbound phone calls being made by our telemarketing department. Those numbers are lower than they should be because of the number of customer issues. We'll bring in some temp help to get those numbers on track. If we don't, then our leads pipeline and business levels will be affected in about six months."

Clicking her way to other facets of the Six Disciplines system, Diane continued, "Here's a graph of customer satisfaction for the past seven years. And here's a graph of employee satisfaction with the company as a whole for seven years, and a breakout for my department." She stopped for a moment, wondering how deeply to go into Hancock's technology tie-ins to the Six Disciplines. After a brief pause, she resumed her explanation.

"There's a lot to learn to master the Six Disciplines Methodologies and systems. Over on the right is the Assistance Manager. Look at this. With a click of the button, I can find any of the key business processes we have in our business and see the steps that we go through to implement them. There are even direct links to the appropriate Six Disciplines screens to complete that particular step. Also, here's a link to a brief video tutorial on how a particular process or function works."

Turning away from her computer screen, Diane summarized, "In a way, the Six Disciplines Methodology is just a structured framework for learning—learning how to make Hancock Engineering a better business."

Steve returned to his chair, impressed with the "nickel" tour he had just been given.

Diane said, "Steve, the point I'm making is that the whole Six Disciplines approach is implementation-oriented. The Leadership Center thinks most businesses don't need more theory or business expertise, but do need assistance in developing more effective execution. The Six Disciplines Methodology and their support and services are structured around that idea.

*The key insight was that the problem wasn't knowing what to do; the real problem was doing it over a long period of time.*

"I won't kid you. Other people have come in here and can't believe how well this organization functions now. Everybody here set goals quarterly and we hit more than 97 percent of them. Everyone has trended measures like these at their fingertips. All of us understand what we're all about and how our work connects to the purpose of the company.

"But it wasn't easy. It takes time. It's kind of like compound interest; you keep doing the right things for a long time and, all of a sudden, you realize you've become a completely different organization. For us, this compounding has been going on for almost ten years, and we just keep getting stronger. I wouldn't go back for anything."

Steve replied: "You have eight people reporting to you. How much time do you spend reviewing status reports and having regular meetings with your people?"

Diane nodded and said, "I spend about an hour or two per employee once a *quarter* to make sure we're on the same page with goals for the quarter. This is the best investment I can make, because from that point forward each team member manages to those goals. Each week, the IP Status reports take me just a few minutes to review.

"I try to have at least a 20-minute weekly meeting with each member of my team, just to talk through any concerns on the goals list. Sometimes, issues turn up and the meetings run for up to 45 minutes. But I've learned that finding a problem early saves many hours later. The bottom line is that this approach doesn't *cost* time, it *saves* time, because people learn to self-manage."

Brian had quietly slipped back into the room. Steve said, "Thanks for that demo. It really helps me see how this works in an everyday implementation. By the way, on those graphs you showed me, where did that data come from?"

*Most businesses don't need more theory or business expertise, but do need assistance in developing more effective execution.*

Diane said, "That's all maintained in the SixBox™. Tracking the plans, business processes and measures makes implementation of the Methodology much easier. The reason so many great books spew out all these wonderful ideas that never get used is that nobody helps you implement them.

"For small businesses in particular, it almost *has* to be all in one box—we don't have the time or ability to integrate all this ourselves. Fortunately, Six Disciplines has not only developed the Methodology, but the systems, services and support to help us stick with it."

Steve thanked Diane again and turned to Brian. "Wow! You've opened up a whole new dimension of possibilities for me, and I'm sure only a fraction of it has begun to sink in! Once again, I appreciate your time *and* Diane's."

Brian said, "Let me walk you to the car, Steve." As they moved through the building, Brian commented, "When we first talked about this last week, I mentioned that the Six Disciplines Methodology was best applied when a business was doing well. I don't mean the business has to be problem-free—no business is. What I *mean* is that the business is solid enough financially and managed well enough that the leadership can focus on a long-term, disciplined approach, instead of just firefighting."

Brian continued, "The book was named right. These are disciplines, and they take a while to develop and get working, but they *do* work if you follow them. I've found the Six Disciplines Leadership Center to be a great resource, and for us a necessary catalyst that makes it all happen. And, I've come to value Susan's input as much as any of my other external advisors, and in some ways *more*. She's helping us do what *no one* else does, which is learning how to get better at building a lasting and successful business."

Steve shook Brian's hand and thanked him again, saying, "This is starting to sink in. If my business is going to continue its current success, we've got to learn how to move from widget building to business building. And just like we need a systematic approach for printing a job correctly, we need a systematic approach for working on the business as well. I can't wait to go back and explain this to our team! Thanks again."

. . .The beginning

# Appendix

# Notes

## Chapter 1

1. Michael E. Gerber, *The E-Myth Revisited* (New York: HarperCollins Publishers, Inc., 1995), page 2.
2. Stephen R. Covey, *The 7 Habits of Highly Effective People* (New York: Simon and Schuster, 1989), page 18.
3. Lewis Carroll, *Alice's Adventures in Wonderland and Through the Looking Glass* (New York: Signet Classic Printing, 2000)
4. Robert S. Kaplan and David P. Norton, *The Strategy-Focused Organization* (Boston: Harvard Business School Press, 2001), page 13.
5. Ibid, page 1.
6. James C. Collins and Jerry I. Porras, *Built to Last* (New York: HarperCollins Publishers, Inc., 1997), page 23.
7. Kaplan and Norton, op. cit., page 1.
8. Gerber, op. cit.
9. Peter M. Senge, *The Fifth Discipline: The Art and Practice of the Learning Organization* (New York: Bantam Doubleday Dell Publishing Group, Inc., 1990), page 12.
10. Ibid, page 218.

## Chapter 2

1. US Census Table 2a Employment Size of Employer Firms, 1999; Establishment and Employment Changes from Births, Deaths, Expansions, and Contractions, 1999-2000.
2. Gerber, op. cit.
3. Anonymous.

## Chapter 4

1. Collins and Porras, op. cit., page 78.
2. Collins and Porras, op. cit., page 77.
3. American Express Website, http://home3.americanexpress.com/smallbusiness/resources/starting/bizplan
4. Senge, op. cit., page 275.
5. Michael E. Porter, "What is Strategy?" *Harvard Business Review*, reprint 96608, 1996, page 78.
6. Collins and Porras, op. cit., page 221.
7. Porter, op. cit., page 70.

## Chapter 5

1. Robert S. Kaplan and David P. Norton, *The Balanced Scorecard: Translating into Action* (Boston: Harvard Business School Press, 1996), page 306.
2. Michael Hammer, "Reengineering Work: Don't Automate, Obliterate;" *Harvard Business Review*, reprint 90406, 1990.
3. Kaplan and Norton, op. cit., page 55.
4. Kaplan and Norton, op. cit., page 215.

## Chapter 6

1. *Performance Cycle Guidebook*, Franklin Covey Co. 1997, page 17.
2. Bennet P. Lientz and Kathryn P. Rea, *Achieve Lasting Process Improvement* (San Diego: CA: Academic Press, 2002), page xvii.
3. Theodore Levitt, *Marketing for Business Growth* (New York: McGraw-Hill, Inc., 1974), page 16.

## Chapter 7

1. Kaplan and Norton, op. cit., page 1.

## Chapter 8

1. Reference unknown.
2. Levitt, op. cit., page 73.
3. Senge, op. cit., page 4.
4. Scripture taken from the *New American Standard Bible*, copyright 1960, 1962, 1963, 1971, 1972, 1973, 1975, 1977, 1995 by the Lockman Foundation. Used by permission.

# Resources

Local Six Disciplines Leadership Centers were formed solely for the mission of helping small businesses achieve lasting excellence by applying the principles in this book. There are a number of resources available to assist you in this on-going endeavor. Please refer to our web site: **www.SixDisciplines.com** for up-to-date information.

A small sampling of the resources include:

❑ Electronic copies of the forms, examples and checklists used in this book

❑ Training classes on the use of the Six Disciplines Methodology

❑ Private assessment of organizational readiness

❑ Certified facilitators to assist in effectively utilizing the Six Disciplines Methodology in your organization

❑ The SixBox™. To make things easier for small businesses, much of the software and learning materials needed to automate implementation of the Methodology, including measure tracking, are included "in the box"

❑ Learning resources for more effectively applying the Methodology in your organization

# Index

# Acknowledgements

**Jesus Christ**—the architect of the universe and everyone in it. He has developed and is executing the "ultimate business plan." He gives meaning to everything I do.

**Rhonda Harpst**—my friend and life partner. You're the best part of my day, every day!

**James, Anna and Jordan Harpst**—may you some day have the joy in your children that I do in you.

**Joe and Norma Harpst**—from Dad, I learned the value of honesty and hard work. From Mom, I learned creativity and taking initiative. Every day I appreciate you more.

**Jack Ridge and Vernon Strong**—my business partners and faithful friends. Jack believed before anyone else and put up the seed money to start it all. The adventure continues!

**Wonderboy, CanMan, StickMan and Shademan**—the memories never leave me!

## The Six Disciplines Team

What a team! I've never seen a team that fits together as well as this one. We're doing *amazing* things together.

**Joe Longo**—partner and soul mate on what Six Disciplines is all about—*lasting excellence*. Knows small businesses cold and has the rare quality of knowing how to simplify things.

**Neil Teatsorth**—who continues to build the Six Disciplines team and has a passion for building high quality organizations.

**Randy Minder**—who leads our technical team in developing the great tools for making Six Disciplines easier for small businesses.

**Matt Lauth**—the mastermind behind our learning and portal strategy. It's all about learning! His years at Solomon made me realize he has one of the best combinations of technical, managerial and business experience around. Thanks for your leadership!

**John Crawford**—Long time, faithful contributor at Solomon. John has the knack for getting things done and building winning teams. I am grateful that he is on the Six Disciplines team now.

**Debora Edds**—who helps me wherever, whenever and however I need it. Thanks much.

**Jim Cline**—our technical guru who can find and fix anything. Genius at work.

**Wendell Giedeman**—our expert in reporting, measures and information management. Can't manage it if you don't measure it!

**Matt Hauser**—architect of our very friendly and awesome user interface.

**Casey Leichty**—the fastest learner in the group—can take on anything, anytime. We couldn't have done it without you. And the best is ahead.

**Russ Thompson**—mastermind behind our whole applications strategy. Don't know how you keep it all straight. Nobody has ever done what you did on this project.

**Scott May**—A former Solomon team member who has a wealth of customer, publisher and consulting experience. A great addition to the Six Disciplines team.

**Cory Wetherill**—spooky ability to test software—"It ain't excellent until he says it's excellent." Great job!

**Bryan Hunt**—EIS Group. Keeps our infrastructure working, especially my laptop.

**John Navratil**—first one who helped shape the Six Disciplines concept. John is a consummate analyst and a friend. I like the way your mind works!

**G.A. Sullivan**—headed by Eric Brown, a great team of people who helped shape our technical strategy.

**Sam Allred**—friend and champion of business excellence and leaving nothing to chance.

**Doug Huffman**—an attorney who defines what it means to be a trusted advisor. I don't do much without talking to Doug first.

**John Howell**—best marketing mind on the planet. Impossible to describe how much I've learned from him. Launched the Solomon brand and built our international business. Major contributor for 20 years.

**Don Gaylord**—foremost expert on project accounting anywhere. Absolute highest standards of quality.

**John Antman**—invested years in helping us pull this whole thing together. You name it and John helped do it!

**Jim Stritzinger**—great counsel on many of the key decisions we made. Jim is the most enthusiastic person I know. Always can do!

## Book Assistance

**Lynn Child** of Aardvark, **Terry Terhark** of The Right Thing, **Johnny Warren, Bryan Taylor** and **Ray Tyler** of Cornerstone Management, **Lindy Lopez** of Research for Action, for your incredibly valuable input from reading drafts of the book.

**Willy Mathes, Bob Kelly, Patricia Draznin**, and **Jay Marquart** for your valuable guidance. A special thanks to Willy as the lead editor for knowing how to draw out of me what I was trying to say.

**George Foster** and **Barry Kerrigan** for doing a great job of designing the cover and the interior of the book.

## Solomon Team

What a group. There has been no more exciting and fulfilling time, for me, than the 20 years spent with this group of people. I've learned so much from you. This whole industry has been partly shaped by your creativity, passion and commitment. The Solomon business, the Six Disciplines business and this book would never have been possible without your blood, sweat and tears. Thank you from the bottom of my heart for the privilege of working with you. Space doesn't permit acknowledging you all, so I'm just going to mention the few I spent the most time with over these 20 years.

**Brian Clark**—no one contributed more to the character of Solomon. He's the model of patient persistence in doing the right thing. I'm continuing to understand his wisdom, years after the fact. Brian was the key to our successful turnaround in the 90s.

**Harold Morgan**—the ultimate people person. He helped us at a critical time and we will never forget how he cared.

**Eric Kurjan**—best people leader we had. Willing to take on anything and always did it well.

**Bob Sprague**—an advisor and friend. His belief in what we were doing at Solomon caused him to almost single-handedly raise several million dollars in funding.

**Dave Lehman**—only one willing to make the move. We built our Findlay sales team around Dave.

**Leland Strange, Dave Johnston**—great board members, advisors and friends. What a joy to work with people you trust.

**Steve Dennis**—he and his team made our whole company better. Great at business management process.

**Ray Parsons**—man of great integrity, passion for the distribution business.

**Pat Fitzhenry**—best there is at marketing programs. Always successful in every venture undertaken. Never got him to move to Findlay.

**Mike Rupe**—Mike helped us strengthen our management approach and team, preparing us for a high growth future.

**Mickey Linn**—great market analyst, understands what it takes to grow a business.

**Mark Granville**—loyal, hard working. Always stuck to it, no matter how hard the sledding.

**Dave Graham**—built our services business and set the tone for years to come.

**Pat Shannon**—always had the trust of our channel partners.

**Robert Deshaies**—continues to grow in his professional capabilities. Gradually taking over Microsoft™.

**Jan Galvin**—kept me on track for years. Thanks, Jan.

**Gretchen Thompson**—First hire. Absolutely gifted developer.

**Rick Mortensen**—Second hire. The most knowledgeable, innovative person on customization that I know of. Laid the foundation for much of our technical leadership.

**Florene Nelson**—did the work of three people before her departure. She got us off the ground!

**Skip Reardon**—Fifth hire. Wow, Skip! You've done it all! You've done everything I've ever asked. You're amazing in your knowledge of this industry.

**Pat Gibson**—Sixth hire. Great technical mind. Built much of the technical foundation on which Solomon was based.

**Lee Melinger**—a bundle of energy and creativity. Lee uprooted his life in California and contributed a great deal to our success.

**Deb Core, Karen and Bill Archer, Sue Farquharson, Tom and Pat Hartman, Larry Hoos, Peter Berton, Karen Peters, Holly Hunter, Diane and Dan Wienczkowski, Ruth Ann Ellerbrock, Elaine Rettig, Sharon Hoepf, Kathy Hemmer, Deb Montooth, Tim Hitchings, Dan Fleming, Gail Leatherman, Dianne Althaus, Denise McDaniel, Lisa Inniger, Sharon Keeran, Bill Savard, Claudia Smith, Steve Fetters, Dave Bowsher, Kathy Adams, Dave Reddick, Joyce Kirchner, Tawana Weidman, Pat and Dave Busch, Tom Higginbotham . . .**

And the list goes on. Please forgive me for the names I've forgotten. I don't have room to name the more than a thousand people who've worked for Solomon over the years. But the names above are some of the early contributors who laid the foundation. Thanks to you all!